Comparative Ethics Series/
Collection d'Éthique Comparée: 2

Comparative Ethics Series/
Collection d'Éthique Comparée

As Religious Studies in its various branches has spread out in recent years, it has met with a newly emergent discipline: Comparative Ethics as the study of moralities as cultural systems, rather than as the philosophical investigation of particular moral issues. To study a morality as a dynamic whole in its social nature and functioning requires a context in which other instances of a comparable kind are considered. Moral action-guides and religious action-guides have historically been brought together in mixed, moral-religious or religious-moral systems. The different paths followed by moralities as cultural systems in the varying contexts demand comparative study.

The series embraces three kinds of studies: (1) methodological studies, which will endeavour to elaborate and discuss principles, concepts, and models for the new discipline; (2) studies which aim at deepening our knowledge of the nature and functioning, the scope and content of particular moral systems, such as the Islamic, the Hindu, the Christian, and so on; (3) studies of a directly comparative kind, which bring differing moral systems or elements of systems into relationship.

COMPARATIVE ETHICS

Volume 2

Methodist Education in Peru

Social Gospel, Politics, and American Ideological and Economic Penetration, 1888-1930

Rosa del Carmen Bruno-Jofré

Published for the Canadian Corporation for Studies in Religion/Corporation Canadienne des Sciences Religieuses by Wilfrid Laurier University Press

1988

Canadian Cataloguing in Publication Data

Bruno-Jofré, Rosa del Carmen, 1946-
  Methodist education in Peru

(Comparative ethics series ; v. 2)
Bibliography: p.
Includes index.
ISBN 0-88920-954-5

1. Methodist Episcopal Church – Education – Peru –
History.   2. Methodist Episcopal Church – Missions –
Peru – History.   3. Church and education – Peru –
History.   4. Social gospel – History.   5. Politics
and education – Peru – History.   I. Title.   II. Series.

LC577.B78 1988   377.6′0985   C87-094116-X

© 1988 Canadian Corporation for Studies in Religion/
     Corporation Canadienne des Sciences Religieuses

88 89 90 91 4 3 2 1

Printed in Canada

Methodist Education in Peru has been produced from a manuscript supplied in
camera-ready form by the author.

Cover design by Michael Baldwin, MSIAD

Order from:
Wilfrid Laurier University Press
Wilfrid Laurier University
Waterloo, Ontario, Canada   N2L 3C5

*To my father Luis Bruno
who introduced me to the
mysteries of history in
my early childhood.*

*To my mother Rosa Baier
for her love and unfaulting
faith in my work.*

TABLE OF CONTENTS

LIST OF ILLUSTRATIONS

MAP

FIGURES

TABLES

Introduction and Acknowledgments

This book is in answer to numerous questions posed, during 1976 and 1977, by inquisitive and politically minded young people of the Methodist Church of Peru and the Peruvian Office of the Ecumenical Union of Latin American Youth (ULAJE). The work was entirely written in Canada in 1982 and 1983. As a historian, I was offered the great opportunity to explore a little-known historical problem and to have access to a rich, still sealed, and unorganized collection of documents. I felt a great responsibility in providing answers that were at the same time scholarly and useful. In this sense, I always had in mind E.J. Hobsbawm's words: "the historian's business is not praise and blame, but analysis." I am aware that some of the conclusions will motivate contrasting reactions. It is my hope that this work will make a contribution to the ongoing discussion on the writing of the history of Christian churches in Latin America.

I could not have carried through this work without the help and encouragement of the authorities of the Methodist Church in Peru. I encountered, however, tremendous problems with the primary sources, which were both widely dispersed and fragmented in quality. For example, it was a painful and almost impossible task to obtain curriculum material and educational sources to develop further the influence of Social Gospel and Progressivism on Methodist education.

I had the opportunity to use, for the first time, the collection of official correspondence of the American Mission in Peru without restrictions. The authorization was provided by the late bishop Dr. Wenceslao Bahamonde and his successor bishop Marco Ochoa Amoretti. They also volunteered material from their personal libraries and made extensive comments on their experiences. The collection was in the form of packages of documents containing mail as well as non-classified documents. Many of the documents were badly damaged. Rev. Elton Watlington carefully collected all the sources available. He also moved part of the Methodist Library from Huancayo to Lima (the library in the episcopal house was not organized at the time). Mrs. Hayes, in charge of the Wolfe Memorial Library and the Vertical Archive helped in providing printed material and documents from the mid 1930s and 1940s. Mrs. Oilda de

Carrasco, principal of Colegio Maria Alvarado (formerly Lima High School), allowed me to have access to the files of the school and gladly collaborated on my work. Regrettably, we could not find early documents in the school collection. Aby Salazar, secretary to the bishop, helped in numerous ways during the searching process and later when I wrote the draft. She also discovered that many sources I had consulted were no longer there.

The bibliographical search was completed thanks to the efficiency of the Interloan Library Service of the Calgary Public Library and the University of Calgary and the dedicated work of Mrs. Judy Pelchat. I acknowledge the kind collaboration of the Library of the General Commission on Archive and History of the United Methodist Church in the United States, which was moved from North Carolina to Drew's University collection of Methodistica while my research was in progress.

I am grateful to Dr. John Macdonald, with whom I have had a long intellectual interchange—sometimes a fiery one; this has extraordinary enriched my intellectual resources. And I wish to recognize the help given me by Dr. Evelina Orteza y Miranda. Her incredible blending of professional expertise and personal moral support has enlightened and enriched my career.

I would like to thank the direct or indirect help I received during these years from my friends Guido, Elisabeth, Richmond, Bonnie and others that I do not mention by virtue of momentary neglect. Also my thanks to Dr. Alberto Ciria for his positive and always encouraging comments.

My profound gratitude to Dr. Harold Coward of the Canadian Corporation for Studies in Religion. His efficient treatment of my manuscript facilitated its publication.

The manuscript was typed and prepared for publication by the Education Research Centre of the University of Lethbridge. I acknowledge the effort and dedication of Dr. Myrna Greene, Mrs. Beulah Sinclair, and Mrs. Isabel Groves, who made possible the physical production of this manuscript. Last but not least, my thanks to the acting Dean of the Faculty of Education, Dr. Robert Anderson for his continuous support.

Finally, I would like to thank my dear husband Ricardo and my daughter Ana. It has been their love, help, support and encouragement that has enabled me to complete this work.

This book has been published with the help of a grant from

the Canadian Federation for the Humanities, using funds provided by the Social Sciences and Humanities Research Council of Canada.

CHAPTER I

Protestantism in Peru During the Nineteenth Century

The Introduction of the Lancasterian System

Peru has a long history of its own, the continuity of which was broken by the Spanish conquest with the destruction of the Inca Empire and the consequent subjugation of the Indian population.[1] The Roman Catholic Church was then introduced into the country and readily became an ideological force serving and legitimizing the colonial order. It played a directly relevant role in the disintegration of the pre-Hispanic social organization and in the introduction of transplanted Spanish institutions which were combined with fragments of the previous social structure.

Peru today still has a predominantly Roman Catholic population. Besides the official version, there is also a Catholicism of a special kind with roots in the conquest itself[2] that is known as popular Catholicism.[3] Valcarcel explains it by delving into the subjective aspects of the process of colonization:

> When the foreign domination became inevitable, the Indian, astutely, appealed to the skilled use of simulation. Not being able to reject frankly and haughtily the predominant and decisive religious values, he feigned to accept them. He became a Catholic, received baptism and was an assiduous practicant; he took part in rituals and feasts but his heart remained firmly attached to his ancient gods. He incorporated surreptitiously and clandestinely his own liturgy in that of the Church.[4]

Protestantism did not reach Peru in colonial times, in spite of the contact with merchants, particularly English smugglers. (The Inquisition had been established in Peru in 1569 under Felipe II.) During the eighteenth century,[5] however, foreign books, magazines, and especially authors like Condillac, Rousseau, Voltaire, and later, particularly at the beginning of the nineteenth century, Adam Smith and Benjamin Constant increased their currency in the intellectual milieu of the Spanish colonies. The success of the American Revolution also had great influence on intellectual and political life. A spirit of cultural renewal and even critical consciousness emerged in the colonies and generated a different cultural atmosphere.[6] Thus, by the time of the wars of independence, educated and aspriring Creoles had been long acquainted with Protestantism and with modern political and economic ideas. French philosophy and English liberalism were, broadly speaking, the main sources for Latin American revolutionaries looking for theoretical foundation, first for their aspirations of liberation from Spain, and thereafter, for the organization of political and economic life. In the case of Peru, political independence came, for the most part, as a result of external forces, with the army from the south led by San Martin and that from the north led by Bolivar, moving into Peru, rather than as a consequence of an internal movement.

In the first years of the independence period (which opened with the declaration of independence in Lima, on July 28, 1821), in spite of the lack of consolidation of the triumph over Spain there was within the imported liberal atmosphere an initial acceptance of biblical teaching at a popular level. This teaching was itself linked to the first attempt to organize public education.

Whatever their political differences, the leaders of the emancipation in Peru (liberal republicans, in particular) made a serious effort to use imported liberal juridical and ideological elements to construct what they saw as a new order, in which education would have a special role.[7] Jorge Basadre, the famous Peruvian historian, synthesizes the whole question as follows:

> The men who founded the Republic were generous, kind, patriotic; but they lacked a consciousness of Peru's position in time and space. . . . They believed they were inventing a new country and ignored the fact that this country had the enviable privilege of having an old culture. They talked of the Colony as if it had only been a long period during which time the oppressed Peruvian had dragged along his ominous chain. If they thought of the Incas, it was when using a rhetorical figure.[8]

For example, the constitution promulgated by the first Peruvian Constitutional Congress in 1823 (the first of many attempts to write a constitution) was an expression of doctrinaire faith in liberalism (liberal republicans enjoyed a large majority) and hence was largely inapplicable to Peru.[9] It was based on popular sovereignty to the extent that Articles 4 and 5 say: "The Nation does not have the faculty to promulgate laws that negatively affect individual rights. . . ."[10] All the usual guarantees—civil liberties, personal security, freedom of the press, freedom of commerce and industry, and personal freedom (slavery was suppressed)—were included except for religious freedom;[11] the Constitution stated "The Apostolic Roman Catholic Religion is the religion of the state and the practice of any other is excluded."[12] (It should be noted that a third of the Congress delegates were in favour of religious tolerance.) This omission of a guarantee of religious freedom already shows the strength of the conservative forces within the Catholic Church, and gives an early indication of the role this church would play in the future. Instruction was considered in this Constitution to be a common need that the republic owed equally to all its individuals (Article 181),[13] and consequently universities were to be established in the departmental (provincial) capitals as well as elementary (monitorial) schools in the small villages.[14]

It is also noticeable that the leaders of the independence movement in Hispanic America, who sponsored the introduction of the Lancasterian system, were mostly Masons (Jose de San Martin, Bernardo O'Higgins, Bernardo Monteagudo, Simon Bolivar, Vicente Rocafuerte, among many others). Masonic affiliation did not prevent, however, strong political differences as expressed in the polemic between republicans and monarchists (in the last instance between liberals and conservatives). In Peru, the Lautaro Lodge was founded by San Martin in 1821.[15] Its roots were in the Gran Reunion Americana which was founded by Francisco Miranda, who himself had been initiated in the Lodge to which Washington and Franklin had belonged. Miranda originally founded the Gran Reunion Americana in London, with branches in Paris, Madrid, and Cadiz. The Reunion Americana was the place where most of the leaders received "masonic light." The Order did not have specific religious affiliations: universality was the watchword in everything from fraternal love to science, philosophy, and politics; the object of worship was God as the "Great Architect of the Universe," the superior cause of life, and a building, ordering, revolutionary force.[16] In practice, masonic ideals were challenged by the complexities of Latin American reality. New issues as well as internal conflicts were generated along with the formative process of the new national states. The sometimes tortuous process of secularization of the institutions illustrates the variety of approaches and policies carried out by masonic leaders.

James Diego Thomson and the Lancasterian System

The organization in Peru of Lancasterian schools (the first public schools in the country) was characterized by the use of pupil or child monitors, strict discipline, memorization, and Christian but not denominational teaching. This took place under the direction of the Scottish Baptist lay-reader James Diego Thomson, agent of the British and Foreign School Society, who was also working with the British and Foreign Bible Society. It was part of the effort to open up Peru to "progress and civilization", two ideals of the time that went back to the eighteenth century and became related to the universalism that had surpassed the economic sphere—particularly in England, the international industrial leader and hegemonic economic centre—to penetrate the ideological sphere. This universalism had as a point of departure the idea that the international division of labour would provide economic prosperity for the world.

Thomson describes in a number of letters how Jose de San Martin, the Argentinian general who was the Protector of Peru at that time, welcomed him in Lima in 1822. For example, he writes:

> my expectations have been all fulfilled, and more than fulfilled. San Martin is most decidedly a friend to general, to universal education. I hope none of the members of the Committee of the British and Foreign School Society will be offended, but rather gratified, when I say that they are not more friendly to this object than San Martin.[17]

He does not make any reference to San Martin's political stands which had already generated strong opposition among liberal republicans and were manifested in his monarchic proposals and in his understanding that only the educated could exercise political rights. Article 2 of his decree on citizenship said, "Those nationals will be citizens who have a degree or public license in a science or in a liberal art or a profession that provides an annual income of 500 pesos." When he created the Orden del Sol to honour citizens who had been of great service to the country, he created a school exclusively for the children of the members of the Orden. At the same time, however, he sponsored universal education, which included reading, writing, the teaching of the religion recognized by the state, and the learning of a trade.[18] (The class ingredient converged with the project of universal education as it did in contemporary European liberalism of a conservative bent.) Nonetheless, Thomson was not able to realize that two distinct political positions, Peruvian conservatism and Peruvian liberalism—both equally separated from reality—had been already established and would endure for the generations ahead.

From the decree of July 6, 1822, signed by Bernardo Monteagudo and published in the *Lima Gazette* (as reproduced by Thomson in his letter of July 12, 1822), it is learned that the entire public educational system in Peru was to be organized to follow exclusively Lancasterian principles. Article 4 says, "At the expiration of six months all the public schools which are not conducted according to the system of mutual instruction shall be shut [down]."[19] The central or principal school was authorized to begin operating, under Mr. Thomson's direction, at St. Thomas Convent. Formal education had been under the control of the Catholic Church throughout the period of Spanish rule, and had been extremely restricted. Indian children and mestizos could attend parochial schools where they were mainly taught the Roman Catholic catechism.[20] In 1825, when Thomson had already left, General Simon Bolivar, a dominating figure in the fight for independence who had completed the liberating campaign against Spain's counterattack, ordered that the Lancasterian system be extended throughout the Republic and Normal Schools established in the capital of each department.[21] A decree differentiating elementary from secondary schools followed, carrying with it the creation of secondary schools in different parts of the country; the Colegio de Educandas in Cuzco was the first secondary school for girls in Peru and was open to all social classes.[22]

Thomson introduced the Bible as a textbook and emphasized the New Testament. The British and Foreign Bible Society provided the Bibles and New Testaments. Reward and praise for discipline were prominent in Thomson's letters. Teaching had a non-denominational character with a powerful moral dimension. Nevertheless, there was a strong liaison between Thomson and the British Foreign Bible Society:

> Whilst, however, I hold myself forward in the eyes of
> South America a promoter of education and an instructor

of youth, I consider myself in all respects as the servant of the British and Foreign Bible Society.[23]

In 1822, he sold 500 Bibles and 500 New Testaments in Lima with the collaboration of Catholic priests—whom he called liberals.[24] The Bibles were copies of the Catholic version translated into Spanish by Scio de San Miguel, so the clergy working with Thomson could hardly be accused of being heretics.[25] There was, however, strong opposition to Thomson's work by conservative priests.

Thomson's explanation of the way he used the New Testament in the classroom is illuminating:

> Each part of these lessons I cause to be read repeatedly in the classes, until the children can read them readily. By the time they can do so, the substance of what they have read, and the instruction contained in it, is tolerably imprinted on their memory. Children, you know, have a habit of repeating to themselves what they have been saying or reading frequently.[26]

In fact, he firmly believed in the power of the scriptures as much as in education as a means of liberating people from ignorance and facilitating movement towards progress and happiness under the law. Laws and constitutions had in his understanding prime importance in the organization of the state.[27]

While assessing his own experience and reviewing the state and progress of education in South America, Thomson writes in 1826:

> I have no hesitation in saying, that the public voice is decidedly in favour of *Universal Education.* I never heard, even once, what is still to be heard elsewhere, "that the poor should not be taught."[28]

Thomson, acting as the agent of the British and Foreign School Society, was active in expanding the Lancasterian System not only in Peru, but also in Argentina, Chile, Ecuador, and Colombia.[29] (There were also monitorial schools in Mexico and Venezuela.) It is important to notice that the Society in England, as Carl Kaestle writes,

> gained its support from a melange of reform whigs like

Mill, Bentham, and Francis Place, dissenting ministers like Rowland Hill and Quaker philanthropists like William Allen and Joseph Foster.[30]

The ideas of Bentham and Mill and their preoccupation with political reform and extended education, as well as the principles of political economy as expounded by Smith, Ricardo, and Say, were known in a number of Latin American countries. Courses in political economy were created at universities in Brazil in 1808 and in Buenos Aires in 1823.[31] Sergio Bagu notes that the Argentinian Rivadavian group enthusiastically assimilated the reformist passions of Jeremy Bentham.[32] Thomson leaves eloquent mention of these influences when he refers to Bernardino Rivadavia:

> For some years past he has resided in London and Paris; and the time he has spent in these places has been well employed. He has studied and is now practising the soundest principles of political economy. . . . A fine emulation will be carried on, and is already begun between Buenos Aires and Lima.[33]

The economic plan implemented by the Rivadavian group attempted, in Sergio Bagu's words, to create an organic national economy of a capitalist type while departing from a colonial structure.[34] It was a unique experiment in the Latin American context at that time. What had been achieved in Great Britain with great spontaneity, says Bagu, the Rivadavian group attempted to reproduce by means of state initiation, meanwhile thinking that private interest could be motivated to assume the main role.[35] Accordingly, the necessity of providing practical knowledge that could be directly applied to economic planning led both to the preoccupation with specialized education and to the expansion of basic education, the latter based on the monitorial system.[36] Although the Rivadavian group found inspiration in British economists and philosophers, it faced obstacles in its attempt to win over to its plans the network of economic interests delineated by the British Empire.[37] There were no economic projects of this nature in Peru. Thomson's prediction did not come true.

Thomson's ideas, as displayed in his letters, appear to be connected particularly with the utilitarian movement (a version of nineteenth-century English liberalism). From this perspective, education is relevant because the reasonableness of each individual counts in the search for his or her "real" interest and happiness, and education makes people see that "real" interest is bound up with the common interest. These considerations are circumscribed by the political sphere in which legislation had the greatest place in dealing with the harmonization of interests.[38]

Thomson's concern (particularly a missionary one) not only with creoles and mestizos but also with indigenous people, the Quechuas and Aymaras, and even with the inhabitants of the Amazonian region, is to be understood within this ideological context, which was alien to Peruvian historical reality, without disregarding the emphasis given to educational extension by the Protestant Reformation.[39] Evidence of this concern was that while in Peru he was able to effect the translation of the entire New Testament into Quechua and even prepare the Gospel of St. Luke for the press.[40]

His faith in the Bible as a source of inspiration was shared by many liberal Latin American political leaders, some of whom were accustomed to drawing a sharp contrast between Spanish obscurantism and the development of science and industry in Protestant countries.[41] This attitude was also in line with the supportive sympathies expressed by Great Britain—which had already been building its commercial network in the Spanish colonies—towards the independence movement. However, this respect for the Bible and Protestantism in Great Britain and the United States was largely a personal matter and involved great contradictions. Protestant historians overrated the achievements of Thomson's missionary enterprises while underestimating the role of the Roman Catholic Church within the social and political context of the time. A promising interpretation has been advanced by Jean Pierre Bastian who suggests that "the liberals admired Protestantism outside Latin America and, in particular, in the United States, but they were afraid that with its presence in Latin America they would lose their own identity."[42] The question of building nation states became highly complex due to the lack of ideological points of reference rooted in the Latin American reality.

Thomson proudly reproduces an article entitled "Public Education" written anonymously by a Chilean political leader and published in the Chilean *Public Gazette* on August 4, 1821. The role of education in the process of political participation, as the progressive bourgeoisie and utilitarian philosophers, in particular, understood it in England, appears impressive in the following paragraph:

> Ignorance is one of the greatest evils that man can suffer, and it is the principal cause of all his errors and miseries. It is also the grand support of tyranny, and ought, therefore, to be banished by every means from that country which desires a liberty regulated by laws, customs, and opinion. None can be happy unless he study religion, morality, and his own rights, unless he improve the knowledge of those who have preceded him.[43]

Having remained in Peru for more than two years, Thomson left in September of 1824, when Lima and other provinces were again under Spanish occupation. Simon Bolivar, who drove the Spaniards out for the last time, attempted to continue the development of monitorial schools, but he left the country in 1826 in the midst of a political crisis that would continue unresolved until 1845.[44] Monitorial schools legally existed until 1850 when Ramon Castilla signed a new regulation, the Reglamento General de Instruccion Publica.[45] During those long years, between 1826 and 1850, public instruction was characterized by lack of central direction and confusion in the plan of studies, with most elementary teaching being left, due to governmental indifference, under the control of the Catholic Church.[46]

Expectations, hopes, and dreams for formal education and its influence on the building of a new order in Peru clashed with the limitations imposed by the economic, social, and political conditions. The Jacobin egalitarian dreams also had a short life among the leaders of the new republic.

The Peruvian productive centres (mining centres) linked to the international system were already declining or even paralyzed before independence and this, along with the shortage of marketable products and the inconvenience created by distance, particularly for products like sugar, resulted in Peru's commercial isolation. (This situation was quite different from the cases of Argentina and Chile.) Consequently, latifundia developed, strengthened by the liberal legal structure—which was itself mainly inspired by the Napoleonic Code and the Roman Law that broke Indian communal land holdings—and opened the way to political and economic parochialism, while mercantile activities were quickly controlled by foreigners mainly with English associations.[47] Since no class, dominant group, or coalition was able to impose an institutional system at national level that expressed its hegemony, *caudillismo* became the main political form of government, having as its institutional framework a liberal political and legal apparatus.[48] As Basadre put it:

> the war for independence and the wars that followed (1821-1845) generated a social vacuum, which was not the case with other countries like Chile where there was an essential continuity. The revolutions escaped from the hands of the colonial nobility. The military, together with part of an educated middle class belonging to liberal professions, such as lawyers and priests, and with only a fraction of the dominant class, took command of the country in a disorderly fashion.[49]

The Roman Catholic Church, while stressing conservatism, remained the most cohesive institution of the country, a source of power and political legitimation in the midst of the political struggle.

In considering Thomson's ideas and assessments and the fate of monitorial schools in Peru a main issue arises: the idea of a formal universal education that would complement the kind of government described by James Mill (who supported the Lancasterian system) became anachronistic in a *caudillista* political setting based on predominant precapitalist relations of production that did not require innovation. Thomson was not able to understand the Peruvian historical context. There was no similarity here to the situation in which a bourgeoisie or industrial middle class, while assuming the right to represent a proletariat, may nevertheless allow it some say in events. Neither the Peruvian landowners, nor the limited middle class which Basadre mentions, nor the foreigners controlling commerce were in search of social legitimation.

Missionary Efforts in the Late 1800s

During the period of wars and *caudillismo*, and particularly between 1829 and 1845, there was no place for the establishment of Protestantism. The British and Foreign Bible Society found little opportunity for Bible distribution. The American Biblical Society, in spite of sending Bibles and New Testaments, did not extend

formal work to the west coast until 1883,[50] and the establishment
of the Methodist Church was a consequence of this expansion.
However, English penetration was manifested from the early days of
independence in its control of the main financial and mercantile
activities.   The leading commercial houses of London that were
linked to exports were represented in Peru and formed an English
syndicate; while foreign residents were the intermediaries, evident
English influence was exerted over the fragile governments through
its commercial contacts.[51] English business interests became more
prominent in 1841, when the commercialization of guano began,
and later, with the building of railways.   It was natural then that
the first Protestant church in Peru was an Anglican church
founded in 1849 for English speaking people.   It was protected by
the English law of consular chaplaincy, and since the Constitution
did not allow for the public exercise of any religion apart from
that of Roman Catholicism, the community had duly obtained
permission from the President.   The congregation also included a
small group of Americans as well as some German Lutherans.
Later, in 1886, with the support of its communities (foreign
residents), the congregation built both a regular church and an
elementary school registered, in the interest of legality, under the
title of the Anglo-American Society for Primary Instruction and
Debate.   However, this initiative was limited to the city of Lima,
in spite of the existence of important English colonies in Arequipa,
Tacna, Mollendo, Trujillo, and, of course, Callao.[52]

In contrast to the Anglo-American Society, the South
American Missionary Society, founded in London in 1852,
attempted to extend its religious and educational work to
Peruvians, although its primary concern was still to minister to
British subjects living in Peru. (This society has its antecedent in
the Mision Patagonica created by Allen Gardiner in 1844.)   Its
mission began in 1864 in Callao, where there was an English-
speaking community of 1,000 people.   A church and a school for
boys and girls were soon organized.   Reading, arithmetic, English,
the Bible, and Christian morality were taught to eighty pupils,
twenty of whom were Peruvians.   Bible classes were held in
Spanish.   The Roman Catholic Church strongly opposed this new
burst of activity.[53]

Since the missionary effort was initiated in the midst of the
guano boom, it is not surprising that Evangelical activities were

also expanded to the Chincha Islands, where 1,000 Englishmen worked alongside the Peruvians and Chinese.   The Pacific Steam Navigation Company provided the missionaries with a boat to travel between islands.   Work also began in Tacna and Arica, two southern cities where a good number of English merchants had established themselves for commercial purposes.   From the British firm administering the railways the missionaries obtained free fares on the train from Arica to Tacna; the waiting room of the railway station in Arica was used as a chapel.   All of this work was eventually discontinued for many reasons, the most significant of which was the lack of financial means.[54] Even contributions from the English merchants were not a reliable source of income.

The mission organized by William Taylor was an independent effort.   Taylor was an American Methodist Minister but the Methodist Episcopal Missionary Society was not yet ready to open missions on the Pacific coast; the principle he urged was that missions could be developed with all the funds raised in the places where they were established.   This proved to be extremely hard in Peru.   Taylor arrived at Callao in 1877; but as he did not find a helpful social milieu, he decided to go further south to Mollendo, Arica, and Tacna while his brother stayed in Callao. Although he did not find much initial interest on the part of the English merchants, he succeeded in securing help for the establishment of a church and school in Mollendo, a school in Tacna, and a school and church in Iquique.   There was a special endeavor to carry the Gospel to Peruvians.   However, illness, the beginning of the war with Chile in 1879, and unstable economic resources ended this missionary attempt.   The station in Callao, organized in 1879, barely survived until 1887.[55] Beginning in 1884, however, a Presbyterian mission organized a school in Callao and held religious services in both Spanish and English.   The Reverend David Trumbull who had been in South America, mainly Chile, from 1845, insisted before the American Presbyterian Board of Missions upon the need to create a missionary station in Callao. The work was abandoned within two years; again, many promises of financial support did not materialize;[56] also, a number of English-speaking residents moved elsewhere.   Furthermore, the Presbyterian Board refused to assume a permanent financial responsibility, and the number of Peruvians attracted either by Evangelical schools or religious services was still very small.

Early Protestant missions, whether attempting to minister to English-speaking residents or to reach Peruvians, failed to take root in Peru in spite of the substantial English presence. These missions had mostly to rely on local donations since American missionary societies were not yet prepared to intervene. However, both the mission led by William Taylor and the Presbyterian mission established in neighbouring Chile found possibilities of developing permanent religious and educational work among Chileans.[57] (The Presbyterian church for Chileans was well established in the middle 1870s in Santiago and Valparaiso.) A review of the characteristics of the Peruvian economic and social milieu and the special position of the Roman Catholic Church will help to explain the causes for the failure.

Guano was the first great product for exportation that opened Peru to the international market of the nineteenth century. (The "guano age" extends from 1840 to 1880.) Since no group of local landowners and merchants was financially able to undertake its local exploitation and marketing overseas, the guano exploitation fell into foreign hands. The surplus from the commercialization of guano was first used to strengthen the state bureaucracy and to organize the army. But under the administration of Ramon Castilla, in 1850 the law of *consolidacion de la deuda interna* was approved; this law expanded the internal debt by recognizing past claims (i.e., loss of properties during the war of independence, compensation to owners of slaves who were sent to the war, and other claims). The law allowed merchants, landowners, and military men to receive the equivalent of 5,000,000 British pounds.[58] A commercial landowner class then developed economic strength by means of financial speculation in connection with the expansion of the internal debt and later, as consignees of the guano trade with England (1862), and by profiting from the production of sugar and cotton.[59]

The application of new capital to the guano business did not have a significant impact on the Peruvian economy; instead it allowed the creation of a parasite, rentier class.[60] The guano trade, particularly with England, allowed for the accumulation of large fortunes. Yet, guano businessmen were not able to transform the Peruvian economy, destroy its colonial basis and finance the economic development of Peru.[61] Instead they were concerned with speculation and partial investments in coastal plantations (in response to a favourable market situation), becoming financiers, and being submissive to the international market.[62] The actual attempt to change direction did not appear until 1871.

The guano merchants had not been equipped with a political infrastructure, although they were politically influential on the military statesmen.   This lack of political structures facilitated the access to power of Colonel Jose Balta (1868-1871) and Nicolas de Pierola, who became the Minister of Hacienda; under this administration, the guano trade with Europe was taken away from the national consignees[63] and, paradoxically, the major railways began to be constructed.   This project had been proposed by an articulated sector of the commercial-landowner class concerned with the economic future, in particular by the modernizing elite involved in guano trade.[64] In 1871, that elite created the Civil Party (civil as opposed to military statesmanship) in order to build a political organization at a national level that would allow direct control of the state and consolidate the economic power of the commercial-landowner class on a durable basis.[65]

The Civil Party, the first organized political party in Peru, took power in 1872 and tried to carry out a modernizing project, a project that Anibal Quijano characterized as ambivalent, simultaneously national and pro-imperialist.[66] However, as Yepes del Castillo asserted, it was too late.[67] The imbalance of payments generated by importations consumed the guano income, the guano trade was in foreign hands (Dreyfus and Co.), and sugar and cotton prices drastically fell in the international market. As a result, the government had to suspend payment of the public debt in 1876.   The war with Chile in 1879 put an end to the *Civilista* projects, and its outcome—the defeat of Peru and the loss of important economic resources—was, in the opinion of some authors, a consequence of its economic vulnerability as well as its political disarticulation.   In this historical context, and in particular in the failure of the guano capitalists to transform Peru, a tentative explanation is found for the limited ideological and institutional space for Protestant religious proselytizing and the expansion of Protestant educational work.   This interpretation is reinforced by the evidence that during the second half of the nineteenth century the Chilean economy had begun to work out its transition from mercantilism to capitalism while its landowners, businessmen, and mine owners constituted an integrated national class, articulated in a consolidated state.[68] Protestant missions continued in Chile without interruption, in spite of some difficulties derived from local support, even during the war with Peru (1879-1884). They found the essential social support, notwithstanding the opposition of the Roman Catholic Church.

In Peru, within the framework given by a strong seigniorial mentality, the Roman Catholic Church had the institutional power to exert profound influence on the ideas and attitudes of all social classes, particularly through education and by means of religious sanctions linked to daily life. It was the centre of the social order. Ramon Castilla (1845-1851 and 1855-1862) was not successful in his attempt to undermine the influence that the Roman Catholic Church had on education;[69] and the Church, in alliance with landowners, opposed Manuel Pardo (1872-1876) in his proposal for educational changes as being too practical and too liberal, in spite of the inclusion of religion in the primary school curriculum.[70] In practice, primary education remained under the control of the Church-dominated municipalities.

The permanence of the colonial character of Peruvian society—in the context of an economy that did not allow for relevant changes in the relations of production—also left little space for extensive ideological developments, specific to the process of cohesion and self-identification of a social class, a class fraction, or a social movement within the society. There was little inducement for the expectations created by such different doctrines as traditional Protestantism or by Protestant schools. In addition, strong feelings against foreign merchants who controlled commercial activities in the cities grew among the popular classes as they became steadily more impoverished during the second half of the nineteenth century, creating one more obstacle for the missionaries.[71] Missionary enterprises required a measure of spontaneous popular support, and also local financial subvention, in order to have any degree of success.

References

[1]The Viceroyalty of Peru was organized in the sixteenth century, becoming an important colonial centre as a consequence of the mining exploitation.

[2]Reference is made here to the singular content the Roman Catholic Christian faith acquired as a consequence of the way Peruvian people experience their faith in their daily lives as well as to the cultural characteristics that the different ethnic groups introduced into religious practices.

[3]Jeffrey L. Klaiber, S. J., *Religion and Revolution in Peru 1824-1976* (Indiana: University of Notre Dame Press, 1977), p. 2.

[4]Luis E. Valcarcel, *La Ruta Cultural del Peru* (Mexico: Fondo de Cultura Economica, 1945), p. 165.

[5]"The predominance of Scholasticism lasted until the eighteenth century.   Then, America began to feel the impact of ideas and currents that were contrary to scholasticism and very representative of the new direction European thought took beginning with the Renaissance.   This was due in part to internal factors, such as the liberalizing policy of the ministers of Charles III and the work of writers of a reform spirit, like Father Feijoo. It was also due to such factors as travelers and scientific expeditions that were operating within the territories under Spanish domination."   Augusto Salazar Bondy, *Sentido y Problema del Pensamiento Filosofico Hispanoamericano*, with English translation, Occasional Publication No. 16 (Lawrence: Center of Latin American Studies, University of Kansas, 1969), p. 2.

[6]"At the same time, educational and cultural institutions were renovated in those cities that served as viceregal or seats of the 'audiencia'; the so-called Caroline Colleges and the 'Friends of the   Country'   societies   appeared;   and   cultural   reviews   of unquestionable value were published.   An awakening of critical awareness and a first hint of national and American consciousness are   perceptible   in   this   period.   This   cultural   atmosphere   is equivalent, at least superficially, to what is known in Europe as the period of the Enlightenment.   And the doctrinal link is clear, for the enlightened Hispanic American ideology is nothing other than the transplantation of the philosophy of the European, especially the French Enlightenment." Ibid., p. 3.

[7]"The type of state that arises with the Republic is the one called   the   'liberal state'.   Its   fundamental   characteristics   were:

popular sovereignty regulated by a Constitution, division of powers, an elected Executive and Legislature, and Executive very limited in its action, a tendency toward a passive type of government, zeal in guaranteeing the individual face of the state as much in the political sense by the individual guarantees as in the economic sense by inhibiting the action of the state with reference to social and economic relations." Jorge Basadre, *La Multitud, la Ciudad y el Campo* (Lima: Editorial Huascaran, 1947), p. 156, cited by Ernesto Yepes del Castillo, *Peru 1820-1920. Un siglo de Desarrollo Capitalista* (Lima: Instituto de Estudios Peruanos, 1971), pp. 39-40.

[8]Jorge Basadre, *Historia de la Republica del Peru*, 2 Vols. (3rd edition, Lima: Editorial Cultura Antartica, 1946), Vol. 1, p. 13.

[9]There were five constitutions from 1823 to 1838, three of them were liberal (1823, 1828, and 1834) and two authoritarian (1826 and 1836). The liberal constitutions were the product of Constituent Assemblies. In 1839, there was another constitution, *La Constitucion de Huancayo*; in 1856 and 1860 there were new constitutions. In all of them, with the exception of the Constitution for the Confederation with Bolivia (1836) which does not mention religion, Roman Catholicism was considered the religion of the state. Ibid., pp. 154-155. Francis Stanger, "La Iglesia y el Estado en el Peru Independiente" (Doctoral dissertation, Facultad de Filosofia, Historia y Letras, Universidad Mayor Nacional de San Marcos, Lima, 1925), Cuadro de la Evolucion Religiosa de las Constituciones del Peru, no page number.

[10]As Jorge Basadre points out, it should say State instead of Nation. Jorge Basadre, *Historia*, Vol. 1, p. 30.

[11]Ibid.

[12]Francis Stanger, "La Iglesia y el Estado," *Cuadro de la Evolucion*, no page number.

[13]The term individual, instead of citizens, is in line with the requirement stated in the Constitution that in order to be a citizen it was necessary to read and write. However, it was stated that the requirement would not be enforced until 1840, given the high level of illiteracy in the country.

[14]Jorge Basadre, *Historia*, Vol. 1, p. 30.

[15]The Lautaro Lodge participated from 1821 onwards in the

independence movement in Peru; it worked for the consolidation of the Republican form against San Martin's project of establishing a monarchy; it opposed the imperial form of Bolivar and defended the Republic.   (Notice that the order reacted against policies carried out by some of its own members.)   A.L.G.D.U., *Liminar de los Anales Masonicos de la RESP . log . SIMB . Concordia Universal No. 14 Apuntes Sinopticos al Conmemorar Cien Anos de su Fundacion* (Callao, Peru: Talleres Graficos Quiros, 1949), p. 47.

[16]Ramon Martinez Zaldua, *Historia de la Masoneria en Hispano-America.   Es o no una Religion la Masoneria?* (2nd edition, Mexico: Costa Amic, 1967), p. 11 and p. 117.

[17]Letter of James Diego Thomson dated Lima, Peru, July 12, 1822, in his *Letters on the Moral and Religious State of South-America, Written during a Residence of Seven Years in Buenos Aires, Chile, Peru and Colombia* (London: James Nisbet, 1827), p. 38.

[18]Roberto MacLean y Estenos, *Sociologia Educacional del Peru* (Lima: Imprenta Gil, 1944), pp. 134-135.

[19]Letter of James Diego Thomson, dated Lima, July 12, 1822, in his *Letters on the Moral*, pp. 39-43.   The *Gaceta* of Lima refers to *Gaceta del Gobierno.*

[20]Cameron D. Ebaugh, *Education in Peru* (Washington: U. S. Office of Education, Bulletin 1946, No 3), p. 3.

[21]General San Martin resigned in September 1822 and left Peru.   Thus, he opened the way to his political counterpart, General Simon Bolivar.   The Congress, faced by a Spanish threat and a chaotic political situation, delegated the executive power to a triumvirate (governing junta).

[22]Cameron D. Ebaugh, *Education*, p. 4.

[23]Letter of James Diego Thomson, dated Santiago de Chile, October 8, 1821, in his *Letters on the Moral*, p. 15.

[24]Letter of James Diego Thomson, dated Lima, December 2, 1822, in his *Letters on the Moral*, pp. 66-67.

[25]Wenceslao O. Bahamonde, "The Establishment of Evangelical Christianity in Peru 1822-1900" (unpublished Doctoral dissertation, Hartford Seminary, 1952), p. 29.

[26]Letter of James Diego Thomson, dated Lima, March 1, 1824, in his *Letters on the Moral*, p. 111. "These portions were recited in schools, and premiums were awarded according to the accuracy of the recitation, and the clearness of the views which the children gave in their own language, of what they had recited." Letter of James Diego Thomson addressed to the Committee of the British and Foreign School Society, dated London, May 25, 1826, in his *Letters on the Moral*, p. 282.

[27]Letter of James Diego Thomson dated in Lima, December 1, 1823, in his *Letters on the Moral*, p. 108.

[28]Letter of James Diego Thomson addressed to the Committee of The British and Foreign School Society, dated London, May 25, 1826, in his *Letters on the Moral*, p. 291.

[29]"In 1807 a small group of philanthropists had rallied around Lancaster to extricate him from the considerable debts he had accumulated and to promote his system of education. In 1811 this organization took the name The Royal Lancasterian Institute and solicited public subscriptions. In 1813 it became the *British and Foreign School Society*, the name it retained into the twentieth century." Carl F. Kaestle, *Joseph Lancaster and the Monitorial School Movement* (New York and London: Teacher College Press, Columbia University, 1973), pp. 19-20. James Thomson does not differentiate Ecuador from Colombia since Ecuador became an independent state in 1830 when the Southern Provinces of Colombia declared themselves independent. What is today the Republica Argentina constituted the core of the Provincias Unidas del Rio de la Plata. Buenos Aires was the political and economic centre.

[30]Ibid., p. 21-22. The emphasis is mine.

[31]Bagu, Sergio, *El Plan Economico del Grupo Rivadaviano 1811-1827. Su Sentido y Sus Contradicciones, Sus Proyecciones Sociales, Sus Enemigos*, (Rosario, Argentina: Instituto de Investigaciones Historicas, 1966), pp. 20-21.

[32]Ibid., p.20.

[33]Letter of James Diego Thomson dated Santiago de Chile, May 9, 1822, in his *Letters on the Moral*, p. 31.

[34]Sergio Bagu, *El Plan Economico*, p. 107.

[35]Ibid., pp. 107-108.

[36]Ibid., pp. 34-35.   "Mutual instruction, which today draws so much interest in the most cultured peoples of the world, has been improved and spread much more than could have been expected in the midst of the great conflicts that have incessantly surrounded the government.   A considerable number of primary schools for the education of children of both sexes have increased from those that existed before in the city and in the country." *Respuesta a la Circular del Poder Ejecutivo de la Provincia de Buenos Aires de 20 de Agosto de 1827 y al Mensaje del mismo de 14 de Setiembre de 1827*, Item 4, September 24, 1827, in Sergio Bagu, *El Plan Economico*, Seccion Documental, No. 163, p. 247.

[37]Sergio Bagu, *El Plan Economico*, pp. 108-109.

[38]"With   James   Mill,   as   with   Bentham,   we   find   a combination of laissez-faire economics with a reiterated demand for political reform.   As every man naturally seeks his own interest, it is not surprising that the executive does so.   The executive, therefore, must be controlled by the legislature.   But the House of Commons is itself the organ of the interests of a comparatively small number of families.   And its interest can not be made identical with that of the community in general unless the suffrage is extended and elections are frequent.   Like other Benthamites, Mill also had a somewhat simple faith in the power of education to make men see that their 'real' interests are bound up with the common interest.   Hence political reform and extended education should go hand in hand."   Frederick Copleston, S. J., *A History of Philosophy*, Vol. VIII, *Modern Philosophy. Bentham to Russell*, (New York: Image Books, 1965), Part I, p. 35.

[39]Letter of James Diego Thomson dated in Lima, November 25, 1823, in his *Letters on the Moral*, pp. 101-103.

[40]Letter of James Diego Thomson dated in Guayaquil, October 5, 1823, in his *Letters on the Moral*, p. 165.

[41]James Thomson acknowledges these feelings.   He also reproduces a report of Mr. Rocafuerte, Charge d'Affaires in England from the Government of Mexico, delivered in a speech at the Twenty-first Annual Meeting of the British and Foreign School Society, May 15, 1826.   James Diego Thomson, *Letters on the Moral*, p. 292.
    Vincente Rocafuerte was born in Guayaquil, Ecuador.   He had an outstanding diplomatic background, including his position in the Mexican government before becoming the president of the Republic of Ecuador in 1835 until 1839.

[42]Jean Pierre Bastian, *Breve Historia del Protestantismo en America Latina* (Mexico: CUPSA, 1986), p. 95.

[43]Letter of James Diego Thomson, dated Santiago de Chile, August 6, 1821, in his *Letters on the Moral*, p. 9.

[44]"Factors other than the opposition of liberally-inclined intellectuals contributed to Bolivar's failure as Peru's chief executive.   His approval of the creation of Bolivia as a separate republic within an envisioned Confederation irritated many Peruvians who felt they were deprived of territory that was rightly theirs.   Moreover, Bolivar was a foreigner who had a low regard for Peruvians in general and tended to surround himself with other foreigners as advisers.   A rising desire among Peruvians for self-government clashed with Bolivar's attempt to rule through a bureaucracy whose senior members were mainly Colombians and Venezuelans and with his dream of an Hispanic-American Confederation."   (Bolivar decided to leave Peru.)   Frederick B. Pike, *The Modern History of Peru* (New York-Washington: Praeger, 1967), p. 63.   Pike downplays—as most North American historians do—Bolivar's vision of the relevance of achieving a degree of unity among former colonies and his early awareness of the danger posed by the United States.

[45]Cameron D. Ebaugh, *Education*, p. 5.

[46]Roberto MacLean y Estenos, *Sociologia Educacional*, pp. 196-203.

[47]Ernesto Yepes del Castillo, *Peru 1820-1920*, pp. 39-41.

[48]Ibid., p. 42.

[49]Jorge Basadre, *Historia de la Republica del Peru*, Vol. X (Lima: Ediciones Historia, 1964), Chapter CXCVIII, p. 4729.

[50]Wenceslao O. Bahamonde, "The Establishment of Evangelical Christianity," pp. 52-58.

[51]Ernesto Yepes del Castillo, *Peru 1820-1920*, pp. 45-46.

[52]Wenceslao O. Bahamonde, "The Establishment of Evangelical Christianity," pp. 58-61.

[53]Ibid., pp. 61-66.

[54]Ibid., pp. 72-73.

[55]Ibid., pp. 80-84.   Goodsil F. Arms, *El Origen del Metodismo y su Implantacion en la Costa Occidental de Sud-America* (Santiago de Chile: Imprenta Universitaria, 1923), pp. 20-21.

[56]Wenceslao O. Bahamonde, "The Establishment of Evangelical Christianity," pp. 85-88.

[57]Goodsil F. Arms, *El Origen del Metodismo y su Implantacion*, Part II, pp. 20-68.   Reginald W. Wheeler, Robert Gardner McGregor, et al. (members of a commission appointed to visit Chile and Brazil by the Board of Foreign Missions of the Presbyterian Church in the U. S.), *Modern Missions in Chile and Brazil* (Philadelphia: The Westminister Press, 1926), Chapter XIII.

[58]Heraclio Bonilla, *Guano y Burguesia en el Peru* (Lima: Instituto de Estudios Peruanos, 1974), pp. 23-39.

[59]Ibid., p. 50.

[60]Ibid., p. 33.

[61]H. Bonilla writes that the national merchants who replaced foreign firms in the commercialization of guano could not be considered a bourgeoisie and even less a national bourgeoisie. National consignees were devoted to speculative commerce and when they applied part of their capital to agriculture (cotton and sugar) they became a rentier class.   These merchants were highly dependent on the international market.   Also, their economic strength was not great enough to avoid the London economic market and hence they had to resort to the English House, Thompson Bonar, which became a powerful ally.   Ibid., pp. 44-45.

[62]The economic development of Peru existed as a historical possibility, but did not in fact occur.   The internal accumulation of finance capital was not transformed into industrial capital.
    Guano capitalists established the first domestic financial houses: between 1862 and 1869 five banks were opened; commercial and financial capital merged.   The banks did not provide a source of funds for Peruvian industrialization; they were not conceived of as means but as ends in themselves.   Bonilla finds the reasons for the unproductive investment of capital in the peculiar Peruvian economic, social, and political structure.   In fact, economic growth would have required considerable modifications in the prevailing colonial structure.   Also, speculative investments were stimulated by the large government deficit and high interest rates. Large amounts of money were lent to the state, and further sums

were devoted to the importation of luxury goods.

However, the new capitalists invested money in coastal plantations of sugar and cotton; this was a response to the rise of prices of those commodities during the American Civil War and the Cuban political crisis.   Bonilla says, "It is easy to understand the instability of that kind of development in which the internal production is subjected to the fluctuations of the international market."   Ibid., pp. 49-50.

[63]In 1868, when Pierola became Minister of Hacienda, the financial situation was disastrous.   The external debt reached Soles 45'000,000 and the budget had a deficit of Soles 17'000,000. Abuses by guano merchants, the external deficit and popular discontent were justifications offered for removing the guano *consignment* from national businessmen.   Balta and Pierola did not have links with the guano business.   Ibid., pp. 69 and 72.

[64]Enlightened members of the commercial-landowner class, conscious of wasteful public expenditure, began to think about the productive utilization of guano profits.   This concern was the first step toward the harmonization of the economic and political interest of those constituting this class.   This class had acquired economic power by the law that expanded the internal debt in 1850, and had further established itself by participating in the financial operations of consolidation and conversion under Echenique (1851-1854).   Although a fraction of this class had begun to participate directly in the guano business from 1862 onwards, making huge fortunes, a modernizing group considered that the state should use the guano surplus to set the basis for further development.

The main political and economic ideas of the modernizing elite (basically integrated by guano businessmen) were published in *La Revista de Lima* from 1859.   Manuel Pardo, who would be the first Civilista president in 1872, was a main contributor.   The proposals included the need to diversify the economy, augment production of export goods other than guano, increase commerce, protect Peruvian industry, and attract foreign capital.   The building of railways was considered fundamental.   Ibid., pp. 53-65.

[65]Order was a fundamental aim of the Civil Party and representative democracy was the slogan which served to manipulate urban masses, to limit military intrusion and to secure the government for the dominant group.   Ernesto Yepes del Castillo, *Peru 1820-1920*, p. 105.

[66]Anibal Quijano Obregon, "Imperialismo, Clases Sociales y Estado en el Peru: 1895-1930", in Raul Benitez Zenteno

(Coordinador Seminario de Oaxaca), *Clases Sociales y Crisis Politica en America Latina* (Mexico: Siglo XXI, 1977), p. 128.

[67]Ernesto Yepes del Castillo, *Peru 1820-1920*, p. 107.

[68]Anibal Quijano Obregon, "Imperialismo, Clases Sociales y Estado," pp. 113-150. (It includes a comparative analysis of Chile and Peru; see pp. 125-131.)

[69]Ramon Castilla tried to build the structure of institutionalized power; order was the major concern to secure continuity of the guano business. He promoted important educational changes in 1850 and 1855; in particular he attempted to distinguish between public and private education and tried to develop vocational training. His goal was national integration. Ernesto Yepes del Castillo, *Peru 1820-1920*, pp. 95-96; Roberto MacLean y Estenos, *Sociologia Educacional*, pp. 208-215, 222-227.

[70]Manuel Pardo, the *Civilista* president, included popular instruction, decentralization, fiscal equilibrium, and the reorganization of the army in the program he read before the Congress in 1872. The creation of Normal Schools, the Faculty of Political and Administrative Sciences at San Marcos National University, and the School of Engineers (there was also an incipient attempt at industrialization) indicated changes in the approach to education. Anibal Quijano Obregon, "Imperialismo, Clases Sociales y Estado," pp. 128-129; Ernesto Yepes del Castillo, *Peru 1820-1920*, p. 184.

[71]Ernesto Yepes del Castillo, *Peru 1820-1920*, Chapter II, particularly pp. 60-63.

CHAPTER II

The Establishment of the
Methodist Episcopal Church

Socio-Economic and Political Conditions, Late Nineteenth/Early Twentieth Centuries

The first steps towards the establishment of Protestantism on a permanent basis in Peru were made after the war with Chile by the American Biblical Society in Buenos Aires, which had become interested in working in the countries situated on the northwestern coast of South America. The result was the foundation in 1889 of the Methodist Episcopal Church in Peru, a Spanish-speaking church for Peruvians, by an agent of the Society, and the organization of the American Methodist Episcopal Mission in 1891. In the latter year the first Methodist school opened its doors.[1]

The establishment of the Methodist Church in Peru touched off a struggle, particularly bitter between 1889 and 1891, over religious freedom. Peru was at the time recuperating after the war with Chile; a brief examination of political and economic conditions of the time illustrates the difficulties and opportunities of Protestantism.

The years between 1884, when the war ended, and the revolution of 1895 were spanned by the so-called "second militarism" which, in the midst of chaos, took charge of reconstruction. During the war the guano-based economy had collapsed, affecting all productive sectors, and the *latifundistas* had extended their concentration of power by taking over burned *haciendas*. Hence, landowners became the dominant political force, with predictable consequences: strong political and economic parochialism and a weak state.[2] However, this period was a transitional one, not only because of internal discontent, especially among merchants and industrialists (both agglutinated in the Democrata party), but also because of changes in Peruvian economic relations with international centres of power which brought on heavy repercussions in the productive base. In fact, while Great Britain increased its domination by direct investments, other European countries and the United States, in particular, bought their way into Peru. While the Peruvian political scene was still offering a debate between *caudillos*, foreign capital progressively took over the main productive resources of the country (coastal plantations, mines, railroads, export trade, textile industry). Local producers were left with production for local markets and secondary exports.[3]

The revolution of 1895 brought about necessary institutional changes, in particular the creation of a coherent state apparatus, and also provided a basis for ideological re-accommodation. At economic levels, the revolution opened the doors to foreign capital even wider; at political levels, it allowed for the progressive organization of the Civilista hegemony. This second Civilismo was, in Yepes del Castillo's words, the political expression of the export model of insertion in the new international system; the Civilista aristocratic elite acted as a political intermediary between the Peruvian people and the representatives of foreign capital, and, of course, reaped an economic reward.[4]

During the war, the bankruptcy of the banking circuit, which had been nourished by the guano economy, dragged down the coastal plantations, which had now lost their sources of capital. A great number of plantations were taken over by foreigners: English, German, and Italian immigrants (like Larco), and companies like Grace. All of these invested large sums in the organization of the haciendas and introduced modern practices, with security provided by foreign capital. Three groups emerged with the most power: Grace (Cartavio Sugar Company), Gildemeister (Sociedad Agricola CasaGrande Ltda), and Larco (Hacienda Roma).[5]

The social consequences of these changes were felt most immediately by large and small proprietors who had lost their land to big agro-industrial business, but also by urban merchants who had to compete with foreign firms that were also involved in retail trade. (Peter Klaren examines this period of social displacement closely in his analysis of the origins of the American Popular Revolutionary Alliance (APRA) and its anti-imperialist content.[6]) At the same time, there emerged a proletariat linked to agro-industrial activities. This proletariat was mainly composed of dispossessed Indian peasants who lost their lands as a consequence of the expansion of the foreign companies.

Investments of an imperialist[7] and capitalist nature were concentrated in primary production, in the form of economic enclaves,[8] and were meagre in industrial production. Agriculture (as we have already seen), mining, petroleum, railways, and textiles were the main activities to which investments were applied. Between 1890 and 1920, the main capitalist investments were established under the control of four large corporations: Cerro de Pasco Copper Corporation, Grace and Company, International Petroleum Corporation, and Peruvian Corporation (the first three were American; the last, British); along with these there were other lesser companies, like Duncan Fox and Co. (British).[9] The famous Contrato Grace, signed in 1889, had set the scene for a large increase in foreign investments and tied the economy first to England and later to the United States.[10] As a consequence of these developments, there grew up a proletariat formed by those working in the extractive export centres (mining, petroleum, and, as previously mentioned, agro-industrial). However, pre-capitalist forms of production continued; not only did landowners, most notably in the Sierra, continue to exploit great masses of peasants under semi-servile and semi-feudal conditions, but the imperialist companies also profited from pre-capitalist forms of production.

Subsidiary economic activities particularly linked to foreign investment fostered a proliferation of banks, insurance companies, financial and commercial offices, transportation services, and other such businesses, while public administration also became more complex. However, local small- and middle-size businesses providing services found limitations to their growth, not only because of the character of the investments, which favoured the establishment of economic enclaves,[11] but also because of direct foreign competition. In fact, at the end of the century the import houses had begun to sell on a retail basis and European outlets had opened in Lima that competed with existing small business, and particularly with shopkeepers.[12] Meanwhile, a symbiosis of interests was taking place between foreign businessmen and their Peruvian intermediaries and associates; the Lima Chamber of Commerce, founded in 1888, was a practical expression of that symbiosis and a useful means of exerting influence on governmental decisions.[13]

The development of the Peruvian manufacturing industry was very slow; investment in this sector of the economy was scarce and a system of free trade and free enterprise—an orthodox liberal economy in Baltazar Caravedo's terms—did not favour local enterprises. However, the textile industry was very important and was sustained by foreign capital. The most important companies were Vitarte Cotton Mill and Inca Cotton Mill (owned by Grace), El Progreso and La Union (owned by Duncan Fox), and La Victoria (owned by the Prado family). The food processing industry and the perishable goods industry also had room to grow, and many immigrants, especially Italians, were active in it. Thus, by the end of the century there was a noticeable industrial proletariat, especially in Lima, Callao, Vitarte, Arequipa, and Trujillo.[14]

The Civil Party came to power in 1904 (in fact it had been an important political force since the revolution of 1895). The Civilistas, who found ideological support in the positivist ideas of the time, saw social order as a necessary condition for the development of capitalist economic institutions within the context of a system of free trade and free enterprise. (The economic model emphasized exportation.[15]) Thus, the laws regulating commerce, mining, banks, and agriculture were reformed;[16] the new regulations made it even easier for foreign capital to own or control the main products of exportation. The Civilistas themselves had important ties with English capital because of their banking associations and their economic base in the agro-exporting sector. The surplus that remained in the country was shared by a small group connected to the export business, while manufacturers, the middle class, artisans, and proletarians suffered economically from the limitations of the liberal economic policy.[17]

The above describes the basic matrix of the Peruvian socio-economic formation[18] as encountered by missionaries when they began their religious and educational activities towards the end of the century. This matrix can be characterized by its uneven and combined character; in spite of capitalist dominance, pre-capitalist forms of production (as well as pre-capitalist social institutions) continued, in a degenerating way, and combined with capitalist forms (for example, the practice of enganche in the mining centres).[19] The structure of the state has been conceptualized by Anibal Quijano as hybrid, containing contradictory but nevertheless complementary components; at once bourgeois and seigniorial, it contrived to articulate the various interests, whether capitalist or pre-capitalist, of the dominant classes.[20] The Roman Catholic Church, always an ally of the landowners, played an important political role because of its long-term identification with the

Peruvian state and its influence on social life and popular opinion. The Civil Party would be able to control the state and act as a political mediator between foreign capitalists and the Peruvian people until a revision of the economic model and a political re-accommodation became urgent.

The characteristics of the Peruvian socio-economic formation analyzed here help to explain the sometimes conflict-ridden relations between the Methodist Mission and the representatives of the state apparatus and the attraction that Methodist schools, with their emphasis on the teaching of English and commercial subjects, had for many Peruvian middle-class parents.

The Foundation of the Methodist Church and Mission

The American Biblical Society asked Francisco Penzotti—who had already been in Peru—to establish an agency there and expand the work to Ecuador, Bolivia, and Chile. However, when he came to Callao in July 1888, he initiated a new attempt at evangelization; he preached in Spanish to Peruvians, organized classes for teaching the Bible, and set up a small church which was the first Evangelical congregation organized in Peru for Spanish-speaking people.[21] Catholic authorities immediately began harassment to such an extent that the nascent congregation was prevented from using the chapel (originally built by the South American Missionary Society with the help of the English community, and lent to Penzotti by its trustees). Catholic priests, alarmed by the attendance, threatened to dynamite the building and the Methodists were asked to vacate it.[22] An old warehouse was then restored by the members of the congregation and on August 31, 1889, they celebrated the first preaching service at the new location; it was a private service and invitations brought together more than 170 people.[23] The Methodist Church in Peru was officially organized as a branch of the American Methodist Episcopal Church (North) by the Superintendent of the Mission of the Methodist Episcopal Church in South America early in 1890, and was part of the South American Conference of Buenos Aires, Argentina, until 1900.[24] The mission in Peru was organized in 1891.

The Catholic Church now used its power and political influence to induce the civil authorities to take action against Penzotti. The Church also organized a campaign throughout its own press, accusing Protestants of being foreign agents and

distributing pernicious literature.   In January 1889, when Penzotti
went to Arequipa to sell Bibles, the local Bishop accused him of
introducing immoral books, and personally ordered that he (along
with two Peruvian associates) be arrested.   He remained in jail,
without a charge being laid, for ninety days, but was treated well
by the prison authorities.   The three were then released, thanks to
the efforts of the Italian Ambassador and pressure on the President
of Peru by powerful liberals supporting Penzotti; no trial resulted.[25]
Having returned to Callao, Penzotti was still pursued by the
Church, and at its instigation, a Callao judge ordered his second
imprisonment.   Penzotti was placed on July 26, 1890, in Casas
Matas, the old fort Real Felipe in Callao. In spite of the fact that
Penzotti had organized private services in agreement with the
Constitution, he was accused of leading religious services other than
the Catholic service and of conducting baptism and marriages.[26]

Penzotti's treatment aroused considerable anger in the United
States, since he was an official representative of the American
Methodist Episcopal Church, and a letter that he wrote while in
jail was published in the *New York Herald*.   The American Biblical
Society appealed directly to the Secretary of State and asked for
his intervention, whereupon he instructed the American consul in
Lima to proceed unofficially to do everything possible to gain
Penzotti's freedom.   Meanwhile, the British and American
consulates in Lima were being flooded with letters of outrage.[27]

In Peru itself the case aroused considerable public argument
and sharply divided the press.   The emergent Civilistas saw this
evidence of the lack of religious freedom as threatening
modernization and discouraging potential immigrants.[28]   (The
proportion of foreign-born was already high in Lima and Callao.)
Penzotti's congregation was constituted, however, by Peruvians, a
number of them artisans. Still, the extent of the disagreement
between the Church and the civil authorities was now rapidly
becoming apparent and reflected the transitional political character
of the period.   Penzotti was found innocent by three different
courts; the Church, stubbornly fighting a rearguard action, appealed
the verdict on each occasion; but his congregation continued to
meet without further trouble under the guidance of the first
converts, Illescas, Noriega, and others.   Penzotti was also treated
with great consideration by the governor of his prison.[29]

The Peruvian masonic lodges not only used their publications to defend religious freedom but went further, providing the two lawyers who assumed responsibility for Penzotti's defense.[30] The lodges were strongly influenced by the new political and economic interests working in Peru, and one finds on their membership lists the names of W. R. Grace, Civilistas like Alejandro Deustua, and a number of Italian immigrants.[31] One of their important goals was in fact religious freedom, which they hoped to achieve by presenting to Parliament a petition to reform Article 4 of the Constitution, as it was stated in *La Revista Masonica de Peru.*[32] Penzotti gained his freedom on March 28, 1891, when the Supreme Court finally judged that he had not violated the law. The decision meant that "private" worship and the distribution of Bibles could be carried on in Peru without risk of arrest. Religious freedom had been granted *de facto* if not *de jure* (the divisive issue of constitutional change was avoided). Penzotti, having won his victory, returned to Buenos Aires. He was to become a "paladin of freedom" for Protestants in Peru. The Missionary Society of the Methodist Episcopal Church (North) continued his work; it organized the Methodist Episcopal Mission, and established the general headquarters in Lima. Dr. Thomas B. Wood, an American missionary and an eminent Mason, came to Peru from Argentina where he had been directing the theological seminar he had founded in 1889.[33] From this point on, the creation of schools and the struggle for civil rights were the central issues in Methodist work. The Laws of Civil Marriage of December 23, 1897, and November 23, 1903, were important achievements for Methodists.[34]

Protestantism's Place in the Late Eighteenth-Century Ideological and Intellectual Structure

A quotation from a great Peruvian thinker, Augusto Salazar Bondy, describes the social atmosphere during the last fifteen years of the nineteenth century.

> A collective psychology, stained with disenchantment and bitterness, and at the same time, wishful for new reasons for hoping is the yeast of the project of national life that begins to stir up in those years the efforts of the Peruvian community. In this process, philosophical thought is inserted as a singular expression of the crisis and also as a new weapon with which the leading groups of the country

seek to approach the crisis.[35]

The psychological and intellectual milieu described above is vitally expressed by Manuel Gonzalez Prada in his writings; he was a severe social critic during the period of reconstruction and was described as "the social consciousness of Peru."[36] His views followed a tangled path from radical and anti-Catholic social protest, while under positivist influence, to anarchism. They influenced a later generation of progressive intellectuals, and also later political movements (the APRA leaders considered Prada an intellectual mentor).[37]

The University of San Marcos meanwhile became the disseminating centre for new intellectual perspectives, and especially for positivism. At the end of the century, Prado, Cornejo, Capelo, Villaran, and Manzanilla—all members of the Civil Party—were among the intellectuals who spread the notions of scientific method, order, and progress. As Salazar Bondy writes:

> In the final decades of the century, the tendency of the Hispanic American intelligentsia was to turn towards another doctrine, or complex of doctrines, formed by the Positivism of August Comte in France, and various other contemporary currents of thought, such as Naturalism, Materialism, Experimentalism and Evolutionism. . . . In this period, the popularity of Comte was equalled if not exceeded by that of Spencer. Through his teachings, evolution was imposed as a universal explanatory principle, applied to realms of both physical nature and society. In the latter case, it was used equally to justify the predominance of the bourgeoisie and the claims of the proletariat. Nevertheless, Positivism was fundamentally a philosophical doctrine adopted by the upper classes of Hispanic America in the period of establishment and consolidation of international capitalism in our countries.[38]

The last sentence applies with force to positivism in Peru.

It should be added that Peruvian positivists, who favoured the building of a capitalist society in Peru, were admirers of Protestantism and praised especially its ethical judgments. This positive assessment may be partially explained from the peculiarities of positivism as elaborated in Peru (having there a broader meaning than in Europe).[39] Carlos Lisson, dean of the Faculty of

Letters at San Marcos from 1885, urged Peruvians to acquire habits of hard work and those values generally associated with the Protestant ethic.[40] This ethic was a topic on which Peruvian positivist thinkers were particularly warm. Even Gonzalez Prada, in spite of his anti-religious stand, considered the Protestant schools to represent a moral advance over Catholic education.

Within Civilismo, there were also to be found intellectuals of a more idealistic bent, such as Alejandro Deustua and Francisco Garcia Calderon, who, beginning in 1900, led the "spiritualist reaction."[41] These writers, in spite of their aristocratic standpoint (which included an elitist approach to education), also had good relations with Protestant missionaries.

By the end of the nineteenth century the organization of the Peruvian proletariat had already begun, mainly in Lima and the big cities. Bakers, typesetters, textile workers, and longshoremen went on strike, while within the Mutualista movement there were leaders who organized in 1896 and 1901 the first Workers' Congresses, in which working-class social aspirations were strenuously articulated. The most combative of these labour leaders were later in touch with anarchist ideas.[42] Social critics also attacked the conditions of the peasantry and the Indian population. Writers, artists, and politicians became concerned about the Indians' misery and exploitation. Two women novelists stood out for their audacity in denouncing the exploitation of the Indian population: Clorinda Matto de Turner (1854-1909) and Mercedes Cabello de Carbonera (1845-1909). In 1909, Dora Mayer (1868-1959), Joaquin Capelo (1852-1928) and Pedro Zulen (1889-1925) founded the Asociacion Pro-Indigena, to give a voice to the Indians' needs.[43] Imperialist penetration deepened the exploitation of Indians and the process of dispossession from communal and family lands. This led to widespread peasant rebellions and fed the Indigenista Movement.

Methodists arrived in Peru at a time of material and ideological reconstruction, and opened a way for other Protestant churches that came during the last decade of the nineteenth century. Methodist missionaries and other Protestants who were established in Peru preached a spiritual reconstruction, which presented Protestantism as a dynamic force working "for good" within both the individual and the society; the Roman Catholic Church, in their view, was spiritually quiescent. The approach manifested universality; however, a review of the Methodist missionary activities will reveal that the universality was within the limits of a triumphant "North-Americanism."[44]

Conclusion

In spite of the restrictions on religious freedom set out in Article 4 of the State Constitution, Methodist missionaries obtained, at the beginning of their work, support and legitimation from influential Civilistas, including politicians who would eventually hold high political office, and also their intellectual allies. As a case in point, Dr. Thomas Wood participated directly in the creation in 1899 of the Escuela Tecnica de Comercio, a commercial training school for boys. The school, directed by Wood, worked under the auspices of the powerful Lima Chamber of Commerce. In 1903 members of the national cabinet became members of the board of trustees.[45] The imprisonment of Penzotti, the constant harassment of the Methodists, the long struggle for the achievement of freedom of religion, and the threat in 1923 of a Concordat with the Vatican by the pro-American administration of Augusto Leguia must all be understood within the context of the uneven character of the Peruvian socio-economic formation.

The political aspects of the missionary work were not limited to the junctural co-operation with the Civilistas. The ideological interaction of the Methodists—and other Protestant denominations—with Peruvian social classes and their attempts to participate in the social movements of the early 1920s are discussed later; particular attention is paid to the doctrinal basis for Methodist practice and its political implications in the missionary field. This analysis, along with a close examination of the theoretical guidelines of the missionary policy as applied in Peru and the organizational aspects of the Mission, will establish a base from which to study the Methodist educational work. In the long run it was the ability of the Mission to provide progressively run schools which offered instruction in skills greatly in demand as a consequence of the penetration of foreign capital, that secured its continuing influence.

References

[1]Wenceslao O. Bahamonde, "The Establishment of Evangelical Christianity in Peru, 1822-1900" (unpublished Doctoral dissertation, Hartford Seminary, 1952), Chapter V. See note 21 regarding the date of the foundation of the Methodist Church in Peru.

[2]Baltazar Caravedo Molinari, *Burguesia e Industria en el Peru 1933-1945* (Lima: Instituto de Estudios Peruanos, 1976), p. 32.

[3]Ernesto Yepes del Castillo, *Peru 1820-1920, Un Siglo de Desarrollo Capitalista* (Lima: Instituto de Estudios Peruanos, 1971), pp. 127-132.

[4]Ibid., p. 184.

[5]Ibid., pp. 134-135.

[6]Peter Klaren, *La Formacion de las Haciendas Azucareras y los Origenes del APRA* (Lima: Instituto de Estudios Peruanos, 1970), p. 29.

[7]The imperialist epoch of capitalism is characterized by the phenomenon of surplus capital, in the hands of the monopolies of the imperialist countries, which seeks new fields of investments. The export of capital becomes an essential trait of the imperialist era.

[8]Economic enclaves: the concentration of imperialist capitalist investments in the production of primary products organized in enclaves. These enclaves are not organically connected among themselves in the dependent country's internal economy, but are individually connected to the metropolitan capitalist economy. Anibal Quijano Obregon, "Imperialism and International Relations in Latin America," in Julio Cotler and Richard R. Fagen (editors), *Latin America and the United States: The Changing Political Realities* (California: Stanford University Press, 1974), p. 68.

[9]Anibal Quijano Obregon, "Imperialismo, Clases Sociales y Estado en el Peru: 1895-1930," in Raul Benitez Zenteno (Coordinador Seminario de Oaxaca), *Clases Sociales y Crisis Politica en America Latina* (Mexico: Siglo XXI, 1977), pp. 116-117.

[10]This contract was signed with W. R. Grace and Company, a firm with large and expanding interests in Europe and the

United States. In the latter country, for example, it controlled the Lincoln Bank, the New York Life Insurance Company, and industrial enterprises (e.g., Ingersoll Rand). The contract gave up the control of railways and the guano exploitation. The Company also received a number of concessions related to free navigation in internal waters (for example, Lake Titicaca). In 1890, the Peruvian Corporation was set up in order to facilitate the new arrangement. This company got important land concessions in the jungle. Grace was able to control the railways, while having a large share in mining exploitation, plantations, textile industry, etc. Ernesto Yepes del Castillo, *Peru 1820-1920*, pp. 136-140.

[11]Ibid., pp. 135-138.

[12]Ernesto Yepes del Castillo, *Peru 1820-1920*, pp. 133-134.

[13]Ibid.

[14]Denis Sulmont, S., *Historia del Movimiento Obrero en el Peru (de 1890 a 1977)* (Lima: TAREA, 1977), pp. 24-25.

[15]Ernesto Yepes del Castillo, *Peru 1820-1920*, pp. 184-185.

[16]Ibid., pp. 201-204.

[17]Baltazar Caravedo Molinari, *Burguesia e Industria*, pp. 34-37.

[18]Socio-economic formation refers to the totality of a given concrete historical context.

[19]The central consequence of the imperialist character of the capitalist relations of production is the organic articulation of capitalism and pre-capitalism, in the process of capitalist accumulation. Anibal Quijano Obregon, "Imperialismo, Clases Sociales y Estado," pp. 116-119.

[20]Ibid., pp. 138-139.

[21]The dates differ greatly, depending on the source. The congregation began its development in 1888. July 10, 1889 is the date of foundation provided to the author by Oficina Episcopal de la Iglesia Metodista del Peru. Paul E. Kuhl places the foundation of the Methodist Church in Peru in 1888. Paul E. Kuhl, "Protestant Missionary Activity and Freedom of Religion in Ecuador, Peru, and Bolivia" (unpublished Doctoral dissertation, Sourthern Illinois University, 1982), Chapter 2. Kuhl is currently

doing research on Penzotti's work.   Francisco Penzotti, *Spiritual Victories in Latin America: The Autobiography of Reverend Francis G. Penzotti* (New York: American Bible Society, 1916), pp. 43-44. Wenceslao O. Bahamonde, "The Establishment of Evangelical Christianity," pp. 94-96, and Appendix I, p. 146.   Bahamonde was the first Peruvian minister to become a bishop.   See also: *Presencia de la Iglesia Metodista en nuestra Patria y su Contribucion* (Peru: 1964).   This is a booklet prepared by the church to celebrate its 75th anniversary.

[22]Wenceslao O. Bahamonde, "The Establishment of Evangelical Christianity," p. 96.

[23]Ibid., pp. 96-97. Ines Milne, *Desde el Cabo de Hornos hasta Quito con la Biblia* (Buenos Aires: La Aurora, 1944), pp. 129-130. A.T. Vasquez, "Datos Historicos de la Iglesia Metodista Episcopal," personal testimony (Lima, September 1937). Vasquez also situates the events in 1889.

[24]Information provided by Rev. Elton Watlington. Wenceslao O. Bahamonde, "The Establishment of Evangelical Christianity," pp. 99.

[25]Wenceslao O. Bahamonde, "The Establishment of Evangelical Christianity," pp. 101-105.

[26]Ibid., p. 105.

[27]Ibid., pp. 110-111.

[28]The articles published in *Revista Masonica del Peru* are illustrative.   See for example: Casimiro Medina and Jose B. Ugarte, "Dictamen," *Revista Masonica del Peru*, XI, No. 125 (Lima, March 31, 1892), pp. 60-62.

[29]Wenceslao O. Bahamonde, "The Establishment of Evangelical Christianity," p. 108.

[30]"The brothers Jose Maria Vivanco and Jose B. Ugarte were named for the defense of the accused, the presbyter Penzotti, before the court of crime in Callao and the court of this capital, respectively.   The first complied with his mission with the zeal and talent that had won him credit in his noble profession; the second found it impossible to respond to the the honour received, in being named defense lawyer by the court, and this duty happily fell to Alberto Quimper who has harvested immeasurable laurels with his brilliant presentation before the tribunals of justice in this defense."

"Seccion Official," *Revista Masonica del Peru*, X, No. 113 (Lima, March 31, 1891), p. 58.

[31]A. L. G. D. A. U., *Liminar de Los Anales Masonicos de la RESP. .LOG. SIMB. ., Concordia Universal No. 14. Apuntes Sinopticos al Conmemorar Cien Anos de su Fundacion* (Callao, Peru: Talleres Graficos Quiros, 1949), p. 79.

[32]"Seccion Oficial," *Revista Masonica del Peru*, X, No. 113 (Lima: March 31, 1891), p. 58.

[33]Wenceslao O. Bahamonde, "The Establishment of Evangelical Christianity," pp. 116-117. A. T. Vasquez, "Datos Historicos," p. 1. "Rasgos Biograficos del Reverendo Dr. Thomas B. Wood," *El Mensajero Cristiano*, IX, No. 120 (Lima: March 15, 1923), p. 2.

[34]It had been usual to allow for the inscription of civil marriages of non-Catholic foreigners in the Civil Registry. However, when an increasing number of Peruvians, mainly Protestants, married in this way, ecclesiastical authorities exerted pressure on the government to suppress the practice. Thus, non-Catholic couples could enter into legal marriage only by becoming Catholics. When on May 30, 1895, Dr. Thomas Wood's daughter Amy married Mr. F. A. Hazeltine, in the Methodist Church of Callao, the marriage, although recorded in the Civil Registry, was therefore promptly nullified by the government responding to ecclesiastical demands. The case became a public scandal, and led to a movement for a law of civil marriage. The law was promulgated on December 23, 1897. However, in May 1899 President Pierola regulated the application of the law in such a way that Protestants were almost in a similar situation to that of the years before 1897. On November 23, 1903, the Congress approved another law stating that it was enough to obtain authorization for a civil marriage, if one of the contracting parties stated that he or she had never belonged to the Roman Catholic Church. Wenceslao O. Bahamonde, "The Establishment of Evangelical Christianity," pp. 122-123; A. T. V., "El Matrimonio Civil," *El Alba*, No. 33 (Lima, February 1920), no page number.

[35]Augusto Salazar Bondy, *Historia de las Ideas en el Peru Contemporaneo, El Proceso del Pensamiento Filosofico*, Vol. I (2nd edition, Lima: Francisco Moncloa Editores, 1967), Introduction, no page number.

[36]Jeffrey L. Klaiber, S. J., *Religion and Revolution in Peru, 1824-1976* (Indiana: University of Notre Dame Press, 1977), pp.

24-44.

[37]For a detailed analysis see Hugo Garcia Salvatecci, *El Pensamiento de Gonzalez Prada* (Lima: Editorial Arica, 1972).

[38]Augusto Salazar Bondy, *Sentido y Problema del Pensamiento Filosofico Hispanoamericano* (with English translation), Occasional Publication No. 16 (Lawrence: Center of Latin American Studies, University of Kansas, 1969), p. 4.

[39]"In Peru the philosophy of Spencer was recognized and exalted as the most genuine realization of Positivist ideals. This is a characteristic peculiar to the Peruvian movement that needs to be taken into account for a correct understanding of its sense and process. It is known that Spencerism was only partially Positivist. In Peru, on the contrary, it results in genuine Positivism. The denomination 'Positivism' used by the men of the time, has among us a broader meaning than in Europe. It covers at the same time the Positive Philosophy in the strict sense and all forms of Naturalism including Materialism and doctrines of transition towards Spiritualism of the type expressed by Fouillee, Guyau or Hoffding. Many of our philosophers could then declare themselves Positivist while frankly embracing the Catholic faith. For that reason it was also relatively easy for most of them to abandon, in their maturity, the illusions of Positivism—as Juan Manuel Polar described them—and be enrolled in Bergsonism." Augusto Salazar Bondy, *Historia*, Vol. I, p. 6.

[40]Carlos Lisson, *Breves Apuntes sobre la Sociologia del Peru en 1886* (Lima, 1886), p. 45, cited in Frederick B. Pike, *Modern History of Peru* (New York—Washington: Praeger 1967), pp. 160-161.

[41]For a detailed analysis see Augusto Salazar Bondy, *Historia*, Vol. I.

[42]Denis Sulmont S., *Historia del Movimiento*, pp. 27 and 31.

[43]Cecilia Bustamante, "Intelectuales Peruanas de la Generacion de Jose Carlos Mariategui," *The Canadian Journal of Latin American and Caribbean Studies*, VII, No. 13 (1982), pp. 115-117.

[44]The author prefers to use North-Americanism instead of Americanism. See note 11, Chapter 3, for a clarification of the term.

[45]Wenceslao O. Bahamonde, "The Establishment of Evangelical Christianity," Chapter V; *Annual Report of the Missionary Society of the Methodist Episcopal Church for the Year 1903* (New York), p. 406. See also Paul E. Kuhl, "Go Ye Into All the World and Teach Arithmetic to Every Creature: Thomas Bond Wood and the Methodist Schools in Peru, 1891-1902", paper delivered at an Interdisciplinary Conference on Latin America and Education sponsored by the Center for Latin American Studies of Tulane University, New Orleans, Lousiana, April 28-30, 1983.   In 1916, this school was declared of "national utility" by an act of Congress and was subsidized by the government, it being stipulated that the school would continue "under the immediate supervision of the Chamber of Commerce and with the same organization it had from its foundation."   *Anuario de la Legislacion Peruana*, Vol. I (Edicion Oficial, Legislatura 1916), p. 4.

CHAPTER III

Social Gospel and the Mission

Social Gospel Doctrines, the American Methodist Church, and the Methodist Mission

The establishment of Methodist missionary work in Peru was undertaken by the Methodist Episcopal Church (North) during 1890 and 1891. At that time, all Protestant churches in the United States were responding to the challenge presented by the emergence of an industrial society and the scientific achievements that had put in question a literal reading of the Bible. In the 1880s, the churches moved slowly from an almost unbroken front in defence of the status quo to limited social criticism. This response was certainly not homogeneous, and the 1880s are considered part of a longer period of awakening and discussion running from the late 1870s to the middle 1890s.[1] The details of this change go beyond the limits of this study, but the following material examines the disputed issues and their importance.

Unrestricted competition based on the tenets of classical economics, the relationship between labour and capital, the prevalent business ethic, and the problems of urban life were the main issues and many ministers felt that it was imperative to address them. Henry May put it as follows:

> For a generation, slums and depressions, farmer protests and labour parties had been pictured by church theorists as necessary, incidental flaws in the inevitable improvement of society. The events of 1877, of 1886, and 1892-1894 were, however, impossible to ignore and difficult to explain away. Optimistic theory had to be reconsidered in the light of burning freight cars. Spokesmen of religion were forced, like editors and professors, to answer the question why, in the home of Christian progress, desperate men were refusing well-meant advice, defying authority, organizing, and battling with the determination of despair.[2]

Social crisis, labour conflict, the evident gulf between classes and the awareness of the separation of the church from the labouring masses were all decisive ingredients in the attempt to reconsider the social dimensions of Christianity.

May distinguishes three theological approaches, all of them

motivated by the social crisis and based on the belief in a Christian solution. These are: conservative social Christianity, progressive social Christianity (the Social Gospel), and radical social Christianity. He uses the expression "social Christianity" for all of the attempts to find Christian solutions for social problems, varying from conservative to radical approaches.[3]

Social conservatives are characterized as defensive and apologetic instead of being complacent like their more conservative predecessors. Suspicious of trade unions, they did not challenge contemporary economic assumptions. There would be a degree of reform, but on a voluntary, individual basis.[4]

Important sectors within the churches as well as whole denominations remained conservative and separated themselves from the issues of social concern, thereby reinforcing traditional moral views, and devoted their effort to individual reformation. However, an articulate group moved beyond defensive modifications to constitute a new school of theology that was later known, particularly from the 1910s onwards, as the Social Gospel School, and exerted a great influence on American thought. In tracing the origin of the Social Gospel, Charles H. Hopkins paid particular attention to what he calls the "progressive orthodoxy" that paved the way to an ethical Christianity by replacing the dualism sustained by the old orthodoxy of "this world versus the other world."[5] May describes Social Gospel as only moderately progressive, refraining from following radical paths that could separate its representatives from the mass of their Protestant contemporaries.[6] Radical Christian groups, on the other hand, rejected the basic existing social and economic organization, promoting solutions that were mostly very shocking for their contemporaries, but courageous in any case. Good examples are Theodore Borvine, who in 1884 recommended following the Christian communism of the apostles, and Hugh D. Pentecost, the Christian anarchist who, standing alone among Christian ministers, denounced the hanging of the Chicago anarchists as murder.[7]

The Social Gospel doctrines (progressive social Christianity) will be examined here because they reached the missionary field and were closely related to the educational theories that Methodists enunciated and tried to develop. Social Gospel leaders did not limit their concern to individual regeneration but also demanded social changes and became indebted to contemporary secular proposals for change. Their demands were not radical, however, and many scholars characterize Social Gospel as a middle-class creed. In fact, its churches had become middle-class institutions.[8] In spite of the vagueness that may be implied by describing a doctrine as a middle-class creed, this brief characterization is in line with the Methodist missionary policy in Peru and in particular with the policy developed by the interdenominational Committee on Cooperation in Latin America, whose activities were supported by the Methodist Mission.

May considers that the importance of Social Gospel in the development of American thought lies in its effect on the ideas of the progressive middle class. It failed either to convert conservatives or to attract the support of organized labour.[9] Protestant churches had a history of poor relations with labour organizations; it had taken so long for the churches to recognize labour problems that Social Gospel preachers had a hard time convincing labour leaders of their sincere concern for labour issues. The appearance of the Social Gospel was not an isolated ideological phenomenon. American progressivism and the Social Gospel appear closely related in spirit.[10] Moreover, the liberal reformist criticism worked out by Social Gospel leaders is not far from the basic ideas about the individual and society to be found in pragmatism, which was the dominant school of American philosophy at the time. For example, their loose, non-classist conceptualization of society, with "brotherhood" as the basis (i.e., the conciliation of classes through mutual co-operation), is within range of the modes of societal life as presented by John Dewey. It should be added that the Social Gospel doctrines as applied in missionary work contained all the ideological elements, in their full messianic character, that from a very early period formed the collective conviction of the "manifest destiny" of the United States and of the "superior" contributions to humanity of the American people. From the Latin American perspective, this is known as "North-Americanism."[11]

Although its antecedents can be traced to the 1870s, the Social Gospel lacked a systematic formulation until the 1890s. By 1895, the doctrines of the Social Gospel were almost completely formulated and had penetrated the major denominational and interdenominational organizations.[12] (The conservative social Christianity with which the Social Gospel co-existed followed a parallel course of development.) Episcopalians and

Congregationalists were the early leaders, while initially the Methodists lagged behind.[13] In the Methodist Episcopal Church (North), social action was mainly channelled by the Methodist Federation for Social Service, organized in Washington on December 7, 1907, by five socially-minded ministers: Elbert R. Zaring, Herbert Welch, Frank Mason, Harry Ward, and Worth Tippy.[14] (Ward and Mason were associated with the missionary activities in Latin America; a significant number of letters addressed to the Methodist mission in Peru were signed by one or the other of them.) These ministers tried to stimulate the down-to-earth study of social questions while at the same time pressing for a practical social engagement that would bring the church in touch with the less-favoured groups.[15] Antecedents to the request for social involvement go back to the celebration of the Methodist Centennial in 1884; social issues again appeared at the General Conference of the Methodist Episcopal Church in 1892, 1896, and 1904.[16] Finally, in 1908, the Federation for Social Service became official, and the "Social Creed of Methodism" was then adopted. In the statement, "The Church and Social Problems," which preceded the Social Creed, there was a proclamation which concerned the ultimate solution of all the problems affecting the social order and which asked for fraternity, reconciliation, and co-operation.[17] The Social Creed did not differ significantly from the formulations of progressives, populists, and other moderate reformers. Among many demands, it included those for equal rights and complete justice for all people in all stations of life, for the protection of the workers from dangerous machinery and occupational disease, and for the abolition of child labour.[18] In 1912, the Methodist Federation for Social Service became an executive agency of the Methodist Church aiming to rally forces within the church to the Social Gospel cause. Rev. Dr. Harry Ward, one of the most enthusiastic and radical of the Social Gospel leaders, was secretary of the Federation.[19]

The organization of the Federal Council of the Churches of Christ in America, in 1908, had meant the official recognition of progressive social Christianity by the main American and Canadian denominations. The common denominator of the Council was social action.[20] From the beginning of the century, most denominations organized agencies and committees for social action and began to engage in intense educational activities. However, this did not imply the acceptance of Social Gospel doctrine by all communicants or even by all the ministers of the churches represented in these new organizations.

Two characteristics of the Social Gospel became explicit very early: its interdenominational dimension and its worldly preoccupation with humankind beyond national boundaries. Foreign missionary activities were relevant to the aims of the Social Gospel doctrines and Latin America was a promising field. The guiding idea was that "the missionary himself must carry a Gospel which could be distinctively alive to the needs of society, as well as to those of the individual."[21] There is an illustrative paragraph in an article "Missions and the Social Gospel" published in the *International Review of Missions* in 1914:

> We have the same and the only Gospel. Our confidence lies in the fact that it is sufficient not only for individual Jews and Gentiles, but also for transforming the reconstructive forces of our social order in so far as they can be transformed, and of destroying those elements of our social order that are incapable of being transformed into agencies of fraternity.[22]

The ethnocentric approach characterizing this article, which mainly refers to missions in non-Christian countries, makes a strong impression, as does the presentation of the Gospel as the ultimate source of solutions for the grievances afflicting the world. Protestant Christianity is assumed to be the best religious doctrine.

The Student Volunteer Movement founded in 1906 was not an organization, a fact that the Chairman, John Mott, made clear, but rather a movement having as its basis "a common declaration of life purpose".[23] It was an integration of American and Canadian students devoted to foreign missionary service, the primary function being that of recruitment. The work was carried out in collaboration with the mission boards, the Young Men's Christian Association, and with other student Christian religious societies.[24] This movement owed its origin to the influence of the Social Gospel doctrine on colleges and schools.

The Young Men's Christian Association was itself to be of some importance in the missionary field. In the case of Peru, the Roman Catholic Church made the YMCA a prime target in its attack on Protestantism, in spite of YMCA's ecumenical character.

A pamphlet published by the YMCA in Peru explained its goals:

> the well rounded development of young men, providing
> opportunities, during leisure hours so as not to interfere
> with their studies or work, to increase their knowledge,
> develop character and fortify health, all in a Christian,
> homelike, respectful and *genuinely democratic* atmosphere,
> and in accord with the Good Samaritan example, without,
> in its eagerness to do good, taking note of any differences
> in creed, race, or nationality.[25]

Missionaries and native workers met in the World Missionary
Conference in Edinburgh in 1910 to outline the different forms of
missionary work.   In order to secure permanent co-operation and
co-ordination among the various missionary agencies engaged in
missionary work, the Continuation Committee was formed.   This
Committee began publication of the *International Review of
Missions.*   With respect to this review, Mott said, "Workers,
scholars and statesmen will have the opportunity to influence
missionary policy, and constructive Christian statesmanship will be
promoted."[26] A detailed reading of a number of articles makes it
clear that, in an historical context, both the Committee and the
journal were working for the organized expansion of Western values
and institutions, especially those of American or English origin.[27]

The Latin American Missionary Field and the Committee
on Cooperation in Latin America

The conference held in Edinburgh did not deal with Latin
American missionary activities, on the grounds that Latin American
countries were,

> at least nominally, Christian and proper use of the current
> terminology and a truly scientific method of survey would
> exclude Latin America from consideration along with non-
> Christian lands, because of essential differences of the
> problems to be considered.[28]

The delegates interested in Latin America reserved the
privilege of holding a subsequent conference entirely dedicated to
Latin America—this would be the Panama Congress on Christian
Work in Latin America held in that city in 1916.[29] The reports of
this congress document missionary practice; they are also the most
detailed source for the educational conceptions at the basis of

missionary school activities.

The preparation for the Panama Congress included the Conference on Missions in Latin America, which was held in New York in 1913 and attended by representatives of thirty different organizations. A committee of five, appointed to work out a plan to achieve co-operation, was called the Committee on Cooperation in Latin America.[30] It was enlarged by inviting each board working in Latin America to elect its own representative to the Committee. The Panama Congress made the Committee a permanent body and it was to become the most influential and active organization working in Latin America. Its office was in New York.[31]

The Committee on Cooperation consisted of an American, a Canadian, and a European section; the latter included a representative from each European mission.[32] (It is noticeable, however, that Canadian missionary societies did very limited work in Latin America[33] and that the European section was actually British and its existence basically nominal in spite of its willingness to co-operate in attending the Congresses.)[34]

The main means used by the Committee were "the creation of educational institutions and the production of healthy literature."[35] The goal was to build solidarity ties within the American continent. This solidarity was understood as "the cordial fraternity of all the republics, of beneficial and educational forces that were devoted to save souls and alleviate the ailments of the body."[36] In order to achieve this inter-American solidarity, a solidarity that had as a point of reference the United States, the Committee tried to obtain the co-operation of well-known intellectuals and to exert influence on the national leadership of the countries concerned. In this it was broadly successful, particularly through the agency of *La Nueva Democracia*, a magazine to which the "most relevant writers and politicians" were invited to contribute. It became an important journal of opinion, in which philosophical, political, and literary questions were discussed, and reached a large and influential audience.

The basic question arises from the preceding description. It is divided into two parts here. Was the attempt at unity and solidarity an expression of "North-Americanism," a paternalistic approach to Latin American people, whom missionaries wanted to uplift and redeem by supplanting their own cultures? And was it an expression of imperialist ideological penetration that occurred along with the dominance of American capital in Latin America?

This study provides a positive answer to this question, particularly by analyzing the actual religious and educational work and its results. However, it is hoped that the reader can be dissuaded from undertaking a reductionist reading. The missionary work (both Methodist activity specifically and the work of the Committee on Cooperation) was carried out from 1910 onwards by reform-minded people. Their approaches ranged from very mild to radical, although within the framework and mainly with the acceptance of a capitalist society that happened to be ruled by an imperialist bourgeoisie. The Christian doctrine, as Social Gospel understood it, had inherent universality that justified carrying Christ and his Gospel to other peoples, and it also had a social message. The religious and social discourse was, however, impregnated by both triumphant expansionism and the reformist language of American progressivism. A letter concerning the Methodist meeting held in Detroit in November 1921, with representatives from the world ministry in attendance, contains an illustrative paragraph (the letter is signed by Frank North Mason):

> the great world program of the church must be brought back more evidently to its central place in popular thinking . . . . Americans do not need to be entertained by further recitals of differences between other people and themselves, their attention should be focused on things which they as triumphant Christians have in common with others around the world. They need to know the exhilaration of conquest which as Christians—as Methodists—they have in common with people of other nations and other races.[37]

On the other hand, the interaction with Latin Americans would also influence missionary policies. From the early 1920s, they encountered the emergence of new social and political movements along with growing nationalism, Peru being an example. Missionaries did not remain alien to these changes as was manifested by their relations with Victor Raul Haya de la Torre. Meanwhile, the advocacy of Protestantism as the religious aspect of Pan-Americanism became an enduring and somewhat contentious issue from the late 1910s. Reverend Samuel Guy Inman, secretary of the Committee and founder of *La Nueva Democracia*, was its most notable preacher.

The writers and politicians who collaborated by preparing articles for *La Nueva Democracia* and working with the Committee on Cooperation in Latin America acted as intermediaries between this Committee and their own nationals at various levels.   An assessment of the influence of *La Nueva Democracia* prepared by the Committee on Cooperation in 1933 said:

> the magazine through the years has been able to fundamentally change the attitude toward the Evangelical Church and toward the Christian movement in the United States of many leaders in Latin America. It is a constant influence, working month by month in the offices of the presidents, cabinet members and congressional leaders, in educational centres, among the students of faculties of state and evangelical schools, and in groups of open-minded pastors and laymen of evangelical churches, offering to all of these the Christian solution of present-day questions.[38]

The Advisory Board of *La Nueva Democracia* included in 1925 the following names: Dr. Baltazar Brum, Dr. Jose Vasconcelos, Don Juan B. Huyke, Dr. John A. Mackay, Dr. M. Marquez Sterling, Prof. J. Navarro Monzo, Dr. Tulio Cestero, Gral Aaron Saenz, Prof. Federico de Onis, Srta. Gabriela Mistral, Dr. Juan Uriarte, Don C. Silva Cruz and Dr. Ernesto Nelson.[39] To this we need to add a long list, encompassing four decades, of contributors, relevant intellectuals like the Argentinian Francisco Romero or the writer Enrique Banchs and Peruvian Aprista leaders like Luis Heysen and the writer Luis A. Sanchez.   It would be simplistic to think of all these writers as colonized intellectuals consciously serving the interests of imperialism.   Rather, a significant number of those writers and politicians believed in the liberal system and expressed their views—in many cases anti-imperialist and anti-oligarchic as well—through this channel.   (In the case of the Peruvian leader Haya de la Torre, he and the executives of the Committee on Cooperation shared, from the late 1920s, a faith in the potential leadership of the middle-social sectors.[40])

Many American scholars consider that by 1920 Social Gospel doctrines had already died or at least had lost their initial energy.[41] It is even suggested that the Social Gospel preachers spoke for only a handful of church members during the 1920s.

The point such authors make is that social criticism and dissenting views decreased in the Prosperity Decade, while most churches embraced materialistic standards, the techniques of the business community, and most extensively its language. However, Miller discusses this topic in detail and, after examining primary sources dated in the third decade, such as sermons, reports, and statements of position, he arrives at the conclusion that the Social Gospel was far from dead, and that churches maintained their interest in social matters, although the strength and influence of Social Gospel doctrines and the audience in the U.S. for progressive preachers had indeed declined.[42] With reference to the Methodist Episcopal Church (North), Miller points out that the Federation for Social Service, founded by Social Gospel leaders, continued its critical approach to current social and economic issues. In 1922 and 1926 the Federation organized conferences on "Christianity and the Economic Order." Miller also finds that the reports from the General Conferences of this church and their agencies included social and economic criticism.[43]

At an interdenominational level, the committees and organizations, especially those associated with missionary activities and those created during the second decade or even earlier by Social Gospel preachers, were still under their control. The Committee on Cooperation in Latin America increased its influence, in particular through *La Nueva Democracia*, and not only during the 1920s, but also during the 1930s. As a marginal comment, it should be noted that business language had penetrated everywhere during the 1920s and corporative efficiency was highly regarded even by Social Gospel preachers.

The Panama and Montevideo Congresses

The Committee on Cooperation organized two Inter-American Congresses (which included South America), the Panama Congress, held in 1916 when Social Gospel doctrines reached their highest point of popularity, and the Montevideo Congress, held in 1925 at a time when the appeal of Social Gospel doctrines had noticeably diminished in the United States. (The La Habana Congress held in 1929 covered Central American countries and the northern part of South America.)

The reports from the Panama Congress indicate preoccupation with the legitimation and justification of Evangelical work in Latin America.   The growing American interests in Latin America, noticeable at both economic and diplomatic levels, were stated as the imperative reason for the organization of the interdenominational Congress; the Panama Congress had a North American orientation while the earlier Edinburgh Conference, although international in scope, had an European orientation.   The participants worked on the description of aims and characterization of ideals, as well as on a basic definition of education; formal education activities were considered fundamental to the missionary enterprise.   The reports are enlivened both with "North-Americanism" and its inherent expansionism, and with a bright optimism derived from the faith in progress through co-operation and conciliation, to which Christianity was essential since the goal was to build the Kingdom of God also on earth.[44]

From these documents it can be concluded that the Roman Catholic Church, the powerful historical Church in Latin America, was regarded as the main hindrance to ecumenical "co-operation and unity." Social Gospel leaders, who considered themselves to be the carriers of modern ideas and high civilizing approaches, understood that co-operation with institutional Catholicism was impracticable and tried to enlist the support of Roman Catholics as individuals.   The Committee was in fact successful in attracting the interest of some well-known Catholics with views more progressive than those of their Church, the social policy of which remained extremely conservative in Latin America at least until the 1930s. The case of Gabriela Mistral, the Chilean writer, is one example.

A paternalistic and ethnocentric approach permeates the reports of the Panama Congress.   However, missionaries were already aware of what they called "the Latin fear of the overwhelming of their civilization through political and commercial aggression."[45] (The American progressive trait is present in the intermittently critical attitude towards agents and corporations working in Latin America.) "As conspicuous offenders, the United States are in the process of mending their manners in respect to the Latin American nations."[46] Preachers of an ethically engaged church, they thought of themselves as bringing the best of America to their vocation, and felt that distrust could be overcome by the constant display of tact, sincerity, simplicity, and charitableness.[47]

At the Panama Congress, although there were Latin Americans and a few Europeans participating, the perspective was that of the American missionary. "The largest element in the Panama Congress was from home churches in the United States . . . . . The Congress was English rather than Latin."[48] All the reports of the commissions were printed and presented in English only. The table of contents of volumes I and III have suggestive and illustrative titles that show the missionaries' referential framework; for example, "The Evangelical Churches and the Social Gospel," "The Aim and Message of the Evangelical Churches," and "The World Movement toward Cooperation and Unity."

The reports from the Congress on Christian Work in South America (held in Montevideo in 1925) do not provide enough material with which to review the doctrinal discussion. However, the influence of the Social Gospel appears powerful. It is most noticeable that at the Montevideo Congress much more attention was given to problems arising out of missionary practice in Latin America. Two reports attract notice, "Social Movements in Latin America" and "The Indians." According to the introduction to the report on social movements:

> The task of this commission has been to study the social movements as they exist in South America today and the attitude and relationship of the Christian forces toward these movements, also to face the question of their responsibility in the future.[49]

The report deals with issues such as "Some Major Social Problems," "Social Welfare Movement," "The Organized Labour Movement," "The Student Movement," "Feminist Movement," "Movement Toward International Friendship," and "A Wise Social program for the Evangelical Churches."[50]

The report on Indians, largely informational, illustrates further the characterization of the Social Gospel doctrines offered here. The discussion is not only paternalistic; but contains strong overtones of racial prejudice as well. The description of the Indians from Peru and Bolivia, particularly the Quechuas, reads as follows:

> In some districts, where suitable clay is available, they make very good pottery, these achievements indicate some degree of intellectual capacity. Judging from his general appearance, his physiognomy, his behavior and work, some have considered the Quechua Indian far above the

Australian black in the scale of intelligent beings, perhaps above the Kaffir and Hottentot and the North American Indian, but below the Maori of New Zealand. It has to be remembered, however, that while the Maori has had a chance to show in school and college what he is made of, the Quechua Indian has not.[51]

If we take into account the history of missionary enterprises inside the United States, particularly those organized by the churches of the northern industrialist region, and the racial divisions within the churches (in spite of stated good will), the description reproduced here is not surprising. The underestimation of other cultures and their achievements was a persistent trait of missionary work, European or American, from colonial times in Latin America. The point here is that even reform-minded preachers working in foreign missions in Latin America were trapped in this ideological framework.

It is also observed that in the report intelligence is measured by the ability of the Indians to adopt Western values and the ways of an alien culture. This is not only in line with the official American discourse that justified foreign policy at political and economic levels by claiming to bring progress to the "younger brothers" of the South, but also with the evolutionary concept of change as promoted by missionaries in Latin America.[52]

Bishop Francis J. McConnell, a representative of the Methodist Episcopal Church (North) and a supporter of the Social Gospel, closed the congress with an address that underlined the feeling that Latin America was the promised land for Social Gospel preachers. Although his use of reformist language was pronounced, he was nevertheless aware of difficulties revealed at the Congress. One of the paragraphs from the address says:

So true it is that we have assumed the soundness of the social policies announced here that we would do well to remind ourselves that the real conflict in the Christianization of the social order is to be won or lost over concrete issues. The victory over the forces which would exploit the labour, or the resources, of any class for the benefit of any other, or over the forces which would unfairly gain control of the riches of one country for the upbuilding of another, or over the forces which for any reason would plunge nations into war, cannot be won by passing resolutions at religious congresses. Victory in any of these directions cannot be reached except as some heroic and prophetic souls are prepared to walk the way of the Cross.   Still, the principles announced here concerning the social spread of the gospel of Jesus have in them terrific dynamic power.   It is of immense significance that there is practical unanimity concerning them.   We have come a long way from the day when such problems were looked upon as outside the realm of religious responsibility.[53]

Although Bishop McConnell played down differences in favour of co-operation and unity, the reports show inconsistencies in the treatment of the issues that go beyond the differences of emphasis (a more moderate or a more radical approach to social problems).   Thus, the report on Social Movements, when dealing with the land tenure system does not go further than mentioning the existence of *latifundia* and its evils (ignorance, servitude, moral and spiritual problems) while the Popular Universities are treated respectfully.   These inconsistencies had complex origins.   The reports were field-oriented, concentrating on problems that had demanded a response from missionaries and leading converts; the responses were determined by the historical context and by the possibilities of expansion and consolidation each mission had.   In addition, the doctrinal framework, which was only superficially coherent, did not help in the building of a coherent social policy for Latin America.   However, at executive levels the discourse continued, hiding along the way actual difficulties.   (*La Nueva Democracia* provides a good example.)

While the Panama Congress dealt with the whole of Latin America, the Montevideo Congress addressed itself only to South America.   A significant number of South Americans, Protestant ministers and laymen, participated in its sessions.   Educationists and writers who sympathized with the Committee on Cooperation attended or made their support known.   (Gabriela Mistral, later awarded the Nobel Prize for Literature, a Catholic who believed in an ecumenical Christianity, had hoped to attend but was not able to do so.)   Spanish and Portuguese were the dominant languages.[54]   Methodist and Presbyterians were very well represented but, in spite of the presence of various denominations, we can hardly say that all the missionary boards working in South America took part.   The Free Church of Scotland (Presbyterian) had an active role through the presence of its missionary in Peru, Dr. John Mackay, who cultivated a close relationship with other missionaries in that country. The Evangelical Union of South America (English) was represented by missionaries working in the field (Peru). Representatives from para-ecclesiastical and non-denominational organizations like the Young Men's Christian Association, Young Women's Christian Association, World Sunday School Association, and Federal Council of the Churches of Christ in America (all of these strongly influenced by Social Gospel preachers) and others like the British and Foreign Bible Society, the Comite Protestant Francais, and the Federation of Evangelical Churches of Spain increased the list of delegates and visitors.[55]

Peruvian Methodist Literature and Doctrinal Issues

Prior to the second decade of the twentieth century there is insufficient documentation to discuss the main doctrinal issues that were introduced to Peruvians. However, we are aware that the early Methodist Mission was interested in social and political affairs, and that it was involved in the quest for civil rights such as civil marriage and religious freedom, two issues of importance for the development of the missionary work.[56] Also, the new church had practical concerns. The good relationship between the missionary Thomas Wood and the Lima Chamber of Commerce has already been mentioned, and the Mission showed an interest in collaborating to provide skills demanded by new business related to foreign capital. The two main Mission schools were founded very early, the Callao High School in 1891 and the Lima High School in 1906. There was missionary zeal in the school work, which was considered especially important for evangelistic expansion.

Doctrinal conceptions, and the current discussion of their implications for political, social, and educational stands, mainly reached ordinary Peruvians through *El Mensajero*—later *El Mensajero Cristiano*—(1914-1924). However, travelling preachers like George Howard, a speaker for the Social Gospel who was knowledgeable in educational theory, also visited Peru. Earlier, controversial populist leader and religious speaker William Jennings Bryan had been invited to address the first meeting of the missionary North Andes Conference held in Lima, in 1910. (Thomas Wood was still in Peru.)[57] *La Nueva Democracia* (1920) was distributed in Peru by Methodists (also by other denominations) among friends and converts, but it aimed to contact educated people and influential progressive leaders. Articles on Social Gospel topics were mostly reproduced in *El Mensajero*. This latter periodical also published lectures delivered by progressive Protestants at important religious or educational meetings. A good example is the address by Webster E. Browning which opened the sessions of the Second Congress on the Child in Montevideo, and which was published in *El Mensajero* in January 1920.[58] The recommendations and conclusions from the two inter-denominational Inter-American Congresses—the Panama Congress (1916) and the Montevideo Congress (1925)—were also discussed.

In analyzing the essential doctrinal ideas that would eventually nourish and condition the approach of Methodist missionaries to Peruvian secular problems, it is soon obvious that one is dealing with an "ethically engaged church." Using a common language and in a historical context, "ethically engaged church" means a church preoccupied with the political and social role of Christianity. From the second decade of the new century, Social Gospel doctrines were being preached by Methodist missionaries to their converts (although, from time to time, they coexisted with more conservative views). Peruvian Methodist literature talked of the immanence of God—who is present everywhere, in nature and in human society and who unfolds himself in human institutions—and of an ecumenical Christianity.

El Mensajero reproduced articles published in *La Nueva Democracia* (which began publication in 1920) and also translations from American periodicals like the *Christian Observer* containing expositions of current doctrinal issues. Particular attention will be paid to one of the articles because it summarizes, although in grandiloquent terms, the main points of Social Gospel doctrine.

Progress, the ascendant march of humanity led by the "new" ideas of co-ordination and co-operation, is at the core of this article, which appeared in *El Mensajero*, in January 1920, under the title *El Movimiento Interdenominacional* (Interdenominational Movement). It says,

> the predominant ideas and impelling sentiments at the present moment are the ideas of coordination and cooperation—to produce better results faster and more efficiently—all infused with the enthusiasm of absolute democracy; a democracy that banished the emphasis on

hated names such as subjects and kings, lords and serfs, rich and poor, capital and work and stresses the comforting words of social justice, human fraternity, and collective service.[59]

The writer includes in his balance of horror not only the World War, social uneasiness in Italy and England, anarchism in Bavaria and Hungary but also "the terrible spectre of Bolshevism in Russia." And in the midst of this historical crisis Christianity was able to bring solutions. However, Christianity needed a different program, different tactics than those employed before the war.

A Christianity that could not offer a unique social program to provide for the needs of humanity; a Christianity that could not present the same Christ or the same salvationist message, would be a Christianity as impotent for solving present problems as it was for avoiding the world catastrophe known as the Great War.[60]

The themes that are touched upon in this article are scattered everywhere in the literature, in letters from the Methodist Board of Foreign Missions to the mission in Peru, and in reports on the Congresses. However, the language became more moderate as the third decade of the century advanced.

On reading the article, one readily notes the emphasis on co-ordination and co-operation and the conception of a pluralist society, politically organized in a utopian, pure democracy based on the conciliation of antagonistic interests. The role of Christianity is to mediate between those antagonistic interests, to become an alternative to socialism, and to preserve the liberal content. The application of the principles of co-ordination and co-operation is based on "the implicit recognition of individual freedom and on the sacred concept of human personality."[61] Here an important point is that progress (historical advance) is achieved by co-operation, and by the solidarity of social forces, and not by conflict. Conflict is considered a "tragic" obstacle to progress. Social Gospel leaders talked of an evolutionary progress that culminated in the Christian ideal as they preached it. This entire process was seen to be embodied in American democracy. A comment on a lecture delivered by Julio Navarro Monzo, the Argentine continent-wide leader of the YMCA, which was published in *El Mensajero* in

1923, provides material to support and broaden our interpretation. It says:

> He [Navarro Monzo] supports the need for optimism and he verifies it in evolutionary progress, believing as present thinkers do that the spirit of struggle in societies and pride in men has generated the great error in the present civilization which is in crisis and at the border of ruin and failure; it becomes urgent to build men capable of humility and kindness. [The idea of perfection in individual human behavior appears outlined in this interpretation.] Thus, as the historian understands, civilization through the slow march of men from the shadowed days of the Stone Age culminates in the Christian ideal, the highest and most perfect ideology, a leading ideology to transform the world; thus, the individual finds in the same doctrine, and particularly in the figure of Jesus, the exemplary and unique leadership to operate the miracle.[62]

Progress is a recurrent literary ingredient in the reports of the Methodist Peruvian Annual Conferences as well as in articles published in *El Mensajero* from early times. For example, a 1917 issue of this periodical states: "the world is progressing and each one is called upon to study in order to see how he can support 'this progress.' " The article continues, "what Peru and the world need are more vital ideas and beliefs and not the prohibition of new ideas and beliefs. . . . Freedom is fundamental to progress."[63] Since, in Peru, the limits of this freedom were set by the Roman Catholic Church, the author is referring primarily to religious freedom. He is also implicitly expressing a basic idea sustained by missionaries: antiquated ideas and institutions were blocking progress; ignorance and superstition, both nourished by the Roman Catholic Church, impeded historic advance. Peruvian grievances were reduced, in the last analysis, to a conflict between old-fashioned ideas and new ideas, between modern civilization and backwardness. Consequently, the single Christian front demanded by progressive preachers was interpreted in a limited way, as the creation of interdenominational co-operation among Protestants, who would then work together to overcome ignorance and superstition. At the same time, from the second decade onward, missionaries transported to Peru the social reformist approach (found, for example, in the Social Creed of the Methodist Episcopal Church (North) that focused, in the United States, on the establishment of a minimum wage, the institution of social security measures, and the abolition of child labour. These reformist stands relied completely on the conciliation of labour and capital obtained by the creation of a dominant Christian ideology which would mean the highest achievement in human civilization. Its political expression would be a pluralist democratic society.

At this point it can be shown how John Dewey's philosophy of history and theory of cultural lag (especially as expounded in *Liberalism and Social Action*),[64] shares important tenets with Social Gospel doctrines and, in particular, their adaptations in Latin America.

Dewey thought that the "conflicts between institutions and habits originating in the pre-scientific and pre-technological age and the new forces generated by science and technology" lay behind the uncertainties and confusion of his time.[65] However, old habits and institutions had stability and strength; hence, he disregarded fast and radical changes in favour of an evolutionary concept of change in which directed action had a necessary place. Conflicting interests could be resolved because

> the method of democracy—in so far as it is that of organized intelligence—is to bring these conflicts out into the open where their special claims can be seen and appraised, where they can be discussed and judged in the light of more inclusive interests than are represented by either of them separately.[66]

Dewey's notion of pure democracy is associated with his pluralistic theory of society and his public service notion of the state. His emphasis on co-operation and on the building of a unifying ideology is remarkable. For example: "And it is no exaggeration to say that the measure of civilization is the degree in which the method of co-operative intelligence replaces the method of brute conflict."[67] The similarities suggest—to the dismay of Dewey's followers—that Social Gospel doctrine as presented to Latin Americans was a religious version of the basic conceptual scheme thought out by Dewey. Furthermore, both Social Gospel preachers and Dewey believed in the objectivity of their intellectual means of approaching reality and constructing solutions to problems. Dewey thought of instrumentalism as uncontaminated by the material reality of democratic America. Social Gospel leaders claimed at the Panama Congress: "our call is to Evangelize, not to Americanize. Any other approach bears unmistakable insularity."[68]

Methodist missionaries encountered in Peru a socio-economic formation characterized by its uneven and combined development and the dominance of imperialist capital. While *El Mensajero* undertook theoretical discussions of the Social Gospel, the attempts of the Mission to secure a place in that uneven formation disclosed a large gap between theory and practice. Moreover, while professing universality, the Methodist periodical's treatment of other topics mostly pertained to the United States and seldom descended to the detailed discussion of Peruvian social and political problems.

In 1920, the first of May, the workers' day, was the occasion for *El Mensajero* to write about the participation of Christian Evangelicals in the struggle for higher wages and better living conditions, as well as for other reforms of a worldly character. After quotations from Ephesians VI:5-6 and James V:4, it urged that capital and labour are interdependent, the prosperity of either being unobtainable without co-operation.[69] Significantly, however, the actual struggles of Peruvian workers and their horrible working conditions, particularly in the mining enclaves where Methodists had churches and schools, were nowhere mentioned. Thus, while receiving assistance from the Cerro de Pasco Company, the Mission neglected to consider the social consequences of the company's labour policy. Instead, a meeting between J. D. Rockefeller and a Mr. Morrison, a representative of the American Federation of Workers, was chosen to illustrate the growing awareness of the mutually dependent relationship between labour and capital; this meeting, it was argued, would lead to a common search for solutions to problems that would consider the needs of both parties.[70] In a historical perspective, this theory of countervailing forces was very easy to adapt to the rule of the rich, to those having power; its exponents did not take into account that co-operation between representatives of capital and labour is given on the basis of antagonistic interests. (Moreover, it could be enforced "collaboration.")

The original Social Gospel doctrines criticized the laissez-faire economics and the rugged individualism that created a setting not only for monopolistic enterprises but also for their moral acceptance; however, their preachers rejected socialist solutions and their "collectivist" implications.[71] Attacks against the Bolshevik Revolution were published in *El Mensajero*, in the Peruvian interdenominational magazine *Renacimiento* (in which Methodists did not participate), and even in *La Nueva Democracia*. Lenin was portrayed as a "tyrant" who did not boast freedom or want it, while the "great democracy of the North" was praised, with particular mention of its role in Europe and in the formation of the League of Nations.[72] And Methodist missionaries took pains to teach the Methodist articles of faith to new converts, particularly with respect to property. Article XXIV says:

> With respect to the possessions of Christians: The richness and properties are not communal nor are the rights, titles and possessions, as some falsely assert. However, every Christian may give charity to the poor with liberality according to his fortune and faculties. . . . Neither the Lord nor the Apostles recommended the community of goods among the believers.[73]

Interdenominational Co-operation in Peru

In spite of the articles published in *El Mensajero*, *Renacimiento*, or *La Nueva Democracia* praising the "interdenominational movement," co-operation among Protestant churches in Peru was not actually accomplished. Individualism and a competitive spirit had penetrated them too deeply. There were even complaints by Methodists working in the Sierra about the competitive policies of other missionaries. There is evidence of co-ordinated activities but, with a few exceptions, they did not last or were motivated by a common urgent concern, such as the achievement of religious freedom or the threat of a new Concordat with the Vatican (1920). The Biblical Institute, organized in 1917 under the direction of the Evangelical Union, the Salvationist Church, the Methodist Episcopal Church, and the Free Church of Scotland (Presbyterian), is a positive example.[74] There was an interchange of literature, and mutual collaboration in publishing religious material, particularly among churches belonging to traditional Protestantism. The merging in 1924 of the Instituto Norteamericano de Varones (Methodist) with the Colegio Anglo-Peruano (Free Church of Scotland) was a great achievement. Co-operation in this case was based on a shared sympathetic attitude toward progressive Protestantism.

The difficulties in arranging for interdenominational co-operation in the field were to some degree a consequence of doctrinal differences. There were in Peru, among Protestants, "fundamentalist" and "modernist" theological currents (the latter current meant "a more general effort to come to terms with secular culture").[75] Among modernist (mainly Social Gospel preachers) there were noticeable differences of emphasis in the approach to social and political issues.

The intervention of Rev. John Ritchie of Lima, Peru (Evangelical Union of South America) in the discussion of the report on "Cooperation and Unity," at the Montevideo Congress, summarized some concrete obstacles. He felt

> that this spirit [of opposition to co-operation] was due to a certain non-essential feature of the cooperative movement. The very title of the report, in his judgment, went too far. Instead of being "Cooperation and Unity," it should have simply been "Cooperation." Union, in any true sense of the word, is chimerical for our generation.

He went on to observe,

> In other ways the cooperation movement has become entangled with ideas or movements which estrange certain of those who are in Christian Works in South America. One of these is its association with Pan-Americanism, which is a matter of international politics. Still another is its relation with notable South Americans who are notoriously unbelievers, not only being in opposition to the Christian Church, but hostile to it.[76]

This is an oblique reference to the Executive of the Committee on Cooperation in Latin America and *La Nueva Democracia.*

However, the Social Gospel was the dominant doctrinal current influencing the Methodist missionary work in Peru from the second decade of the century. Not only are the basic tenets systematically taught and preached; there is also an explicit contention that "Methodism should be identified with the progressive movement originating within Protestant Christianity."[77] Of course, this dominance of one point of view did not mean that orthodox clergymen of the older sort ceased to be Methodists. Nevertheless, the Methodist Social Gospel preachers ranged from very mild reformists to radical prophets like Harry Ward, who even supported the Russian Revolution, particularly when social fervour reappeared in American churches during the 1930s, after the uneasy survival of the Social Gospel during the middle 1920s.

Considerations such as these, the idealism inherent in the Social Gospel doctrines, and the individualist Wesleyian tradition often make it difficult to distinguish conservative from progressive interpretations, particularly in the pulpit. In the educational field, where Social Gospel doctrine is combined with Dewey's pedagogical ideas, the Methodist work gives a better impression of originality and coherence.

Progressive Christianity in the Context of Intellectual and Ideological Changes, 1900-1930

Peruvian positivist thinkers, most of them members of the Civil Party, had a sympathetic attitude toward Methodism and Protestantism in general. Protestant emphasis on discipline, efficiency, and provision of modern skills in commercial subjects were in line with positivist aims, at the end of the nineteenth century, of order and progress. A special attribute of Peruvian positivism has also been mentioned: its ready acceptance of ideas from non-naturalist thought, to the extent, as eventually pointed out by some writers, of evolving toward spiritualism.

In the early years of the twentieth century, as a consequence of both the internal evolution of positivism in Peru and the influences of new European philosophical schools, there was a change of perspective, known as the "spiritualist reaction."[78] In the meantime Nietzsche, Schopenhauer—who had been discovered rather late—William James, and, in particular, the philosophers Boutroux and Bergson became known and finally gained a hearing in the universities.[79] Salazar Bondy makes an important observation about the acceptance of pragmatism by Peruvian thinkers: "This acceptance goes with the conviction that said that the Pragmatism that would survive and nourish philosophy would be that which benefited from spiritualist idealism." Francisco Garcia Calderon would later assume the same position.[80]

The change of perspective was not rapid, and previous philosophical ideas relating to earlier Peruvian versions of positivism remained in circulation for a long time at the University of San Marcos. The commanding personality of Alejandro Deustua led the full development of spiritualism.[81] Two generations, that of 1905 and that of 1920, bore the mark of his influence. By the later year, the philosophical induction of academics meant—using Salazar Bondy's words—the consolidation of spiritualism, with Bergson's ideas carrying particular weight. From a political point of view, this new philosophical perspective provided new bases for the dominant rightist policy.[82]

Among thinkers involved in spiritualism, there emerged a group called Arielistas, after the book *Ariel*, written by the Uruguayan Jose Enrique Rodo. Garcia Calderon, Jose de la Riva Aguero, and Victor Andres Belaunde had found a source of inspiration in *Ariel*, a book that stressed the need to place spiritual values over materialistic ones. The Arielistas revered tradition and placed their hopes in the creation of an intellectual elite. (Rodo's influence was not limited, however, to this elitist group; many Peruvian writers were affected.)[83]

During the third decade of the century, a time when popular masses burst upon the political scene, a group of intellectuals introduced a new approach to the study of Peruvian and Latin American reality. They had been directly or indirectly influenced by Marxism but cultivated an "open Marxism." Their theme of reflection was Peru and they attempted "to give thought a Peruvian identification."[84] From a philosophical perspective, this effort meant the insertion of historical materialism into national thought. However, other philosophical tendencies like pragmatism, Spengler's relativism, and Bergsonism—that nourished rightist as well as leftist political and doctrinal currents—also played their part in this intellectual renovation.[85] Salazar Bondy describes this renovation as an encompassing "movement of ideas" that embraced new artistic and literary currents (e.g., Indigenismo, an interest in Indian topics) and the study of Peruvian history and social themes (i.e., the work of Luis Valcarcel, Jorge Basadre, Luis Alberto Sanchez). Victor Raul Haya de la Torre, Antenor Orrego, and Jose Carlos Mariategui were leading names.[86] Jose Carlos Mariategui, a brilliant Marxist thinker, provided a durable Marxist interpretation of Peruvian historical reality.

The leaders of this movement remained for the most part outside the university environment, although most of them had obtained their education there, and had participated in the university reform (1919). They rejected the structure of the university and the "reactionary" role that it played. They created, then, the Popular Universities, a means for a creative relationship with the working class.[87]

By the second half of the 1920s, the Peruvian working class itself was moving out of isolation, away from its earlier interest in anarchism and towards a greater ideological maturity and higher organizational levels. It tried to build links between its own struggles and those of the indigenous peoples, the petite bourgeoisie, and the middle-social sectors.[88] (The process of organization of the working class culminated on May 27, 1929 with the creation of the General Confederation of Workers of Peru.)[89] By the end of the 1920s, two main political alternatives were already being presented: socialism and *aprismo*. Jose Carlos Mariategui considered that the *clase obrera* (by this he meant the most active and organized element of the working class) and the working class in general (in which he included the Indian masses and workers and peasant proletarians) could be the basis of a socialist force that would grow at the same pace as imperialistic capitalism in the country. Peruvian socialism would have as its special task to find the solution of the agrarian problem, and to achieve an integration of the national economy, which was inarticulated through its subordination to imperialism.[90] Victor Raul Haya de la Torre founded in 1924 the American Popular Revolutionary Alliance (APRA), a broad anti-imperialist front. The dispute between Haya and Mariategui—who initially agreed with Haya on the creation of a popular front—originated in 1928 when Haya made known his plan to transform APRA from a front into a political party under middle-class leadership. In Haya's national reformist proposals, the middle classes (formed by small industrial and mining capitalists, small rural and urban proprietors, merchants, intellectuals, and white-collar workers) had a progressive and even revolutionary role; they would assume political hegemony in a coalition with the proletariat and the peasantry.[91]

Aware of the importance of the ideological changes that were taking place in Peru, the Committee on Cooperation in Latin America had a receptive attitude towards them. It attempted to influence the leaders of the new political and intellectual movements, and gave them access to *La Nueva Democracia*. The missionary agencies working in Peru that supported the Committee, among them the Methodist Episcopal Church and the Free Church of Scotland, acted as a link. From the beginning, the editors of *La Nueva Democracia* did not hide their political sympathies with the leaders of APRA, an attitude which became more explicit in the 1930s, when there was open collaboration between some Methodist missionaries and the Apristas.[92]

There are certainly tremendous contradictions between the ideological ingredients that converged in the formation of the Social Gospel doctrine and the initial motivations of the leaders of the American Popular Revolutionary Alliance as well as the growing nationalist feelings that nourished Peruvian and Latin American literature, art, and politics. In spite of the liberal-reformist content of progressive Christianity, it is hard to speak of a dialogue that resulted in a creative new approach to Latin America or to Peruvian issues. There was instead an accommodation of interests. The contradictions were smoothed over—never resolved—by the attachment to liberal institutions of many progressive writers, by the eclecticism and mystical drives of the APRA ideologists, by the intellectual ubiquity of the Social Gospel doctrines, by the search for sustenance in the middle-social sectors by Committee (including Methodist) leaders, and by the governing desire of many missionaries to take part in new social movements and influence their leaders.

Within this framework it is not surprising that executive members of the Committee on Cooperation, Methodist missionaries, and the missionary from the Free Church of Scotland, Dr. John Mackay, felt quite comfortable supporting their thesis on religious needs in Peru by quoting authors like Francisco Garcia Calderon and Alejandro Deustua. These writers were frequently mentioned, which was understandable, given their non-naturalistic and spiritualistic approach to philosophical issues and Garcia Calderon's special interest in pragmatism and an evolutionary approach to modernization and reform. However, Calderon and Deustua took up oligarchic and even non-democratic political positions that they ultimately justified with their philosophical theories. Thus, their social views differed sharply from those espoused by Methodist missionaries and by Mackay. Missionaries' disregard for these differences can be partly and tentatively explained by the "spiritualistic" affinity and the common paternalistic standpoint. Also, it was in the interests of Protestant expansion to point to useful quotations from influential intellectual and political figures.

The comments that Alejandro Deustua made to Dr. Samuel Guy Inman, when, as Secretary of the Committee on Cooperation, he was visiting Lima in 1921, were reproduced, in various forms, a number of times. They must have pleased American missionaries. Deustua said,

> What Peru needs is idealism carried out practically. Send us from North America your people of ideas and interpreters of the spiritual. We have been great admirers of the United States and this has done us harm in a certain way. Our people have pointed to the Northern Republic as successful because of its practical ability to develop the material. And they have said that if Peru would become rich, it too will become great. We need representatives of your life that will show wherein your true greatness lies, which I am convinced is in your emphasis on the spiritual.[93]

Dr. John Mackay wrote in 1921:

> We share the opinion of Unamuno, Francisco Garcia Calderon and others that the religious problem is the main problem of the country and we contend that its solution would give the key to the solution of other problems. The Renaissance has to be in the soul and be manifested in the newer, or if it is wanted, old type of saint.[94]

The point in common between Peruvian spiritualistic philosophers and progressive Christians was the belief that spiritual rebuilding was the key to the problems of national life. And Methodists were convinced of their ability to offer a religious faith with which Roman Catholicism, tolerant of superstitions and corrupt, could not compete in open argument. It was a faith that had been adjusted to modern capitalist life, and spiritualist philosophers considered themselves modernizers.

This affinity between spiritualist philosophers, who were associated with a rightist political praxis, and progressive Christian missionaries, Methodists in particular, illustrates the somewhat confusing, although pragmatic, missionary policy that allowed for a wide range of allies.

The Organization of the Methodist Church and Its Place Among Other Evangelical Churches

The Methodist Episcopal Church established in Peru was part of the South American Conference based in Buenos Aires, Argentina, from 1891 to 1900. From 1900 to 1910 the Methodist work in Peru came under the jurisdiction of the West Coast South American Conference, based in Chile. (In Argentina and Chile, Methodist work was already well established and schools had been set up.) In 1910, the Peruvian mission became part of the North Andes Mission Conference with Ecuador and Panama. Soon the work in Ecuador ceased. Six years later, Panama separated and Peru alone became the North Andes Mission Conference, renamed during the 1930s, the Missionary Conference of Peru. The bishops who presided from 1900 to 1930 resided either in the United States or in Argentina.[95]

The ecclesiastical structure of the Methodist Episcopal Church in Peru, a missionary branch of the American Methodist Episcopal Church (North), was similar to that of the mother church with its districts, superintendents, and annual conferences composed of lay and clerical delegates from churches in Peru and presided over by visiting bishops. The American bishops appointed the district superintendents, whose task was to co-ordinate missionary work in the field, from among the missionaries in Peru.[96]

In the United States, the Board of Foreign Missions controlled all the missionary work, while the Women's Foreign Missionary Society was mainly concerned with women's education, and bore the responsibility for the Lima High School for Girls in Peru. Aside from the General Conference, which brought together ministers and laymen representing Methodist Episcopal Churches from all over the world every four years,[97] there existed from 1923 the Central Conference "for all the Spanish speaking countries in the New World" and it was attended by delegates from all such countries between Mexico and Chile.[98]

The Methodist Church in Peru was a kind of "colony-church" which transplanted not only a formal organization but also a formalized language and pre-established forms of communication for use among the members and with God. However, one of the objectives of the Central Conference was to increase the financial independence of missionary branches, and especially their ability to maintain an association without constant support from the United States. The central point was to develop churches that did not depend for their sustenance on American money. Bishop G. A. Miller wrote:

> Our great objective is the development of a spiritual, virile, vigorous, active church with self support, self extension and also self direction, but, at the same time, as a strong element within the world movement having its own part in the extension of the Gospel to all the nations. United we will be able to triumph gloriously, but divided we will fall into pieces, and a united church must be integrated by various national unities, each one doing its own part in the development of the universal cause.[99]

Nevertheless, at the end of the 1920s when an anti-imperialist atmosphere prevailed in Peru and the possibility of an autonomous church came up, the missionaries did not consider it feasible for the Methodist Church in Peru to work on its own.

In any case, partial self-support appeared an important and practical aim from the beginning of the missionary work, and the results are often reported at the Annual Conferences. For example, the official minutes for 1916 state that thirty per cent of all the expenses of the Methodist Church in Peru were obtained in the field.[100] These expenses did not include salaries and allowances for missionaries. The amount of money collected locally varied from one year to the next and is difficult to estimate, because the reports of the Annual Conferences held in Peru frequently did not give actual figures. Nevertheless, it is important to notice the scope of the aid from the United States; for example, in 1918 the Board of Foreign Missions approved the appropriation of $150,000 for a Methodist Hospital.[101] The total budget for 1924 for the Peruvian missionary station—including missionaries' salaries—was $27,878.[102] Missionaries' salaries were in fact relatively high in Peru, particularly in comparison with those paid to national pastors, who barely survived, as some letters indicate.[103]

The Peruvian Mission, in spite of having a sizeable number of missionaries (in 1922 fourteen are recorded, not including spouses), was always in need of more staff, especially because of its educational activities and, from the early 1920s onwards, because of its work in the Anglo-American hospital. It relied to an important extent on native converts; for this reason, a Biblical Institute—that worked with many interruptions—was created to prepare helpers and future Peruvian ministers (who could complete their training in another Latin American seminary, like the one in Argentina). Those so trained acted as intermediaries with the Peruvian population and played a decisive role in the Sierra (highlands). There were also Peruvian teachers (in many cases, graduates from Methodist schools with no formal training in education) in the mission schools; some were indeed nominally Roman Catholic, although sympathetic to Evangelical principles. Peruvian converts had responsibilities in editing the periodical publication of the Methodist Episcopal Church in Peru, *El Mensajero*, which ran from 1914 to 1924. Rev. A. Vasquez was the administrator and R. Algorta the director. *Alma Latina* was a publication of the Youth League from Callao; early in 1928 it became the voice of the Evangelical Federation of the Methodist League of Peruvian Youth. Peruvians also wrote contributions for *Incaland*, published in English, nominally every three months, from 1924 to 1941. It was intended for Methodists in the United States and its task was to awaken an interest in missionary enterprise in Peru.

Methodist missionaries aimed to create "new human beings" by instilling the way of life they preached along with the religious principles. But letters containing private comments as well as internal reports and accounts of daily problems prove that previous social experiences and cultural values could not be suppressed and that results were often far from what missionaries considered satisfactory.[104] However, an examination of the articles published in *El Mensajero*, as well as of the reports to the Annual Conferences between 1910 and the middle 1920s, make it clear that most leading Peruvian converts admired American accomplishments and were convinced that they were helping to direct their "brothers and sisters" toward progress. They reduced, in an extremely simplistic manner, the complex Peruvian reality to an ideological conflict between superstition on the one hand, and liberation by conversion on the other. The automatic temporal counterpart of this liberation would be modernity and progress, instead of the existing backwardness.[105] One has the impression of an incomplete acquaintance with the complexities of Methodist doctrine and the Social Gospel, although what is said is certainly consonant with missionary interpretations. It is noticeable, however, that by the end of the 1920s, tensions, owing largely to the growth of anti-imperialist feelings, had begun to show in the hitherto amicable relationships between missionaries and their leading converts.[106]

Methodist missionaries in Peru devoted themselves constantly to the task of outlining their needs. For example, in 1924, one of them enumerated in a long letter addressed to the Board of Foreign Missions three outstanding requirements: the need for young people willing to give their lives to Christian service, the need for the development of schools to train these young people for the ministry, for teaching and for social work, and the need for better equipment and buildings.[107] Sometimes the blame for deficiencies was placed on the Board of Foreign Missions. Missionaries felt that the needs of the North Andes Mission, whether because of its geographical location or for some other reason, were being neglected (among other things, the suitability of new candidates for missionary service was not always fully investigated).[108] The last point of grievance usually arose when outstanding missionaries had to return home, and lively letters and cables were exchanged with the Board of Foreign Missions concerning their replacement.

The main efforts were concentrated in education. (The list preserved in the Methodist Archive in Peru indicates that, except for doctors and nurses, all missionaries were formally prepared for teaching.) As is shown in Figure 1, the educational work of the Mission was already strongly established by 1916 in Lima, Callao, and Huancayo. Numbers attending day school increased year by year, and were held back only by a lack of facilities. There was no religious test for attendance.

Between 1891 and 1930, the Methodist mission founded churches, preaching centres, and schools in the coastal region from Lima and Callao to Ica, in the Sierra, and even in La Merced in the eastern jungle. (See map.) The growth in church membership was very slow, however. In 1908, there were 599 members and converts under probation; in 1909, 637; in 1921, 797; in 1923, 1228; and in 1933, 1368.[109]

The Methodist headquarters in the Sierra was in Huancayo where missionaries initiated evangelistic activities in 1905, one year after the organization of a church and school in Tarma. The Instituto Andino (Andean School) founded in 1914 became the most important school in the commercial city of Huancayo and the surrounding area. The Biblical Institute was also organized in

Map 1

Methodist work in Peru
(1889-1930)

Huancayo in 1917. Visits to San Jeronimo, Concepcion, Sapalanga, Huamancaca Chico, Chupaca, Ahuac, Chongos, Sicaya, Pucara, and Jauja, among other places, were periodically organized.[110] In the Sierra, the mission also founded churches and schools where the American mining enclaves were located or in the immediate vicinity. For example, religious activities in Cerro de Pasco were initiated in 1910; in Smelter in 1917 (when the smelting factory was moved to La Oroya in 1923, missionary activities practically ended in Smelter); a preaching centre was first opened in La Oroya in 1913 and in 1920 a church was inaugurated. Yauli and Huarochiri in the mining circuit were visited by pastors and preachers. Evangelistic work also expanded from the main localities to small villages, following the railways.[111]

On the coast, centres of activity were Lima and Callao. In Lima, the capital city, there were two churches, the Central Church in Lima proper and a church in La Victoria, a district of Lima. The church in La Victoria was the first Methodist church built in Peru. Religious as well as informal educational projects were extended, with differences in intensity and continuity, to Chincha Alta, Ica, and Guadalupe in the south and also to Huaral, Tambo de Mora, and later Chosica.[112]

Religious proselytism was not as successful as the educational work. The Central Church of Lima was, until the early years of 1930, an old and dark building with a capacity for scarcely 100 to 120 people, while the population of the city dramatically increased between 1920 and 1930, especially because of internal migration.[113] (From 1921 to 1930 the census shows an increase of 150,068 people while the number of births was 35,986.[114]) We read in 1924:

> Probably in no capital city in the world where Methodism is at work is our Mission so poorly housed. We have in this great city no property except La Victoria Church in one of the poor suburbs where there is yet not sewage.[115]

The reports from the Callao church—this city was also suffering from demographic pressure—are enthusiastic but do not provide any concrete information.

The Methodist North Andes Mission Conference was supposed to cover all of Peru and Ecuador but "because of agreements, lack of funds and inadequate national leadership, its activities were limited to a strip three hundred miles wide extending across central Peru." The city of Lima was common ground for all the missions that desired to occupy it. The Methodist mission was supposed to be free from competition in the central Sierra, but it complained that agreements were not honored.[116]

The Methodist mission was the pioneering Protestant denomination. In 1890 it was the only denomination with as many as 200 adherents; some years later there were seven mission boards operating with twelve congregations and by 1930 there were fifteen Protestant denominations present, including the American and British Bible societies and one national Evangelical Church. The Protestant constituency at that time was reported to be 14,933 people with 239 organized churches and preaching centres.[117]

There were, among the denominations working in Peru, the Free Church of Scotland (Presbyterian) (which, under the leadership of Dr. John Mackay, worked in close co-operation with the Methodists), the Christian and Missionary Alliance, the Evangelical Union of South America, the Church of the Nazarene, the Seventh Day Adventist Church, and the California Holiness Mission.

The Methodist mission maintained a leading position among evangelical churches at the end of the 1920s, judging by Methodist statements. A report written in 1929 reads,

> In this territory the Methodist Episcopal Church is the leading religious force of the Evangelicals. Here we have 16 charges with 37 preaching places, 11 schools with 15 missionaries and 58 national teachers, one seminary and a great hospital.[118]

The religious expansion of the Methodist Church, as well as of the other denominations, was not in correspondence with the prestige they had gained in the life of the country. Jose Carlos Mariategui concluded his essay on "The Religious Factor in Peru," published in his *Seven Interpretative Essays on the Peruvian Reality* (1928), with an observation appropriate for the time but which proves erroneous if applied to recent decades.

> Protestantism does not penetrate Latin America as a spiritual and religious power, but through its social services (YMCA, Methodist missions in the Sierra, etc). This and other signs indicate that it has exhausted its

possibilities for normal expansion. Furthermore, it suffers from Latin America's anti-imperialism, which suspects the Protestant missions of being strategic outposts of British or North-American capitalism.[119]

Conclusion

One paragraph expresses the entire dimension of the Social Gospel in Latin America and synthesizes all the ideological elements that form this doctrine. The paragraph was part of a report of the Committee on Cooperation in Latin America written in 1933, at a time when social concern had again grown in the American churches and reformist views were re-proposed. A paternalistic and ethnocentric approach toward Latin Americans, an unclear recognition of their individuality, and the desire to build a harmonizing ideology from North to South can once more be recognized. It is difficult to avoid the temptation to see in this desire—or in this vision—an expression of dominance over Latin American people and their cultures.

There are two great challenges for the Christian Church in Latin America. One is the endeavor to carry Christ and his saving Gospel to every individual, which includes not only the great masses of Spanish and Portuguese speaking peoples, but also the millions of Indians who have not yet named the name of Christ. The second challenge is to help mold a continent and a half into a life of new spiritual power with an adequate religion that will appeal to this young continent. It is to be hoped that its place in world life will be one of friendly cooperation with the finest forces in North America to make for a Christian continent which shall throw its influence to the most noble conceptions of a new world.

How goes the movement for larger freedom and unity in Latin America? The organizations united in the Committee on Cooperation in Latin America are interested in this question as well as in the primary problems of giving Christ to every individual in those lands.[120]

References

[1]Henry F. May, *Protestant Churches and Industrial America* (New York: Octagon Books, 1963), pp. 91-112.

[2]Ibid., p. 91.

[3]Ibid., pp. 163-263.

[4]Ibid., p. 163.

[5]Charles Howard Hopkins, *The Rise of the Social Gospel in American Protestantism* (6th Edition, New Haven: Yale University Press, 1961), Chapter III, pp. 55-78.

[6]Henry May, *Protestant Churches*, p. 170.

[7]Ibid., pp. 235-237.

[8]Ibid., pp. 170-171.

[9]Ibid., p. 224.

[10]Ibid., p. 225.   Although British Social Christianity had some effect upon American Social Christianity, the latter was far from an echo of British Christian Socialism.   The American Social Christianity arose out of American conditions and followed American patterns of action.   Ibid., pp. 150-151.

[11]Manifest destiny is not circumscribed to its early historical period but as a persistent ingredient of North-Americanism.   This latter term refers to a manifestation of interwoven ideological and socio-economic processes.   A shared conception of the world, which did not hide a feeling of superiority while justifying expansionist policies, has been an important cohesive element.   At an internal level, the same convictions were useful to justify marginalization and exploitation.   At the beginning of the century there was widespread acceptance of the North American obligation to build a global order.   The first attempts at Pan-Americanism were made between 1889 and April 1890.

[12]Henry May, *Protestant Churches*, p. 182.

[13]Ibid., pp. 182-189.

[14]Charles Howard Hopkins, *The Rise of the Social Gospel*, p. 289.

[15]Ibid.

[16]Ibid., pp. 289-290.

[17]Ibid., p. 290.

[18]Ibid., p. 291.

[19]Ibid., p. 292.

[20]Ibid., p. 302.

[21]Shailer Mathews, "Missions and the Social Gospel," *International Review of Missions*, III, No. 27 (1914), p. 432.

[22]Ibid., pp. 432-433.

[23]"A Quadrennium in the Life and Work of the Student Volunteer Movement," The Report of the Executive of the Student Volunteer Movement for Foreign Missions, presented by Mr. John R. Mott, Chairman, in *Students and the Present Missionary Crisis* (New York:　Student Volunteer Movement for Foreign Missions, 1910), p. 17.

[24]Ibid.

[25]Young Men's Christian Association, *Sirviendo a la Juventud del Mundo* (Lima:　pamphlet, 1944), cited in Wensceslao O. Bahamonde, "Establishment of Evangelical Christianity in Peru." Incomplete materials on developments after 1900, not included in thesis of same title (Lima, 1952), p. 61.

[26]John R. Mott, "The Continuation Committee," *International Review of Missions*, I, 1912, p. 71.

[27]For example:　Tasuko Harada, "The Present Position and Problems of Christianity in Japan," *International Review of Missions*, I (1912), pp. 79-97; W. A. Shedd D. D., "Christianity and Islam, The Vital Forces of Christianity and Islam," in Ibid., I (1912), pp. 294-311; "The Recent Revolution of the Indian Government on Education Policy," in Ibid., II (1913), pp. 430-441.

[28]Panama Congress 1916, *Christian Work in Latin America*, 3 Vols. (New York:　The Missionary Education Movement, 1917), Vol.1, p.6.

[29]Ibid., p. 7.　　[30]Ibid.　　[31]Ibid., p. 9.

[32]The Committee was also authorized to add a number of "co-opted" members not exceeding one half of the number appointed as representatives. Ibid., pp. 33-38.

[33]In 1916, Canadian missionary work was limited to missionary activities in Bolivia that were organized by the Canadian Baptist Foreign Mission Board. There was a kind of indirect participation with the Evangelical Union of South America, an English non-demoninational society based in London, through its North American Council. Ibid., Vol. III, Appendix B, pp. 463-464.

[34]Montevideo Congress 1925, *Christian Work in South America*, 2 Vols. (New York-Chicago: Fleming H. Revell Company, 1925), Vol. 1, p. 8.

[35]J. O. G., "Que es el Comite de Cooperacion en la America Latina?" *El Mensajero*, VI, No. 62 (Lima, June 1920), p. 16.

[36]Ibid.

[37]Letter of Frank Mason North (Board of Foreign Missions) addressed to Rev. Frank Stanger (Lima) dated New York, August 31, 1921.

[38]Committee on Cooperation in Latin America, "Influence of *La Nueva Democracia*," *Report of Secretary* (New York: 1933), pp. 6-7.

[39]Montevideo Congress 1925, *Christian Work*, Vol. II, p.180.

[40]Samuel Guy Inman, who was a founder and editor of *La Nueva Democracia* and the first secretary of the Committee on Cooperation, wrote with enthusiasm on the development of APRA and the Aprista Party in Peru in his writings. This attitude was even more accentuated in the late 1930s and early 1940s.

[41]Robert Moats Miller, *American Protestantism and Social Issues 1919-1939* (Chapel Hill: The University of North Carolina Press, 1958), Chapter II, pp. 17-30.

[42]Ibid., Chapter III, pp. 31-47.

[43]Ibid., p. 36.

[44]The Kingdom of God "was merely the working out of the Divine will through gradual social improvement." Ibid., p. 232.

[45]Panama Congress, 1916, *Christian Work*, Vol. I, p. 129.

[46]Ibid., p. 130.   [47]Ibid., pp. 131-132

[48]Montevideo Congress 1925, *Christian Work*, Vol. I, p. 20.

[49]Ibid., Vol. II, p. 391.

[50]Ibid., Vol. I, pp. 389-455.

[51]Ibid., p. 170.

[52]The United States "invaded" the New World under the name of progress and peace; the new task—that the Old World did not undertake—was to maintain internal order, i.e., to intervene in its internal affairs. Under the presidency of Theodore Roosevelt, the interventionist policy was legalized. The Platt Amendment and the Roosevelt Corollary to the Monroe Doctrine were the new legal resources to justify American intervention. Central American countries in particular would suffer the consequences of this policy.

[53]Montevideo Congress 1925, *Christian Work*, Vol. I, p. 33.

[54]Ibid., pp. 21-29.

[55]Ibid., Vol. II, Appendix, pp. 462-468.

[56]Advocates of Social Gospel doctrines had only occasional hearing in official Methodist circles at the end of the century. "Only in the early twentieth century, when progressive social reform became the creed of much of the American middle class, did Methodists contribute to the Social Gospel movement in proportion to their numbers, discipline and fervency." Henry May, *Protestant Churches*, pp. 188-190.

[57]*Actas de la Primera Reunion del la Conferencia Misionera Andina del Norte de la Iglesia Metodista Episcopal*, Lima, January 1910. W. J. Bryan, populist Democratic candidate, led the Progressive hosts in an attempt to dislodge the finance capitalists from power in Washington in 1896. He was supported by John Dewey. George Novack, *Pragmatism versus Marxism—An Appraisal of John Dewey's Philosophy* (New York: Pathfinder Press, 1975), p. 35.

[58]Webster E. Browning, "La Educacion de la Ninez," *El Mensajero*, VI, No. 57 (Lima, January 1920), pp. 13-14.

[59]J. O. G., "El Movimiento Interdenominacional," *El Mensajero*, VI, No. 57 (Lima, January 1920), pp. 11-13.

[60]Ibid., p. 12.   [61]Ibid.

[62]"Conferencia de Julio Navarro Monzo," *El Mensajero*, XI, No. 122 (Lima, May 15, 1923), p. 11. Julio Navarro Monzo was an Argentinian citizen, originally from Portugal. It is important to notice that the lecture alluded to in the article happended in 1923, before his visits to England and the United States where he entered into a relationship with the Quakers. Navarro's idea of a "New Reform", a Latin American one, was a topic of great contention. On this issue, see Juan A. Mackay, *El Otro Cristo Espanol* (Mexico-Buenos Aires: Casa Unida de Publicationes-Editorial Aurora, 1952), pp. 213-229. This book was first published in English in 1933. At the Montevideo Congress (1925), it was suggested that the Committee on Cooperation secure strong native men like Julio Navarro Monzo or outstanding foreigners like Dr. John (Juan) Mackay to devote their time to lecturing not only among students but among commercial people for the promotion of Christian ideals in business. Montevideo Congress 1925, *Christian Work*, Vol. II, p. 429.

[63]W. O. S., "La Libertad y el Progreso," *El Mensajero*, III, No. 34 (Lima: October, 1917), pp. 4-6; "Progresando," *El Mensajero*, III, No. 31 (Lima: July, 1917), p. 2.

[64]See in particular "The Class Struggle," from John Dewey, *Liberation and Social Action*, included in Joseph Ratner, *Intelligence in the Modern World: John Dewey's Philosophy* (New York: Random House, 1939), pp. 441-449. These ideas are also found in earlier writings, for example in *Human Nature and Conduct* (1922).

[65]Ibid., p. 441.   [66]Ibid., p. 444.

[67]Ibid., p. 445. From an epistemological perspective Dewey's pragmatism did not provide the elements to question North-Americanism at an ideological level or to understand imperialism and its network of exploitation and dependency.

[68]Panama Congress 1916, *Christian Work*, Vol. I, p. 130.

[69]Go Ahead, "El 1ero de Mayo," *El Mensajero*, VI, No. 61 (Lima, May 1920), p. 2.

[70]P. W. O., "Miscelanea. Hechos muy Significativos," *El Mensajero*, VI, No. 60 (Lima, April 1920), p. 10.

[71]For example, one reads with reference to Washington Gladden, a central figure of the Christian social movement: "Gladden's realistic analysis of present society, with his firm insistence on bargaining rights for labour, remained his most distinctive contribution to Protestant social doctrine. He continued to hope for a gradual evolution toward a cooperative social order and rejected with increasing firmness the doctrines of laissez faire. . . . He retained, however, his dislike for political socialism." Henry May, *Protestant Churches*, p. 174.

[72]"El Bolchevismo Desmoraliza al Obrero y Destruye la Industria," *El Mensajero*, VI, No. 66 (Lima, October 1920), p. 11. See also, "Topicos del Mes: La Conversion de los Bolcheviques," *Renacimiento*, X, No. 7 (Lima, July 1921), p. 97.

[73]"Seccion Doctrinal. Los Articulos de Fe," *El Mensajero*, VI, No. 57 (Lima, January 1920), p. 8.

[74]R. A., "El Instituto Biblico," *El Mensajero*, III, No. 29 (Lima, May 1917), p. 2. See also, "El Instituto Biblico," Ibid., III, No. 28 (Lima, April 1917), p. 8.

[75]Harold E. Quinley, *The Prophetic Clergy: Social Activism among Protestant Ministers* (New York: John Wiley and Sons, 1974), p. 32.

[76]Montevideo Congress 1925, *Christian Work*, Vol. II, p. 456.

[77]John R. Mott, "El Programa de los Proximos Cien Anos," *El Mensajero*, VI, No. 57 (Lima, January 1920), p. 9.

[78]Augusto Salazar Bondy, *Historia de las Ideas en el Peru Contemporaneo. El Proceso del Pensamiento Filosofico*, 2nd Edition (Lima: Francisco Moncloa Editores, 1967), Vol. I, p. 147.

[79]Ibid., pp. 147-148.   [80]Ibid.

[81]Deustua developed a theory of general aesthetics based on the intuition of freedom. Under the influence of Bergson and modern philosophies of value, he formulated a general theory of the life of the spirit. Ultimate issues were the concepts of value, order, and freedom. Augusto Salazar Bondy, *Historia*, Vol. I, pp. 151-152.

[82]Ibid., Vol. II, pp. 226 and 307.

[83]Frederick B. Pike, *The Modern History of Peru* (New York:

Praeger, 1967), pp. 203-205.

[84]Augusto Salazar Bondy, *Historia*, Vol. III, p. 308.

[85]Ibid.   [86]Ibid., pp. 308-309.

[87]Ibid., p. 310.

[88]Denis Sulmont S., *Historia del Movimiento Obrero en el Peru (de 1890 a 1977)* (Lima: TAREA, 1977), p. 38.

[89]Ibid., p. 54.

[90]Ibid., p. 54.   It is interesting to notice that both J. Mackay and S.G. Inman wrote with great respect of Jose Carlos Mariategui in spite of their differences.   Mackay, in his book *El Otro Christo Espanol*, refers to Mariategui as a communist militant. He wrote that to visit him at his home and listen to his soft and inflectional voice proclaiming a militant philosophy of life which was in disagreement with the fragile body of its owner, was certainly an inspiring experience.   He went on to say that communism was his religion, which he professed and propagated with the whole passion of his soul.   Mackay made it clear that the reference to Mariategui is relevant because his ideas and influence showed the direction taken by ardent spirits looking for sources to satisfy their religious thirst.   They found the source in revolutionary socialism.   Juan (John) Mackay, *El Otro Cristo* pp. 192-193.

[91]Ibid., pp. 48 and 51.

[92]Luis Alberto Sanchez wrote the preface to *El Destino de America Latina* by Samuel Guy Inman (Committee on Cooperation), Spanish version, 1941.   Sanchez stressed the coincidences between professor Inman's views and APRA proposals, even earlier ones.

[93]Samuel G. Inman, *South America Today* (1921), p. 97 cited in Wenceslao O. Bahamonde, "Establishment of Evangelical Christianity in Peru".   Incomplete materials on developments after 1900, not included in thesis of the same title (Lima, 1952), p. 25.

[94]John Mackay, "Renacimiento," *Renacimiento*, X, No. 7 (Lima, July 1921), p. 101.

[95]"Notas Historicas," in *Actas de la Novena Reunion*, December 5 to 10, 1917.

[96]James Carlton Stanford, "Methodism in Peru 1900-1930" (unpublished Master of Arts dissertation, Chapel Hill, N.C.: University of North Carolina, 1968), p. 2.

[97]"La Conferencia General de la Iglesia Metodista Episcopal," *El Mensajero*, VI, No. 63 (Lima, July 1920), p. 2.

[98]George Miller, "Conferencia Central de la Iglesia Metodista," *El Mensajero Cristiano*, IX (Lima: August 31, 1923), p. 4.

[99]Ibid.

[100]*Actas de la Octava Reunion*, November 30 to December 3, 1916.

[101]*Actas de la Decima Reunion*, November 5 to 10, 1918.

[102]Letter of the Methodist Episcopal Mission in Peru addressed to R. E. Diffendorfer (Board of Foreign Missions) dated Lima, October 6, 1924.

[103]In 1922, salaries and rents for the missionaries in Peru ranged from 1,150 to 2,650 American dollars, assumed to be annual, not cumulative. Letter of the Mission Treasury in Peru addressed to Mr. Chas. E. DeVesty (Board of Foreign Missions) dated Lima, November 22, 1922. The letter contains a complete list of missionaries and their income.

[104]There are many scattered references to the persistence of "poor styles of life" among Peruvian converts and, sometimes, national pastors. For example, the letters between R. Howard Yoder (Lima) and the principal of the Colegio Andino (formerly Instituto Andino, located in Huancayo), from April to December 1939 give an example of poor relations between leading converts. These letters describe actual quarrels.

[105]A Peruvian pastor working in Huancayo said: "The missions in the valley have gained considerably. . . . In those remote villages, the unhappy souls are tied up by heavy chains: ignorance, superstition and fear. The only hope of liberation they have is in the love of their brothers untying them. They will know the truth and the truth will liberate them." *Actas de la Decima Septima Reunion*, January 6 to 9, 1926. We read, "When the day comes that in each Peruvian home from Tumbes to Madre de Dios, from the rich amazonic jungles to the coast, from the poor Indian in his hut lacking hygiene to the magistrate in his

luxurious home, read and study the Bible, then we could have a prosperous, happy, cultivated, civilized, powerful and great country, and wise citizens fulfilling their religious, patriotic and humanitarian obligations, models for other nations like the American Christian statesmen." Senefelder Vallejo, "La Libertad," *El Mensajero Cristiano*, X, No. 153 (Lima: July 31, 1924), p. 7. (The author was attending an American university.)

[106] "The Bishop gave the nationals [pastors] a chance to cast a secret ballot on whether they preferred to carry on the work with or without the help of the missionaries. They voted unanimously in favour of retaining the missionaries. "Nevertheless, the spirit of nationalism is quite strong and should always be taken into account in the administration of the field. There has been restlessness among our hill preachers. There is an Anti-American propaganda being carried on all over South America" "North Andes Mission Conference" in *Annual Report of the Board of Foreign Missions of the Methodist Episcopal Church for the Year 1929* (New York: Board of Foreign Missions of the Methodist Episcopal Church), p. 218.

[107] Letter of the Methodist Episcopal Mission in Peru addressed to R. E. Diffendorfer (Board of Foreign Missions) dated Lima, October 6, 1924.

[108] Letter of the Methodist Episcopal Mission in Peru addressed to Dr. Harry Farmer (Board of Foreign Missions) dated Lima, January 23, 1923.

[109] *Actas de la Primera Reunion*, January 21 to 25, 1910; *Actas de la Decima Tercera Reunion*, December 28 to January 1, 1922; *Actas de la Decima Quinta Reunion*, January 30 to February 5, 1929; *Actas de la Vigesima Quinta Reunion*, December 27 to 31, 1933.

[110] Juan Ritchie, "Apuntes para la Historia del Movimiento Evangelico en el Peru durante el Primer Siglo de la Republica. La Extension del Movimiento de Lima y Cuzco," *Renacimiento*, X, No. 10 (Lima, October 1921), p. 160. *Actas de la Octava Reunion*, November 30 to December 3, 1916; *Actas de la Decima Tercera Reunion*, December 28 to January 1, 1922.

[111] Juan Ritchie, "Apuntes," p. 160; *Actas de la Octava Reunion*, November 30 to December 3, 1916; *Actas de la Quinta Reunion*, December 16 to 21, 1913.

[112] *Actas de la Decima Tercera Reunion*, December 28 to

January 1, 1933; *Actas de la Decima Reunion*, November 5 to 10, 1918; *Actas de la Duodecima Segunda Reunion*, December 2 to 8, 1930.

[113]Letter of the Methodist Episcopal Mission in Peru addressed to R. E. Diffendorfer (Board of Foreign Missions) dated Lima, October 6, 1924.

[114]*Censo de las Provincias de Lima y Callao levantado el 13 de Noviembre de 1931.* Trabajo ejecutado por la Junta Departamental de Lima Pro-Desocupados (Republica del Peru), pp. 267-273.

[115]Letter of the Methodist Episcopal Mission in Peru addressed to R. E. Diffendorfer (Board of Foreign Missions) dated Lima, October 6, 1924.

[116]"North Andes Mission Conference, Peru," in *Annual Report*, p. 218.

[117]Wenceslao O. Bahamonde, "Establishment of Evangelical Christianity,", pp. 14-15.

[118]"North Andes Mission Conference, Peru," in *Annual Report*, p. 218.

[119]Jose Carlos Mariategui, *Seven Interpretative Essays on Peruvian Reality*, Marjory Urquidi, trans. (Austin and London: University of Texas Press, 1971), p. 151.

[120]Committee on Cooperation in Latin America, "The Outreach of Evangelical Work in Latin America," *Report of Secretary* (New York: 1933), p. 3.

CHAPTER IV

Methodists, Religious Freedom, and the Oncenio

The Achievement of Religious Freedom

Protestant missionaries were working in a country where Catholicism reached all social classes, assuming diverse forms that ranged from the traditional ceremonies attended by higher classes and officers of the government to expressions of popular religiosity. Furthermore, Roman Catholicism was the religion of the state, and the public services of other faiths, Christian or not, were banned. Persecution organized by the Catholic Church, such as vandalistic attacks against Protestants and their homes, public protests, and the implementation of religious sanctions, became almost routine in the life of the Methodist and other missions, particularly in the provinces.[1] Sometimes, national and provincial authorities, under the pressure of the Catholic hierarchy, issued orders threatening missionary activities. But they did not follow them up; in fact, the Methodist work, and educational activities in particular, did not suffer any kind of fundamental interruption as a consequence of Catholic opposition. Religious freedom was obviously the main goal that the Protestants wanted to achieve. Hays P. Archerd, the Methodist missionary acting as Superintendent, wrote in 1914

> We want religious freedom to be in the country without the threat of article 100 of the Penal Code; and we want religious freedom to offer to Peru the benefits of moral and religious competition, of real freedom of thought and consciousness.[2]

The Catholic hierarchy used as a leading argument against religious freedom the reasoning that Catholicism was a fundamental ideological element of national unity. In fact, Catholic institutions had been and still were the most cohesive in the country and, by preserving the traditional social order, provided legitimation of the entire socio-economic system, which can be characterized as uneven and combined. The conservative church, a political ally of the land-owners, was indeed a primary link with the colonial past. Catholic conservative social policies were dominant in Latin American countries during this period, a period characterized by the crisis of the colonial Church and the emergence of the socially oriented (reformist) Church, roughly from 1880 to 1930.[3] Official attitudes toward Protestantism followed the changing equilibrium of forces integrating the state, both before and after the achievement of religious freedom in 1915. The Catholic Church became stronger during periods of social or political instability; on the other hand, social disturbances also led to the questioning of its political role.

The campaign for religious freedom actually began in 1913. After Penzotti's acquittal, the Methodist mission, together with other Protestant missions that had been established since the 1890s, continued with the practice of private worship while their schools grew successfully. The incentive to achieve a definite solution emerged when the Roman Catholic bishop of Puno organized and led a mob attack on the Adventist mission which was working among Indians in Puno. The bishop counted on the collaboration of the police and as a consequence six Indians, among them a woman, were taken to jail.[4] These events received great publicity. Meanwhile, Senator Severiano Bezada, from Puno, presented to his Chamber on August 20, 1913, a proposal to amend Article 4 of the State Constitution by eliminating the prohibition of public practice of any religious service other than that of the Roman Catholic Church.[5]

The proposal was approved by both Chambers. As a constitutional amendment, however, it had to be so approved in two consecutive legislative sessions, and final passage was not procured until the spring of 1915. Under severe pressure from the Church, the president refused to append his signature, but he was overridden and the amendment passed into law (Law 2193) in November of that year. Article 4 then read: "The Nation professes the Roman Catholic Apostolic Religion and the State protects it."[6]

Religious freedom was not the simple result of the exemplary work of Protestants in Peru, nor the consequence of direct pressure exerted by Protestant missionaries. When the amending bill was introduced in the Peruvian Congress, Peruvian Protestants organized a pro-religious freedom campaign that, Methodists claimed, was welcomed by the press (except, of course, by Catholic papers) and by "all social classes" to the extent that "we did not need to do anything at all."[7] The organizers gathered signatures in favor of the proposal from all over the country.[8] This supportive social atmosphere was nourished not only by the still-cherished ideas of progress and modernization but also by strong popular criticism, particularly in Lima and Callao, of the political involvement of the Catholic Church.

From the early years of the second decade, the Civilista regime[9] faced growing social unrest particularly within the urban proletariat. Anarcho-syndicalism made its appearance in 1911 and the eight-hour work day was achieved in 1918.[10] There were protests and revolts in the sugar plantations and mining centres.[11] Discontent began to manifest itself among those in the middle strata lacking opportunities for economic advancement and among the small and middle coastal landowners who were losing their land.[12] Moreover, the outbreak of the First World War created new, although temporary, economic stress. The populist policy of President Guillermo Billinghurst, 1912-1914, was a tentative response to social upheavals and also a brief discontinuity in the *Civilista* political patterns. The social agitation was a consequence of the economic model: the prosperity of the country depended on exports from its agro-mining enclaves; the export sector was mainly in foreign hands and the surplus remaining in Peru was distributed among the members of the dominant elite (spent mostly on luxuries) and not used for economic development.[13]

The achievement of religious freedom and the inability of the Catholic Church to prevent it must be analyzed in the historical context that has been summarily outlined above. In practice, both the Roman Catholic Church and the Methodist Church—as well as other traditional Protestant churches—had the ideological space to exert religious and concomitant cultural and political influence. This was done within the setting of an uneven socio-economic formation in which imperialist capitalist penetration was interwoven with pre-capitalist forms and with incipient local capitalism. The Methodists found in the educational field a convenient place to grow. However, the separation of the Roman Catholic Church from the state would remain an important political aim for Protestants in Peru. Methodists argued, always in line with their intellectual framework, that the relationship of the Catholic Church to the state prevented the building of a dynamic moral force and generated instead a religious indifference which inhibited spirituality.[14]

The Attempt to Consecrate Peru to the Sacred Heart

The Oncenio of Leguia: 1919-1930

In 1919, Augusto Leguia, a financier closely associated with American capital became the President of Peru. Paradoxically, in spite of his welcoming attitude towards American capital and especially during the first five years of his presidency, Protestants felt threatened by the influence of the Catholic hierarchy on the government. The proposal of a Concordat with the Vatican kept them especially worried from 1919 to 1924. The threat reached its highest point with the attempted consecration of Peru to the Sacred Heart in 1923.

Leguia's eleven years in government, known as the Oncenio, ran from 1919 to 1930. This era is characterized by a rearrangement of the power structure, which was achieved by means of a close association with American capital. Thus, Leguia was able to broaden the basis of the economic model based on exportation through the active participation of the state. The financial resources for increased state intervention were provided by American loans, which were invested in expanding the state bureaucracy (which in turn increased the internal demand for industrial and consumer goods). This policy was intended to diminish discontent among the middle and popular classes and counter-attack anti-oligarchic criticisms that had been launched against the Civilistas. It led to a fourfold increase in public expenditure and a tenfold increase in internal debt between 1914 and 1929.[15]

This policy amounted to an important break with traditional Civilista economic policy; the Civil Party had been closely associated with the agro-exporting interests and English capital, and adhered to the principles of orthodox liberal economics. Leguia introduced protectionism, which favored the pro-industrial sectors of the native bourgeoisie without interfering with growing American interests in Peru. At this time American capital was mainly concentrated in the mining enclaves while American industrialists were not interested in the introduction of manufactured products.[16]

A broad spectrum of anti-Civilista forces had brought Leguia to power; a reform platform favouring university students, workers, and Indians had been part of his demagogic discourse, summarized in the slogan La Patria Nueva (New Homeland). Once in power, conciliatory attitudes toward the Student Federation and toward workers' committees rapidly gave way to an astute repressive policy. Students, workers, and political leaders were sent into exile in order to prevent popular demonstrations and the creation of political and workers' organizations. However, in spite of the repression, the entire decade was a period of growth and maturation of workers' organizations as expressed in the creation of the General Confederation of Peruvian Workers in 1929.[17] At the beginning of the decade the government had to face the formidable popular protest of May 1923 that prevented the consecration of Peru to the Sacred Heart. At the end of the decade the debate, which can be summarized as dealing with the choice between *aprismo* and socialism, between Victor Raul Haya de la Torre, the exiled leader of the May uprising, and Jose Carlos Mariategui, provided the historical basis for the process of the formation of modern political parties.

Tracing the Popular Uprising of May 1923

The historical foundations of the popular uprising of May 1923 are to be found earlier, especially in the movement for university reform (1919) and the subsequent creation of the Popular Universities, while Leguia's motivations to please the Catholic Church are related to the search for a favourable balance of power within the government, given his dissension with the Civilistas.

In 1917, two years before the university reform movement flourished at San Marcos National University, *El Mensajero* published a comment on the intellectual life in this institution; the influential role of Roman Catholicism on education provides the referential framework. It says

> when those young sons of distinguished families, who receive primary and secondary education at schools controlled by the clergy, leave the clerical atmosphere in order to pursue higher education at San Marcos, they become exposed to the liberal atmosphere that they breathe heavily there. Thereafter, they are no longer submissive instruments of the confessor, but men who know how to maintain freedom of thought and consciousness.[18]

However, the university as an institution was far from being a source of creativity and freedom, in spite of the apparent ideological conflict with the Catholic Church. The prevalent currents of thought had been linked with a rightist political praxis, that of the Civil Party, and remained so in 1917, despite the crisis in the party.   In his essay on public education, included in *Seven Interpretative Essays on Peruvian Reality* (1928), Jose Carlos Mariategui wrote:

> In Peru, for several reasons, the university has been the stronghold of the colonial spirit, the first reason being that under the republic the old colonial aristocracy continued in power.

He adds,

> But this fact has been brought to light only since the new generation, having freed itself of the colonialist mentality or *civilista* historiography, has been able to judge Peruvian reality objectively.   The breakdown of the old class was foretold in 1919 by the "secessionist" character of the change of government.[19]

The movement for university reform is best regarded as a middle-class revolt, taking the form of student protests against the oligarchical selection of teachers, intellectual stagnation, and academic bureaucracy, among other academic concerns.[20]   The decree of September 20, 1919, that created free courses, and Laws 4002 and 4004, with new regulations governing the selection of teachers and the participation of the students in the university council, were temporary achievements.   However, the election of Victor Raul Haya de la Torre[21] as president of the Student Federation of Peru, and especially the resolutions of the First National Congress of Students (under Haya's chairmanship) creating the Gonzalez Prada Popular Universities for the working class, were lasting and influential achievements.   Mariategui worked in the Popular Universities when he returned from Europe in 1923.   The events of May 23, 1923, would reveal the dimension of the new student-worker rapprochement.[22]

> In May [writes Mariategui], the working class and the student vanguard demonstrated how closely they had become allied socially and ideologically.   On that date, in exceptionally favourable circumstances, the new generation played a historical role when it advanced from student unrest to collective and social protest.[23]

The immediate visible causes of the protest, led by Haya de la Torre, were the consecration of the country to the Sacred Heart and the prospective signing of a Concordat with the Vatican, two questions fundamental to the development of Protestant work. Missionaries could not then be indifferent to the popular protests, in spite of having a limited understanding of its real scope.

Protestants began to be alarmed in 1919 when the Vatican proposed to the Peruvian government the formulation of a Concordat which, they understood, would diminish the effects of the reform of the Constitution that provided religious freedom. Leguia took the issue to the Parliament again in 1922. A short article in *Renacimiento* contains the following statement:

> If the Concordat is signed, it will be difficult to promulgate a law improving education, to build good schools for girls, to eliminate ecclesiastical control over school inspectors dealing with discipline or to facilitate civil marriage and divorce. It will allow the nuncio or the bishops to interfere in education and in the promulgation of laws and justice; Colombia is proof of this.[24]

Protestants united beyond considerations of Social Gospel calls for co-operation to face the threat and preserve their existence. "We are glad that in all of this, the Young Men's Christian Association has been closely identified with the evangelical group so far as mutual association and protection are concerned."[25] The Young Men's Christian Association played an important role in the organization of protest and Haya de la Torre, a member himself, rallied support from within this organization. However, active support for the mobilization was not limited to the participation of Protestants, since Masons, anarchists, and many Catholics were also highly involved, while the workers from the Popular Universities and the students of San Marcos were the leading forces of the movement.[26] The protest, having strong socio-economic content although blurred by spontaneism, was directed against both the government and the Roman Catholic hierarchy; but it was not an anti-religious demonstration *per se*. The first manifesto published by the Popular Universities invited all "free men of Peru" to form a united front to block the projected consecration ceremony.

To make a special appeal to working classes, intellectuals,

students and journalists so that they, in support of the
propaganda of the United Front, would seek the adhesion
of all free citizens of Peru to favor the separation of the
Church from the State and the legislation of public
education.[27]

These demands put forward by the United Front Committee,
organized for the protest, were apparently in accordance with
liberal Protestant desires. However, the ideological context differed.
The leaders of the mobilization were those intellectuals, future
politicians and workers attending the Popular Universities,
protagonists of the ideological renovation of Peru during the third
decade.

    The consecration of Peru to the Sacred Heart, regarded by
the Methodists as a step in preparation for the approval of the
Concordat,[28] was prevented by the uprising which was popularly
supported despite the widespread repression used by the
government.[29] The persecution of the leaders, in particular Haya de
la Torre, was intense; however, the Popular Universities, now under
the leadership of Jose Carlos Mariategui, were able to continue
their work until 1927.

    Uncertainty prevailed among Protestants for some months
after the events of May 1923. A letter from the Mission dated in
November of that year addressed to Bishop W. Thirkield of the
Board of Foreign Missions referred to "an extraordinary political-
religious situation just at present and the attempts to crowd out
Protestant work."[30] Another letter dated in the same month reads:

> Just at present it seems to me that the position of all of
> us can be described by saying we are shoulder to shoulder
> with our backs to the wall, waiting to defend ourselves
> against the attacks that may come at any moment.[31]

Methodists misunderstood the political and social situation;
they insisted once more in attributing a dominant and unique role
to the Catholic Church in the state structure and in the
government. The following paragraph selected from a letter
addressed by the Mission to the Board of Foreign Missions in
October 1923 gives an insight into missionaries' views. Thus:

> the President himself is a well-disposed and liberal-minded
> man but he is now in the position where his only real

support is the army and the Church and in face of this he
has had the Constitution changed so as to permit his re-
election for a second term. The Congress is merely a tool
in his hands, so what we really have is a military
dictatorship supported by the priests. Everyone admits
this, the only way of opposing the government in anything
it proposes to do is by popular uprisings such as occurred
in May and these were prevented by arresting and
deporting the leaders.[32]

The lack of reference to the role played by the government of the
United States and the American companies in backing the Leguia
regime is the greatest failing here.[33] Neither is there an explanation
of the personal relationship that Methodist missionaries cultivated
with President Leguia, particularly through the Anglo-American
hospital.

Certainly, as Methodists pointed out, Leguia was close to the
hierarchy of the Roman Catholic Church, and the consecration of
the country to the Sacred Heart could provide seigniorial
legitimization to his government while also appealing to the
religious feelings of the people. It would be a useful resource to
attenuate the political imbalance generated by antagonism with the
agro-exporting sectors. However, he had miscalculated. Repression
was the response to the popular uprising and it was not casual,
given the oligarchic character of the state that did not allow room
for political mediation.

Victor Raul Haya de la Torre and Protestant Missionaries in Peru

Luis Alberto Sanchez and John Mackay have provided well-known
testimony confirming that Victor Raul Haya de la Torre took
refuge at Mackay's house following the events of May 1923. Then
a law student at San Marcos, Haya de la Torre was also a teacher
at the Anglo-Peruvian School, the staff of which also included Luis
Alberto Sanchez and Raul Porras Barrenechea, two politically
committed writers. At the time of the uprising the school was in
the process of being merged with the Instituto Norteamericano de
Varones (North American Institute for Boys), a Methodist school;
this was accomplished in 1924.

Haya de la Torre had been associated with Protestants
through the school where he taught but also through the Young
Men's Christian Association. A detailed letter concerning the May

events reads,

> Some of the bills in his defense [the reference is to Haya]
> happened to bear the printer's mark of the Evangelical
> printing shop and book store run by Mr.   John Ritchie of
> the English Evangelical Union, and an order was issued by
> the government to close his shop and deport him as an
> "extranjero pernicioso" (pernicious foreigner).   Fortunately
> he anticipated the order and explained that the forms for
> the bills were made at the time of the excitement last
> May when there was no question of a revolution and the
> question was purely religious.   So the order was not
> carried out.[34]

Haya was a great favorite with the teachers and students at
the Anglo-Peruvian School.   After his detention by the police it
was declared a centre of revolutionary propaganda and an order
was communicated through the British chargé d'affaires that two
other teachers, friends and sympathizers of his, must be dismissed
at once, or the school would be closed and its leader deported.   At
this point Mackay was on a trip abroad for the YMCA, giving
lectures in Argentina, Chile, and Uruguay, so the order was
complied with pending his return.   On his arrival back in Peru he
was refused permission to land.   Later, however, after a meeting
between the British Charge d'Affaires and the Foreign Minister, the
prohibition was lifted, although his baggage was held in Customs
for seven hours.[35]   Yet in spite of police harassment the Anglo-
Peruvian School as well as other Protestant schools continued their
normal activities.   Diplomatic intervention was always a great help
to missionaries working in Peru.

The relationship between Haya de la Torre and John
Mackay has been alluded to in numerous books and articles.
Nevertheless, Haya de la Torre's exposure to Protestant ideas,
especially Social Gospel doctrine, and his dealings with the
Committee on Cooperation in Latin American have not been
sufficiently explored.   F. Stanger, a leading Methodist missionary,
described Haya in a letter as

> a remarkably talented man (who) has some radical ideas
> but under the influence of Dr. Mackay and the YMCA he
> has modified a good deal and has become a professed
> Christian whereas before he was very anti-religious.
> Everyone who knows him believes in his sincerity and he

has repeated again and again his determination to keep
entirely out of politics and revolutionary plots.   His
ambitions are particularly to benefit the working and
oppressed classes.[36]

When Haya addressed the multitude at San Marcos on the
afternoon of May 23, just before the great demonstration began,

he brilliantly analyzed Christ by exalting the purity of his
doctrine and superiority of his ideals of humanity and
justice which were not in line with the absurd prejudices
and methods in use.

And Luis Alberto Sanchez, from whom the quotation comes, adds:
"the praise of Christ from Haya's lips had such sincerity that even
the most reluctant people applauded."[37] The same thing happened
again at the funeral of the victims of the demonstration, held two
days later.[38]   Haya   emphasized   the   social   dimension   of
Christianity.[39]

Haya de la Torre, after being hidden at Mackay's house, was
arrested (while in jail he was re-elected president of the Federation
of Students in October 1923) and deported to Panama where he
remained briefly (until invited to Mexico by Jose Vasconcelos, the
Mexican Minister of Education).   While in Panama, Haya de la
Torre delivered a number of lectures, one of them at the Methodist
Episcopal Church of the Malecon.   *El Mensajero Cristiano*, the
official Methodist voice in Lima, reproduced comments on Haya's
speech that had been published in *El Nuevo Diario*, a Panamanian
newspaper.   He had been invited to the Methodist Episcopal
Church by Dr. J. Miller, Superintendent of the Evangelical Mission
in the Republic of the Isthmus and in Costa Rica.   The speaker
showed great erudition while "giving an historical overview from
biblical times to our days."   He quoted from the apostles through
Carlyle to Ingenieros to support his argument.   Love, the love
preached by the "Rabbi of Nazareth in Judea" and the one that
Paul took to Europe to reveal to the ignorant masses, was an
important topic in a lecture that had ecumenical scope.[40] Haya's
language here was very similar, at least formally speaking, to that
used in articles published in *El Mensajero* (reproduced from *La
Nueva Democracia*) on the role of Christianity in the contemporary
world.   On his way to Mexico Haya participated in the foundation
of the Jose Marti Popular University in Havana, Cuba, which was

organized according to the model of the Gonzalez Prada Popular Universities in Peru. Shortly thereafter, *La Nueva Democracia* published a summary of his speech on the occasion of its inauguration when he was elected Honorary President.[41] Sanchez includes in his book, *Haya de la Torre o el Politico*, a passage from it:

> The twilight of Capitalist Europe reveals a lively historical lesson: The old social and political organization dies from its thirst for justice; if we help each other, we would be able to install in our New World the desire for a new life, free and belonging to ourselves.[42]

In 1924, Haya, now in Mexico, founded the American Popular Revolutionary Alliance (APRA), a broad anti-imperialist front including workers, peasants, intellectuals, and members of the middle classes. Its program, proposed as a continental one, calls for action against American imperialism, the achievement of political unity of Indoamerica (Haya's term for Latin America), nationalization of land and industries, the internationalization of the Panama Canal, and solidarity with all oppressed countries and classes.[43] From 1928 onwards, however, Haya declared his intention of transforming APRA into a party; thus, the Peruvian Aprista Party (PAP) appeared on the Peruvian political scene in 1931.

There were contradictions between the original APRA proposals, strongly anti-imperialistic and Indo-American, and Social Gospel preaching, messianic and paternalistic and in the end pro-imperialistic, but these were not allowed to interfere with friendly and lasting relations between APRA leaders and the Committee on Cooperation in Latin America. In any case, both believed in the potential hegemonic role of the middle classes. Moreover, qualities praised by Protestant missionaries appear to have been taken up in APRA doctrine, particularly in its mystique, and also in the organizational aspects: the setting of personal examples; the achievement of goals by moral means; the importance of conversion (only Aprismo will save Peru); and the desire to make the Aprista Party an educational force, a way of life (personal transformation was needed in order to transform Peruvian socio-economic conditions). Francois Bourricaud, after analyzing the famous address Haya delivered in Lima in 1931, made a list of the main virtues an Aprista militant was supposed to have.[44] These included the enthusiasm to awaken and convince; discipline, or the need to respect one's obligations to fellow comrades in struggle; realism, marching "with our feet on the sand and looking closely at reality"; and moderation, the avoidance of useless emotional extremes.[45] Although it is not part of this study to examine the early developments of APRA, it seems clear that Haya's acquaintance with evangelical Protestantism was not a negligible influence.[46] Historians who have analyzed APRA doctrine have ignored this source when explaining the origins of the characteristics mentioned above.[47]

The Methodist Mission, the American Embassy, and Leguia

The events of May 1923 as well as the controversy surrounding the proposal of a concordat with the Vatican clearly reveal the close relationship between the Methodist Episcopal Mission and the American Embassy, and indirectly between the Mission and the State Department in Washington.

Beyond the natural anxiety that events in Peru generated at the Board of Foreign Missions, and beyond the search for support among church people in the United States, it can be observed that a clear attempt at exerting pressure through official means was being made. Thus a letter from F. Stanger addressed to Harry Farmer (Board of Foreign Missions) on October 18, 1923, reads:

> I understand that our State Department made some representations to the government of Peru on the matter of this proposed law when it was first reported to you but I do not know just the matter of the communication. I am not even sure that any representation was made but have been told that there was. Just now our ambassador, ex-Senator Poindexter, is away on a trip to the interior so we cannot take the matter up with him. I should think that the State Department should again be appraised of the situation. Peru is now very anxious to keep the friendship of the United States because of the Tacna-Arica arbitration with Chile so a little pressure from Washington goes a long way here. I am not in favor of using this friendship for the control of internal affairs and domestic affairs of Peru, but some of the things done under the present conditions have been so unscrupulous and so daring that a little warning may be a healthy thing.[48]

Another letter unmistakably referred to American loans, when it remarked that Peru was depending too much on the outside world to disregard its opinion.[49] But the most revealing letter is the one that the Board of Foreign Missions sent to the Mission on November 30, 1923. It says:

> The religious and political situation seems to us to be very critical, and we thank you for keeping us advised as to just what is being done.   We sent information on to Secretary Hughes, and he advised us that the whole case had been referred to the Ambassador in Lima.   I hope there will be no further attempt made to promulgate the Concordat, as it would seem that if the matter is pushed, there will be sufficient opposition to raise somewhat of a civil conflict.[50]

The letters quoted above as well as other letters preserved in the collection of the Official Correspondence of the American Methodist Mission in Peru, dated in 1923 and 1924, are strong evidence of Mission opportunism.   On the one hand, Methodist missionaries who, at the time, were supportive of progressive Christian views (incidentally, most of the letters were signed by Stanger) cultivated good relations with those intellectuals and leaders who had begun to question both the Peruvian oligarchic political system and American imperialism.   On the other hand, missionaries tried hard in 1923 to bring American pressure to bear on the Peruvian government, thus illustrating both the inherent North-Americanism of Social Gospel doctrines and the acceptance of an imperialist context in relations between the United States and Latin America.   To complicate matters further, Methodists maintained very good personal relations with Leguia, who, despite his dictatorship, was regarded as a "liberal-minded president" sympathetic to American policies.   This friendship with Leguia was also associated with the ties the Mission had with both the English and the American community.[51] When the Association of the Anglo-American Hospital inaugurated the Casa de Salud in Bellavista, administered by the Methodist Mission, the president attended the tea prepared by the ladies of the English-American community.   The hospital director from 1924, Dr. E. MacCormack, himself a Methodist missionary, became Leguia's personal physician, being granted permission for special visits even after Leguia's overthrow and imprisonment in 1930.[52]

Methodist missionaries in Peru developed throughout the 1920s a dual policy originated by both the search for consolidation and security and the need for broader social support and recognition.   Progressive (Social Gospel supporters) as well as conservative missionaries - sometimes from a political perspective it is not easy to distinguish the one from the other - agreed that American influence was beneficial to the South American republics. Progressives, however, emphasized, within the context of a liberal reformist approach, the importance of influence from "progressive forces in the United States" (they were never specific in their political references).   This approach was the dominant one in the Committee on Cooperation in Latin America.

A statement in the minutes of the Annual Conference of the Methodist Episcopal Church in 1928, a time when *La Nueva Democracia* was publishing many articles by anti-imperialist and even anti-Leguia writers, is an illustrative example of the missionary policies.   It reads as follows:

> There is anti-American propaganda being carried on all over South America.   Nothing succeeds like success in arousing jealousy, envy and opposition.   There is no doubt, as President Leguia says, that the nations of Europe are doing all they can to undermine the influence of North America in South America.   This indirectly affects the work of the missionaries.   It makes people afraid that we are agents of the Government of the north, and that we are working for the economic and political subjugation of Latin America.[53]

Methodists and the Anglo-American Community

The Methodist Episcopal Church in religious terms a representative of traditional American Protestantism, was, in Peru, a conversionist church with the goal of bringing Protestant Christianity to Peruvians.   The church for Methodist foreign residents was organized separately from the beginning, in spite of being under the directorship of the Mission.   However, in 1919 the work with the English-speaking congregation in Callao had been discontinued and the congregation absorbed by the Anglican Church because "only a few people spoke exclusively English in Callao and there was not enough area for two evangelical congregations."[54]

The creation of the Anglo-American Hospital, Casa de Salud

de Bellavista, generated close ties between the Mission and the Anglo-American community. The hospital was opened in 1921, plans having been worked out in detailed negotiations between the community and the Mission a year earlier.[55] The Committee appointed to carry out the proposals consisted of: Mrs. Simpson and Mrs. Rawlings as members of the community, Reverend Walter Lack, and representatives of the following companies: the Cerro de Pasco Copper Corporation; Messrs. Grace and Company; Messrs. Graham, Rowe and Company; Messrs. W. and J. Lockett; and the Peruvian Corporation.[56] The main English and American corporations working in Peru can be easily recognized. In this manner, the Association of the Anglo-American Hospital was constituted; this association bought the building for the hospital. The Mission would be in charge of its direct administration and provision of personnel.

Maintenance of good relations with the Anglo-American community was not entirely easy. A memorandum addressed to the Board of Bishops prepared by the Finance Committee of the North Andean Mission is highly illustrative. It says:

> While recognizing the sincere good will and purpose of Bishop Thirkield, we feel that he does not take the needful attitude toward the Anglo-American community of Lima, and therefore his methods imperil the relations between our mission and that community when at the present time, due to the joint interest in the British-American Hospital of Lima, it is very necessary that the best of relations be cultivated. We feel deeply that in the best interest of our mission, in this and also in other respects, we demand the presence of Bishop Oldham at the upcoming Annual Conference.[57]

The Methodist Mission and the committee representing the Anglo-American community had opposing views on the aims of the hospital. A missionary put it in this way,

> The British-American residents want a hospital for their own use and do not care a fig, the most of them, for philanthropic efforts, while the whole purpose of the Mission is philanthropic.[58]

However, missionaries were able to reach a point of equilibrium—in line with their ambiguous political stands—judging by the documentation concerning life at the hospital and the helpful collaboration the hospital provided to Methodist schools.

The Mission at the American Mining Enclaves

In principle the Methodist teachings in Peru were addressed to everyone, without regard to social conditions, and within an atmosphere of "brotherhood". But the details of Mission practice show that the idea of "brotherhood" was not free from class distinctions and political choices. During the first thirty years of existence (from 1890 to 1920), the Mission, in its pursuit of prestige and influence, assiduously cultivated the dominant classes, including semi-feudal landowners. Testimonies to this policy appear in the reports from Mission schools to the annual conferences in the second decade. Other testimonies support this view. A. T. Vasquez, one of the first converts to become a minister, a man from a working-class background, explained his evangelistic work in Huancayo in 1910 as follows: "I took material for preaching from publications in English; I invited distinguished people belonging to the high society like Priale, Raez and others."[59] Bishop Thomas B. Neely writes in his book *La Iglesia Metodista Episcopal en America del Sur*, published in 1906, that the Methodists had educated poor and middle-class people, but also the youth from the higher classes of society, including the children of presidents and the spouses of senators in some South American republics. He continues, "It has taken men in humble circumstances and it has transformed them into good preachers and useful pastors and has given them social representation and 'entree' into good homes and higher classes."[60] The reader will be left wondering what is wrong with being humble - supposedly he means poor - and what he understood as good homes. The stress on the connection between commitment to evangelical Protestantism and social advancement is striking.

Methodist religious and educational activities in Peru were mainly concentrated in urban areas, reaching people of various social backgrounds and generating (at least in so far as education was concerned) particular interest among the middle class, whose members, together with the Peruvian bourgeoisie, were eager to acquire modern skills, learn English, and imitate foreign styles of life. Mariategui comments colourfully on this imitative trend, using it to illustrate the instability of the political commitment of the middle class, to which APRA had assigned a potential anti-imperialist role:

> In Peru, the white aristocrat and the white bourgeois despise both the popular, and the national, and above all, they think of themselves as white. The *mestizo* petit-bourgeois imitates this example. The *Limena* bourgeoisie fraternize with Yankee capitalists and even with their employees at the Country Club, playing tennis, and at other social functions. A Yankee marries a Creole woman without considerations of race or religion, and she does not feel scruples of nationality or culture when she prefers to marry an individual from the invading race. The middle-class girl also lacks these scruples. The "huachafita" that could "catch" a Yankee employee working for the Grace Company or the Foundation married him with the satisfaction of someone raising her social condition.[61]

However, Methodism, or Protestantism in general, did not become a serious *religious* alternative for either the middle class or any bourgeois sector, including the incipient industrial bourgeoisie (noticeable from 1920 onwards). By the early 1920s, however, the Committee on Cooperation in Latin American (the Methodists were active members) was achieving collaboration with militant intellectuals with a middle-class background who questioned the social and economic system. Thus, a basis was being set for a new source of legitimation.

Testimonies associated with the missionary stations in or near the American mining enclaves provide us with the unique opportunity to compare the Mission social doctrine, as expressed in Methodist publications, with Mission policy in practice.

The minutes of the annual conferences held during the second decade referred to La Oroya, Cerro de Pasco, Smelter, Goyllarisquisga, Yauli, Huarochiri, and other villages found within the mining circuit, as progressive centres.[62] The Mission initiated religious work in the area in 1910; it received material support from both the Cerro de Pasco Copper Corporation (American) and the Peruvian Corporation (British). The latter controlled the railways service.[63] In April 1920 *El Mensajero* acknowledged this co-operation in these terms:

> In Smelter, the school functions under the sponsorship of the American company, and we are pleased to send our

most sincere gratitude to its executives for this generous and philanthropic attitude, which represents their love of mankind.[64]

The old school in Cerro de Pasco was also reopened in 1920 under the protection of the same company.[65] Words of praise were written in *El Mensajero* again when the American company followed governmental regulations and adopted an anti-alcohol policy within the compounds.[66]

This and other evidence of friendly relations with the American company might be taken simply as another example of the Mission's belief, under the inspiration of Social Gospel doctrines, in the importance of conciliation between labour and capital, were it not for the persistent failure to mention the horrible working and living conditions of the mining workers, many of them *enganchados*.

What did it mean to be an *enganchado*? *Enganche* or snaring was a means to recruit a labour force within the pre-capitalist context. The *enganchados* received money in advance upon the commencement of employment, but were forced to shop within the mining compound at the company store (at inflated prices). They were invariably in debt to their employers, and tied to the labour force until they could work off their obligations. As a consequence, the *enganchados* lost the right to determine their own lives.[67] Most *enganchados* were illiterate and also ignorant of their rights; the scarcity of a free labour force led the *enganchadores* to recruit workers even among children. Physical punishment was used and the working "day" lasted thirty-six hours, with occasional breaks to chew coca; the rest period between shifts was for twelve hours only. A high death rate was not uncommon because of accidents or repressive actions intended to discourage rebellion.[68]

In spite of the social dimension of progressive Christianity, the dominant theological current among Methodists, *El Mensajero* was appallingly silent about the labour policies of the Cerro de Pasco Copper Corporation; meanwhile missionaries accepted the co-operation of the company and tried to gain converts among the workers (most of them Indians) and employees. There was a notable tendency to disrupt the equilibrium between the orthodox individualistic approach and social commitment in the evangelistic efforts among mining workers and peasants. This shows that the individualistic components of the Social Gospel doctrines became easily dominant, giving support to rightist political practices. The dominance was partly engendered by the paternalistic character of these doctrines as applied to Latin America (especially the conviction of the superiority of American cultural patterns). But it was also facilitated by the poor preparation of native ministers working in the area (who mainly assimilated the moralizing aspects of the doctrine), by doctrinal disagreements among missionaries, and by a tendency toward the adoption of opportunistic policies in order to gain new converts or to strengthen missionary activities.

Methodist missionaries working in the mining circuit between 1910 and 1930 left many letters, a spiritual literature that describes their impressions. However, they do not contain strong denunciations of the misery and exploitations, nor testimonies supporting workers' protests. A report resulting from a visit to the central mountain district (the document is not dated) which took in Oroya, Smelter, Cerro de Pasco, and included the villages of Huaraucaca and Colquilja, described the people of these places as very humble, ignorant, and economically poor. Yet the visitor conceded that

> I admire them and have a great respect for their faithfulness, and fine Christian spirit. This people of Smelter and Huaraucaca are always eager and anxious to hear the Word of God. And they are not only listeners, but also doers of His Words, for their lives are transformed and changed.[69]

The nature of the transformations and changes is not explained; but it is suspected that temperance was the main issue in this assessment since it was frequently considered a leading cause of moral progress and prosperity.[70]

Methodists and the Indians

At the beginning of the twentieth century, four-fifths of the Peruvian population lived in the countryside; these were mostly Indian peasants under the domination of landowners and *gamonales*.[71] This peasantry consisted of communal landholders, peons, owners of a plot of land, sharecroppers, and other tenant farmers all holding a slightly different peasant status but invariably having to exchange part of their time, their yield, or their money for the right to cultivate a piece of land.[72]

The Methodist Mission originally had considered plans for bringing evangelical Christianity to Peru's Indian peasantry. Thomas Wood even dreamed of the evangelization of the entire territory of the Inca Empire; as a first step he translated St. Luke into Quechua, a language he mastered. The National Missionary Society, an interdenominational Peruvian organization founded in 1916, had as an important goal the spreading among the Indians of the knowledge of the scriptures through publications, missions, and schools, and the supporting of schools already established. The Society went even further when it said that in every school supported by the Society, Quechua should be taught.[73]

Methodist missionary work did not develop in strictly rural areas. The social situation of the Indian peasantry, especially their poverty and "moral state," was mostly attributed by Methodists to the tolerance by Roman Catholicism of alcoholism and superstition, with the consequent furthering of ignorance. (This approach differs from that of contributions published in *La Nueva Democracia* by progressive Peruvian writers.) The Roman Catholic Church, in turn, attributed each rebellion against the expansion of latifundia and *gamonalismo* to the evangelical work being carried out with the Indians. Adventists in Puno, for example, were accused by the Catholic Church of provoking the Indian revolt that shook the north side of Lake Titicaca in 1921; in fact, the Adventists were working on the west side of the lake.[74] In other cases, the priests organized attacks against Protestant missionaries working in the villages;[75] many of these cases affected Methodists.

In spite of the importance of the Indigenista Movement after the second decade and during the 1920s and the consequent public denunciation of landowners and *gamonales* for the victimization of the Indian peasantry, and the occurrence of dramatic peasant rebellions, Methodists in Peru did not elaborate on these matters (although *Renacimiento*, the interdenominational periodical without Methodist representation, clearly denounced the Indians' condition). Because of their special relationship with the Cerro de Pasco Copper Corporation, Methodist missionaries also had little to say about the destructive effects of the La Oroya smelting plant on nearby land, which condemned peasants to proletarianization: a situation that was aggravated by the territorial expansion of the company.[76]

A short article published in *El Mensajero* (articles on Indians are rare in this periodical) and signed by Saulo, a correspondent from Cerro de Pasco, has a strongly paternalistic tone that is interwoven with an underestimation of the ability and intelligence of the indigenous people. Only within this context did the author claim a right for Indians "to participate in the life of civilized people." One of the paragraphs reads:

> Yes friends; If this brother, mentally immature [menor en mente] is forced to take communion, we should work with him with major emphasis, instilling the loving and precious maxims and teachings we received from Christ, the only and blessed friend of the poor.[77]

It continues with a reference condemning Catholic priests. The prejudiced tone of this article is in line with the analysis of Peruvian Indians published in the reports of the Montevideo Congress on Christian Work in South America in 1925.

Conclusion

The involvement of Methodists in the search for civil rights, the progressive educational conceptions found in their schools, their preaching from the second decade onwards of the Social Gospel doctrines, and, in particular, the close ties of the Mission with the Committee on Cooperation in Latin America, suggest that Methodist missionaries in Peru found an ideological space to enable them to play a bourgeois-democratic role. This appreciation can also be extended to other Protestant denominations working in Peru, especially the Free Church of Scotland. This role had its own peculiarity, especially the dual character of the political attitudes assumed by the Mission (i.e., good relations with both Leguia as well as his opponents; a reliance on American pressure during the consecration affair while co-existing with the support of progressive, and even anti-imperialist, views). In fact, the democratic role the Mission was able to play was determined by both the uneven and combined character of the Peruvian socio-economic formation and by the missionaries' democratic conceptions, which, in spite of their reformist content, were not in conflict with imperialism.

References

[1]There are many illustrative testimonies. For example, one reads: "In spite of the tramplings of the Indiada from Huamancaca Chico, due to the insinuation of the priests, the Indians recognized their fault and asked for a friendly reconciliation which was accomplished with fair satisfaction on our part on the 17th of this month."   Letter of Fidel Ferrer addressed to F. M. Stanger (Methodist Mission in Lima), dated Huancayo-Peru, December 19, 1923.   A report dated in 1896 reads: "the parish priest exerts more power than the Supreme Government; this is based on the worn out assumption that the civil power is the secular arm of the ecclesiastic power: thus, it is regrettable that in Peru under the Republic—as it was under the Vice-royalty and the Inquisition—a weak authority obeys the illegal and inquisitorial intimidations of the clergy."   Federico Antay, *Informe desde Julio 17 de 1895 a Enero 12 de 1896* (Lima: Plaza de la Inquisicion 213, Imprenta y Libreria, 1896), p. 36.

[2]*Actas de la Sexta Reunion de la Conferencia Misionera Andina del Norte de la Iglesia Metodista Episcopal*, November 12 to 16, 1914.

[3]Pablo Richard, *Iglesia, Estado Autoritario y Clases Sociales en America Latina*. Documentos. DOCET. CELAM III, No. 10 (Lima: CELADEC, 1975) p. 3.

[4]"Near Puno, in connection with an evangelical mission, there had formed a group of Indians who, by their total abstinence from the use of alcohol and of coca had aroused the admiration of impartial observers; while their growth in numbers provoked the wrath of Dr. Valentin Ampuero, the Rev. Bishop of Puno. On March 3, 1913, this prelate, at the head of a mob, which denouncers calculated to number forty on horseback, and two hundred on foot, marched this crowd to the mission. Arriving there, they committed acts of violence in the building, took six Indian prisoners—one of them a woman—and led them to the Chucuito jail, from which they were conducted by gendarmes to the police station of Puno."   Wenceslao O. Bahamonde, "Establishment of Evangelical Christianity in Peru," Incomplete materials on developments after 1900, not included in thesis of the same title (Lima, 1952), p. 41. See also Francis M. Stanger, "La Iglesia y el Estado en el Peru Independiente."   (Doctoral dissertation, Facultad de Filosofia, Historia y Letras, Universidad Nacional Mayor de San Marcos, Lima, 1925).

[5]*Actas de la Quinta Reunion*, December 16 to 21, 1913.

[6]Wenceslao O. Bahamonde, "Establishment of Evangelical Christianity," p. 42. The opposition of the Catholic Church was strong and the President of the country refused to sign the bill. According to Peruvian practice, a bill became law if, after remaining a specified number of days without being signed by the President of the country, the Congress passed it again.

[7]*Actas de la Quinta Reunion*, December 16 to 21, 1913.

[8]Ibid. Ruperto Algorta was able to raise the interest of the Liberal Centre of Workers in favour of the reform of the Constitution.

[9]The period 1985-1919 is characterized by the dominance of *Civilismo*.

[10]Denis Sulmont S., *Historia del Movimiento Obrero en el Peru (de 1890 a 1977)* (Lima: TAREA, 1977), pp. 31-35.

[11]Ibid., p. 26.

[12]The agro-exporting businessmen used the legal apparatus, the financial services, and the control of water resources to expell small and medium proprietors from their land. Ernesto Yepes del Castillo, *Peru 1820-1920, Un Siglo de Desarrollo Capitalista* (Lima: Instituto de Estudios Peruanos, 1972), p. 132.

[13]"The country had become an agro-mining enclave and the export-import relation constituted the base from where its basic economic mechanism came. A great part of the economic surplus was controlled by foreign capital through exportation; the surplus for investments (which would be able to broaden the productive base and to orient it toward the needs of a growing and impoverished social base) was subjected to direct decisions coming from factors external to the local economy. Thus, part of the surplus (*excedente*) kept in the country, was distributed among the dominant social factions, while the rest remained in the hands of foreign companies." Ernesto Yepes del Castillo, *Peru 1820-1920*, pp. 163-264.

[14]See also, "Carta Abierta al Episcopado Peruano." *Renacimiento*, XXI, No. 5 (Lima: May 1932).

[15]Ernesto Yepes del Castillo, *Peru 1820-1920*, pp. 284-285. See also Baltazar Caravedo Molinari, *Burguesia e Industria en el Peru 1933-1945* (Lima: Instituto de Estudios Peruanos, 1976), pp. 38-46.

[16]Baltazar Caravedo Molinari, *Burguesia e Industria*, pp. 38-46. Leguia's government faced structural pressures, in particular the demographic pressure in urban areas resulting from internal migrations which were a consequence of both the expansion and the industrialization of the "haciendas serranas," especially those located in the south, and the deterioration of the land close to the mining circuit. The government was then forced to embark on a minimal industrialization. The economic policy implemented by Leguia was thus relatively favourable to industrial expansion. This pro-industrial policy moved around four axes: the centralization of the banking system; the tributary guidelines (exporting activities were more heavily taxed—this policy affected the agro-exporting groups); the alliance with pro-industrial forces among the native bourgeoisie; and the construction of highways facilitating regional communications. Ibid., pp. 38-42.

[17]Mariategui actively participated in the organization of the workers. He and his group considered that anarchist trade-unionism had been surpassed by historical circumstances and that its continuation blocked the political development of the proletariat. However, he tried to avoid the ideological divisions that had aborted the initial efforts of organization and centralization. Therefore, he proposed through his articles and speeches at the Popular Universities and at Workers' Congresses the tactic of a single front and proletarian unity. This proposal was first advanced in 1924 on the occasion of the celebration of Workers' Day. On May 17, 1929, the General Confederation of Workers of Peru (CGTP) was organized on the initiative of the Socialist Party of Peru (founded in 1928), a party of workers and peasants. The Confederation of Workers included the main trade-unions of the time; Federation of Drivers, Textile Federation, Graphic Federation, Federation of *Yanaconas*, Federation of Motorists and Engine Drivers, the Unification of Beer Workers at Beckus and Johnson, Society of Stevedores from Callao, and the Federation of Crew Members. Denis Sulmont S., *Historia del Movimiento*, pp. 43 and 54.

[18]"La Universidad Catolica," *El Mensajero*, III, No. 28 (Lima, April 1917), p. 2.

[19]Jose Carlos Mariategui, *Seven Interpretative Essays on Peruvian Reality* (Austin and London: University of Texas Press, 1971), p. 100.

[20]Details of the student movement are not provided here. The reader may consult the following authors: Jose Carlos Mariategui, *Seven Interpretative Essays*, pp. 103-123 and Jorge

Basadre, *Historia de la Republica del Peru*, Vol. X (Lima: Ediciones Historia, 1964), Chapter CLXXXIII.

[21]R. Haya de la Torre was originally from Trujillo, a city on the northern coast. In this region, imperialist companies had displaced small and medium landowners and Indian communities; they also competed with local merchants. Young people from Trujillo, particularly intellectuals from middle-class origins, reacted against the situation. Haya was among these intellectuals. For a detailed analysis see: Peter Klaren, *La Formacion de la Haciendas Azucareras y los Origenes del APRA* (Lima: Instituto de Estudios Peruanos, 1970), Chapter V.

[22]In 1919, Haya became the President of the Student Federation of Peru. In 1920, the Student Congress held in Cuzco approved the creation of the Gonzalez Prada Popular Universities under the direction of the Federation. Popular Universities were evening schools for the working class; they taught courses covered today by formal education, as well as courses related to the workers' organizations and their struggle. The attendance was impressive; for example, in Vitarte, between seventy and four hundred workers of both sexes went to classes twice a week. The Popular Universities published *Claridad*; Jose Carlos Mariategui, who returned to Peru from Europe in 1923, turned Popular Universities into schools for the formation of class consciousness. He also linked the Peruvian proletariat to the international proletariat. There were Popular Universities in Lima, Vitarte, Trujillo, Arequipa, Salaverry, Cuzco, Callao, and other places. Isabel Yepez and Estela Gonzalez, "La Autoeducacion Obrera," *Chaski Boletin de Educacion Popular*, No. 17 (Lima, April 1981), pp. 7-14.

[23]Jose Carlos Mariategui, *Seven Interpretative Essays*, p. 107.

[24]"Una Emboscada," *Renacimiento*, XI, No. 8 (Lima: August 1922), p. 115.

[25]Letter of F. Stanger (Methodist Episcopal Mission in Peru) addressed to Mr. J.C. Field (Board of Foreign Missions) dated Lima, November 9, 1923.

[26]Jeffrey L. Klaiber, S. J., *Religion and Revolution in Peru 1824-1976* (Indiana: University of Notre Dame Press, 1977) pp. 129-132.

[27]Ibid., p. 130.

[28]Letter of F. Stanger (Methodist Episcopal Mission in Peru) addressed to Dr. Harry Farmer (Board of Foreign Missions) dated Lima, October 18, 1923.

[29]"Led by Haya de la Torre and the students of the Popular Universities, several thousand demonstrators marched from San Marcos through downtown Lima toward the principal plaza. Unexpectedly, however, mounted police advanced on the students and workers from the rear, and in the ensuing melee two protesters and three policemen were killed and many wounded.   The day after the confrontation, after calling for a general strike, several thousand students and workers once again took to the streets, this time to protest against the attack by the police on the preceding day.   As they moved through the streets toward the Plaza de Armas they cried such slogans as 'down with the Archbishop' and 'away with Clericalism.'   Once in the plaza, Haya addressed the marchers from the front door of the cathedral."

"The third great protest march, which took place on May 25, was the funeral procession for the two demonstrators who had been killed."

"The brief drama of the consecration of Peru to the Sacred Heart ended that same day when Archbishop Lisson issued a decree suspending the ceremony."   Jeffrey L. Klaiber, S. J., *Religion and Revolution in Peru*, pp. 132-133.

[30]Letter of F. Stanger (Methodist Episcopal Mission in Peru) addressed to Bishop W. P. Thirkield (Board of Foreign Missions) dated in Lima, November 6, 1923.

[31]Letter of F. Stanger (Methodist Episcopal Mission in Peru) addressed to Mr. J. C. Field dated in Lima, November 9, 1923.

[32]Letter of F. Stanger (Methodist Episcopal Mission in Peru) addressed to Dr. Harry Farmer (Board of Foreign Missions) dated in Lima, October 18, 1923.

[33]See James C. Carey, *Peru and the United States, 1900-1962* (Indiana: University of Notre Dame Press, 1964), Chapter III.

[34]Letter of F. Stanger (Methodist Episcopal Mission in Peru) addressed to Dr. Harry Farmer (Board of Foreign Missions) dated in Lima, October 18, 1923.

[35]Ibid.   [36]Ibid.

[37]Luis Alberto Sanchez, *Haya de la Torre o el Politico. Cronica de una Vida sin Tregua* (3rd edition, Santiago de Chile: Ediciones Ercilla, 1936), p. 83.

[38]Ibid., p. 90.

[39]"In his work developing this theme, *The Other Spanish Christ*, Dr. Mackay comments on Haya's discovery of the message of social justice in the prophets and in Jesus. He later made the discovery that in the writings of the Old Testament prophets and in the teachings of Jesus were more incandescent denunciations of oppression and wrong than he or his companions had ever made. It dawned upon him not only that there could be a union between religion and ethics, but that there should be, and that in the religion of the Bible there was. The book began to take on a new meaning." Jeffrey Klaiber, S. J., *Religion and Revolution in Peru*, p. 124. The quotation has been taken from John A. Mackay, *The Other Spanish Christ* (London: Student Christian Movement Press, 1932), p. 194.

[40]The comment concludes in the following manner: "Haya proved that the world is today corrupted and in the same condition it was in when Jesus, the sublime teacher of the Messianic doctrine, came two thousand years ago. The presence of another like him is necessary to bring once again peace to our spirits, harmony to our consciousness, serenity to our life. Thus, it will end the agitation that mankind is experiencing in Europe as in America, Asia and Africa." "El Senor Haya de la Torre: En Panama Pronuncia Bellisima Pieza Oratoria en la Iglesia Metodista," *El Mensajero Cristiano*, IX, No. 136 (Lima, November 15, 1923), p. 8.

[41]Luis Alberto Sanchez, *Haya de la Torre o el Politico*, p. 106.

[42]Ibid, p. 107. The leader of the university reform in Cuba, Julio Antonio Mella, manifested from the beginning a tendency towards social radicalization. There were great political differences between Victor Raul Haya de la Torre and Mella.

[43]Denis Sulmont S., *Historia del Movimiento*, p. 42. The Kuomintang, the nationalist Chinese party created in 1905, and the Mexican Revolution are considered important sources of inspiration for APRA. It is important to point out that, coincidentally, the Methodist mission in China maintained a very good relationship with Chiang Kai-Shek whose wife, educated in the United States, was an active evangelical leader. The social bases of APRA have

been analyzed by the following authors: Peter Klaren, *La Formacion de las Haciendas Azucareras y los Origenes del APRA* (Lima: Instituto de Estudios Peruanos, 1970); Lisa North, "Origenes y Crecimiento del Partido Aprista y el Cambio Socio-economico en el Peru," *Desarrollo Economico*, XXXVIII, No. 10 (1970), pp. 163-214.

[44]François Bourricaud, *Ideologia y Desarrollo, El Caso del Partido Aprista Peruano.*   (Mexico: El Colegio de Mexico, Jornadas No. 58, 1966), p. 17.

[45]Ibid., pp. 17-18.

[46]In a personal conversation with Luis Heysen, *aprista* leader, teacher at the Popular Universities in the early years of the 1920s, and active participant in the dramatic events of May 23rd, he praised Protestant moral standards, and immediately recalled the good relationship with the Committee on Cooperation. He still had at hand old copies of *La Nueva Democracia.*   Dr. Heysen constantly mentioned the Methodists, Dr. John Mackay, and the YMCA during the conversation.   L. Heysen was also a Master Mason.   Personal interview with Luis Heysen, Lima, July 1977.   I was introduced to Dr. Heysen by an ex-Aprista militant, Manuel Carranza Marquez.

[47]For example, Harry Kantor finds a resemblance with Gandhi's ideas.   Harry Kantor, *The Ideology and Program of the Peruvian Aprista Movement* (New York: Octagon Books, 1966), p. 122.   "APRA" is widely used to refer to the Peruvian Aprista Party.

[48]Letter of F. Stanger (Methodist Episcopal Mission in Peru) addressed to Dr. Harry Farmer (Board of Foreign Missions) dated Lima, October 18, 1923.

[49]Letter of F. Stanger (Methodist Episcopal Mission in Peru) addressed to Bishop W. P. Thirkield (Board of Foreign Missions) dated Lima, November 6, 1923.

[50]Letter of Dr. Harry Farmer (Board of Foreign Missions) addressed to F. Stanger (Methodist Episcopal Mission in Peru) dated New York, November 30, 1923.

[51]*Actas de la Decima Tercera Reunion*, December 28, 1921 to January 1, 1922.

[52]Letter of the Methodist Episcopal Mission in Peru

addressed to Dr. and Mrs. Rader dated Lima, January 6, 1932.

[53]*Actas de la Vigesima Reunion*, February 7 to 10, 1929.

[54]*Actas de la Octava Reunion*, November 30 to December 3, 1916.

[55]*Actas de la Decima Segunda Reunion*, February 3 to 8, 1921.

[56]Anglo-American Committee, *Anglo-American Hospital, Report Presented to a General Meeting of the Anglo-American Community on April 5, 1920.*

[57]Memorandum to the Board of Bishops from the Missionaries forming the Financing Committee of the North Andes Mission. Lima, March 28, 1923. Signed by H. P. Archerd (Superintendent Central District), A. W. Greenman (Superintendent Coast District), Dr. Warren L. Fleck, F. M. Stanger (Secretary Financial Committee), Clarence R. Snell, Ruperto Algorta.

[58]Letter of the Methodist Mission in Peru addressed to Dr. Harry Farmer (Board of Foreign Missions), dated Lima, October 5, 1922.

[59]A. T. Vasquez, "Datos Historicos de la Iglesia Metodista Episcopal," Personal testimony (Lima, September, 1937).

[60]Thomas B. Neely, *La Iglesia Metodista Episcopal en America del Sur* (Buenos Aires-Argentina: 1906), pp. 26 and 28.

[61]J. C. Mariategui argued that the nationalist factor was neither decisive nor fundamental to the anti-imperialist struggle in Peru. Jose Carlos Mariategui, "Punto de Vista Anti-Imperialista," in *Ideologia y Politica* (2nd Edition, Lima: Empresa Editora Amauta, 1971), p. 88.

[62]Thomas Wood, the first Methodist missionary in Peru, gained the interest of American businessmen in the exploitation of mining zones there, and a biographical comment published in *El Mensajero* lets us know that the result of his activity was "great and beneficial" for Peru. "Rasgos Biograficos del Rev. Thomas B. Wood," *El Mensajero Cristiano*, IX, No. 120 (Lima, March 15, 1923), p. 2.

[63]*Actas de la Sexta Reunion*, November 12 to 16, 1914.

[64]"Seccion del Centro," *El Mensajero*, VI, No. 61 (Lima, May 1920), p. 13.

[65]Ibid.

[66]"A Nuestros Lectores de Cerro de Pasco y Smelter." *El Mensajero*, VI, No. 59 (Lima, March 1920), p. 18.

[67]Ernesto Yepes del Castillo, *Peru 1820-1920*, pp. 211-212.

[68]Ibid., p.211.

[69]*Visiting the Central Mountain District from Oroya to Smelter and Cerro de Pasco including the villages of Huarancaca and Coquilja.* Internal Report. (Undated, but probably written in the early 1920s.)

[70]The Mission strongly supported the governmental policy against alcohol. (For example, anti-alcohol instruction in schools, Law 2282.) They were also closely in touch with the American and international movement against alcohol. One example is the World League against Alcohol founded in Washington in 1919. The Mission sent a representative, Mr. Ruperto Algorta, a Peruvian convert, to the First Anti-Alcohol International Congress held in Washington in 1920. A diplomatic staff member of the Peruvian Embassy attended the meeting. Ruperto Algorta, "El Congreso Internacional Anti-alcoholico Reunido en Washington, D. C.," *El Mensajero*, VI, No. 67 (Lima, November 1920) pp. 2-3. Mr. William Jennings Bryan was also present. Algorta met him and wrote on his return: "Mr. Bryan congratulated us and had great pleasure in hearing about the anti-alcohol campaign in Peru. He reminisced about the days he had spent in Lima and mentioned well-known names." Go Ahead, "El Congreso Internacional Contra el Alcoholismo," *El Mensajero*, VI, No. 65 (Lima: September 1920), p. 2. *El Mensajero* always included topics on temperance, sometimes up to a whole page. The information focuses a great deal on American policies against alcohol. See for example, "Temperancia: Constitucion de la Liga Mundial Contra el Alcoholismo", *El Mensajero*, VI, No. 61, (Lima, May 1920), pp. 7-8. The struggle of the Protestant missionaries against alcohol was greatly appreciated by many people in Peru. *El Mensajero* reproduced articles published in the main Peruvian newspapers which had positive appraisals on the moral aspects of missionary religion activities. For example, "La labour Moralizadora de los Evangelistas," *La Prensa* (Lima, January 5, 1918) reproduced in *El Mensajero*, V, No. 39 (Lima, March 1918), pp. 11-12.

[71]*Gamonal*: An *haciendado, latifundista,* or other member of the provincial establishment. At once the peasant's landlord and boss.

[72]Denis Sulmont, *Historia del Movimiento,* p. 28. "The new relations established between traditional landowners and modern business leaders allowed for the extraction of the maximum possible benefit from the indigenous people's work by keeping traditional forms of semi-servile and semi-feudal exploitation and by combining these with capitalist methods." *Ibid.*

[73]"Sociedad Misionera Nacional," *El Mensajero,* II, No. 18 (Lima, June 1916), pp. 7-8.

[74]"Sublevacion Indigena," *Renacimiento,* X, No. 11 (Lima, November 1921), p. 162.

[75]One of the most publicized incidents happened in Caraz, in the province of Huaylas, in 1922. "Los Sucesos de Caraz. Documentos para la Historia." *Renacimiento,* XI, No. 8 (Lima, August 1922), p. 123.

[76]Baltazar Caravedo Molinari, *Burguesia e Industria,* p. 39.

[77]Saulo, "El Indigena y el Evangelio," *El Mensajero,* VI, No. 61 (Lima, May 1920), p. 14.

CHAPTER V

The Public School System, 1895-1930

Issues In Educational Policies

At the end of the nineteenth century, there was a clear awareness of the limitations of public schooling. President Nicolas de Pierola said in 1897 in his address to the Legislative Chambers, "Primary instruction is deficient, poorly structured and totally disproportionate to the great expenses that it imposes. Secondary and Superior instruction are very distressing."[1] Criticisms went beyond the schooling system and even touched the ideology of the dominant classes; these came mainly from positivist thinkers. Manual V. Villaran stated in 1900 in his speech on the "Liberal Professions in Peru":

> We are infected with the sickness of the old, decadent countries, with their preoccupation with speaking and writing instead of acting, with "moving words instead of things," an illness that is a sign of indolence and weakness.[2]

Peruvian public education had been characterized by a dominant Spanish influence; consequently literary and rhetorical ideas were emphasized, to the detriment of practical considerations. French influences did not correct the Spanish tendencies but intensified them. (They were manifested in the educational policy implemented by President Manuel Pardo between 1872 and 1876 and also in the Law of Instruction promulgated on March 9, 1901.)[3] British influences inspired the reform of 1902 while American influences were especially notable from 1909 onward and are easily noticed in the law of 1920.[4]

Positivist thinkers examined the functions of schools from the perspective of modern scientific and technological achievement; an education practically oriented was considered the motor for national transformation. Javier Prado, Mariano Cornejo, Joaquin Capelo, Jorge Polar, Pedro A. Labarthe, and Isaac Alzamora are among those intellectuals who interested themselves in education.[5] Prado pointed out the persistence of academicism and colonial scholasticism, and criticized the lack of technical education. He wrote, "memory is developed at the expense of understanding;

passive reception at the expense of fertile spontaneity; stationary imitation at the expense of activity and creative initiative."[6] Prado and Villaran agreed that it was advisable to adopt practical attitudes toward life, to abandon theoretical speculation, and to stress the development of human character through diligent work and industry.

The authors mentioned above emphasized the improvement and extension of primary education and consequently advocated the education of the masses. Villaran developed the most advanced position within the context of a liberal bourgeois conception. In contrast to his fellow positivist thinkers who overvalued education, Villaran argued that economic development of the country must take priority; the increase of "illustration" would depend upon it.[7] Carlos Lisson shared this point of view with Villaran.[8]

Other Peruvian intellectuals, particularly those who were part of the philosophical current known as spiritualism, while stressing the priority of education in the list of national problems, adopted an elitist point of view. Alejandro Deustua and Francisco Garcia Calderon—also the writers Jose de la Riva Aguero and Victor Andres Belaunde—were outstanding exponents of this position.[9] Deustua asserted that the influence of primary education was not significant since those to be benefited—the inhabitants of *punas* and *caserios*—were inherently incapable of improvement; progress was achieved only by a selected minority.[10] Francisco Garcia Calderon, in his turn, argued for the creation of an enlightened elite able to build the nation, an activity that required the establishment of internal order and the development of wealth.[11]

The main issues at stake in this prolonged debate show themselves best in the argument between Villaran and Deustua over educational theory and policy. Villaran, a follower of American trends in education, advocated a vocational-practical approach, which would open the way to capitalist relations of production. Also, he wrote in "The Economic Factor in National Education" in support of his argument that education should be available to all sectors of society.

> An excess of education in the upper class and a lack of education in the lower class would represent the widening of a gap that today separates some classes from others, a situation that favors tyranny and also the iniquity of relations between those who govern and those who are

governed, politically and economically.[12]

Deustua, less interested in economics, postulated an elitist solution while at the same time borrowing from the English model of school organization. In order to sever the illness from its roots, he recommended the reform of the university, the source of national leadership in his view, rather than the primary school.[13] "The capital problem is to educate the leading classes and only science, true science can realize this transformation.[14] Jose Carlos Mariategui understood that beyond the intellectual form of the dispute, "positivism versus idealism," the controversy between Villaran and Deustua reflected conflicting interests within the Civil Party. One side is linked to capitalism, expressed in the liberal bourgeois standpoint defended by Villaran, and the other to feudalism, expressed in Deustua's thought, that "represented the reaction of the old aristocratic spirit more or less dressed up in modern idealism."[15]

Both Deustua and Villaran were directly involved in planning committees that elaborated projects of reform. For example, Deustua had a leading role in the reform of 1902 and Villaran—who in 1909 while working as Minister of Instruction brought a commission from the United States[16]—headed the committee created in 1918 that drew up the first draft of the reform of 1920. However, neither of them could correct the illness they described. As Mariategui put it, with reference to Villaran,

> the educational movement was sabotaged by the continued and widespread existence of a feudal regime. It is not possible to democratize the education of a country without democratizing its economy and its political superstructure.[17]

In fact, four-fifths of the population remained beyond any educational reform.[18]

In 1921, the Popular Universities emerged as part of the struggle for democratization, providing a conception of education within an alternative, informal framework.[19] From 1923, under Mariategui's guidance, workers' self-education was integrated into a major project: the promotion of a workers' culture that would create a collective will able to transform historical reality. In Mariategui's thought, workers' education was associated with their own process of organization at political and trade union levels. Thus, when the General Confederation of Workers of Peru was organized in 1929, the Office for Workers' Self-Education was created.[20] (Popular Universities were closed by Leguia's government in 1927; the political crisis of the early 1930s and the subsequent repression also meant a setback for the General Confederation of Peruvian Workers.)

The Roman Catholic school system was certainly an important segment of the Peruvian school system, since the Roman Catholic Church controlled leading educational institutions and almost everyone involved in political life had been educated at a Roman Catholic school.[21] The Roman Catholic Church considered itself the only church divinely intended and instituted, its two main points of departure being revelation and tradition. The main characteristics of its schools were an emphasis on religious studies and on Latin and Greek, and at the organizational level, the rejection of co-education. In general, it preserved Spanish traditions. Some orders, however, introduced innovations. For example, the Salesians, who arrived in 1891, introduced vocational instruction and were convinced of the importance of physical exercise.[22] Since Roman Catholicism was the Peruvian state religion, the public school system was not unaffected by the practices and policies of Catholic schools.

The Implementation of a Public Educational Policy

The attempts to build a new educational policy took shape under presidents Nicolas de Pierola (1895-1899) and Lopez de Romana (1899-1902); the emphasis on reform was also significant under the *Civilista* government of Jose Pardo (1905-1908) and under Augusto Leguia (1919-1930).

The reforms hoped for by Pardo's government were preceded by the largely nugatory reforming efforts of 1901 and 1902[23] (although the creation of Normal Schools and the establishment of the Schools of Arts and Trades were important achievements).[24] Public education was in such a poor state that a government resolution dated on June 18, 1904 authorized the establishment of *escuelas libres* (private schools) to supplement public primary education.[25] In fact, private schools were already established in considerable numbers at the end of the century, among them those of Methodists. In analyzing Pardo's educational policy particular

notice should be paid, in Basadre's opinion, to the encouragement
of primary education, the improvement of building and equipment,
the establishment of high schools, the introduction of technical
instruction, and the improvement of relations between the
universities and the government.[26] The view taken here is that
Pardo's administration created the basic organizational
infrastructure of the public school system, particularly within
primary education.   By means of Law 162, promulgated on
December 5, 1905, the direction of primary education was removed
from the municipal councils and centralized in the national
government.[27] (In 1901, a directive body had already been created
within the Ministry of Instruction for this educational level,
although municipalities continued the actual direction since new
arrangements never got properly under way.)   The General
Department of Education was organized and a system of national
supervision was created.   Teachers' salaries and school materials
were to be provided by the state.[28] The law also provided for the
establishment of a fund to cover the costs of elementary education;
the resources would come from general revenue (five per cent to be
allocated), from Departmental Councils, and from Municipal
mojonazgo, or taxes on alcoholic beverages (thirty per cent to be
allocated).[29]

In addition, President Pardo signed a decree on January 25,
1905, creating the Normal School for Boys in Lima.   Other Normal
Schools were also established in Arequipa, Puno, Cuzco, and
Trujillo.   (The Normal School for Women had been reorganized in
1904.)[30] There were also other permanent steps towards the
professionalization of teaching, such as the ratification in 1905 of
the law of 1901 that established the rights of primary school
teachers to retirement and *montepio*.[31] (University and High School
Professorships had been considered public careers since 1861.)[32]
Some of the graduates from the Normal School for Boys in Lima
were sent to the United States to improve their skills.   Others
became principals in different parts of the country.[33]

Law 162 provided for free and compulsory education for boys
between six and fourteen and for girls between six and twelve.
The basic instruction included reading, writing, general notions of
universal geography, the geography of Peru, the four arithmetic
operations, the decimal system, Christian doctrine, and physical
exercises (Article 2).[34]

The plan of study for primary schools was issued on June 20, 1906.   The plan laid out a five year program divided into a first stage (the first two years) and a second stage (three years). In the second stage, the curriculum was to include religion, natural and physical sciences, literature, manual work, and courses on agriculture.[35] The plan also recommended that reading and writing be taught simultaneously by using full words rather than by spelling and that arithmetic and geometry be taught by intuitive and practical means.[36]   The Peruvian historian Jorge Basadre considered that the plan was again taking too little account of practical needs and in practice it proved to be too uniform for a country with such a great regional diversity.[37] The persistence of illiteracy—a figure of over eighty per cent in 1915—and the fact that in that same year less than four per cent of the population were enrolled in primary schools, showed that Law 162 had been largely ineffective.[38]

Secondary schools did not receive great attention.   Jose Pardo stated in 1908 that 3162 students attended public high schools in that year, as compared with 1305 in 1900.   In 1915, there were twenty-three schools for boys and three for girls, the latter located in Ayacucho, Trujillo, and Cuzco.[39] The Colegio Nacional de Guadalupe was a thoroughly equipped, well-attended institution patronized by the sons of the political leaders.   The boys of the aristocratic families of Lima went to a school run by French Fathers of the Recoleta.   Catholic schools, of course, were an alternative to public schools.

Foreign professors were hired as part of the attempt to improve public secondary education and professional institutes. They tried to modernize programs and teaching methodologies. For example, a commission from Belgium mostly constituted by professed Roman Catholics associated with the University of Louvaine arrived in Peru in 1903 to work in the *Colegio Guadalupe*.[40] The School of Agriculture, founded in 1901, also had personnel from Belgium.[41] However, these foreign contributions were not integrated into a coherent educational policy at the national level.

These reforms, which established at least in principle an infrastructure for Peruvian education—especially for primary education—were handicapped from the beginning owing to their co-existence with an unreformed and profoundly reactionary economic and political structure. There existed a "democracy" (in which the majority of the population, the Indians in particular, did not have a say) characterized by political favouritism. *Gamonalismo* and "bossism" regularly interfered in the educational activities. In time these circumstances facilitated the development of private schools, in particular Protestant schools, that had only to confront some problems with religious regulations, always finding a suitable solution for them.

A good example of the incompatibility between the law and actual Peruvian practice is to be found in the fate of the primary school inspectorate established under the provisions of Law 162. Abolished in 1915, due to budget restraint and inefficiency, it was re-established (Law 2690) in 1918, in spite of sharp criticism from some quarters.[42] During the debate at the Senate on January 6, 1918, Mariano Cornejo remarked: "The only aim of creating these inspectors was to serve the personal or political interests of those who helped them to obtain the position."[43] Carlos Paz Soldan said:

> It is suitable to point out - and nobody will deny what I shall say because it is present in everyone's awareness - that the objective of that project [the one concerning the re-establishment of the school inspectorate, introduced in January 1916] was to name inspectors for those provinces in which there would be elections to renew one third of the Congress.[44]

Between 1908 and 1919, educational policy seemed to take an erratic course. The whole Civilista political machinery had difficulties in overcoming a crisis of public consensus, particularly visible in urban areas; the Civil Party was also embroiled in its own internal crisis affecting the leadership. But President Augusto Leguia (1908-1912) paid particular attention to primary schools, and provided subsidies to private schools, including Catholic institutions.[45] President Jose Pardo (1915-1919) recognized that education had been "one of the public services more deeply disturbed in these years of agitations and upheavals."[46]

In 1919, the re-appearance of Leguia and what he called La Patria Nueva (The New Homeland) reactualized urgent educational needs. Within the context of a general economic and political policy of open doors for the United States, American influence became so dominant that, at the beginning of 1921, the government contracted with an American commission to fill leading positions in the educational bureaucracy.[47]

Law 2690 (1918) created the committee that, under the leadership of Villaran, provisionally drafted a new law of public instruction. The draft was presented to the executive in September 1919 (Leguia was already president of the country). The Ministry of Instruction, following the advice of H. E. Bard, an American educator, made substantial changes. The new law, known as Ley Organica de Ensenanza, was promulgated in June 1920.[48]

This law called for universal primary instruction and introduced new organizational schemes: the creation of the National Council of Teaching; the appointment of directors of education for the three principal regions of Peru; and the appointment of special directors for various aspects of school administration, for example, curriculum, buildings, libraries, and secondary training centres. The National Council of Teaching was presided over by the minister of education and constituted by the president of the University of San Marcos, two representatives from the University Council in Lima, one representative from the Parliament, and one from the Higher School of Pedagogy. (This council, mostly engaged in curriculum and programs, was later abolished.) The three regional departments of education created to meet regional needs were administered by American educators. Within a year, the three departments were suppressed by the government because of criticism from the Congress and the public, and the entire administrative machinery of public education was centred in Lima. In 1921, twenty-five American educators, experts in different aspects of public instruction were assigned responsibilities within the system. Three years later only one remained in Peru, the rest having been forced to resign because of extensive discontent.[49]

The Peruvian primary school was now divided into General or Common, and Special or Professional. The General or Common consisted of two stages: the elementary stage lasting three years, and a subsequent stage lasting two years in which the knowledge acquired during the first stage was deepened and broadened. Rural schools of first and second grade were also established; they included teaching associated with gardens or farms. The Special or Professional Primary School tried to provide practical skills. Secondary education lasted five years and was divided in the same way: the Special or Professional programs instructed students in agriculture, animal husbandry, and trades. This program could function in an independent building or in annexes of the Common high school.[50]

Secondary education remained in an unfortunate condition. There were not only deficiencies in the program, but a poor preparation of the professorship and a lack of professional security.[51] The frustrated reform of 1930 (Leguia's regime was overthrown in August 1930) tried to introduce new teaching methods and to modernize the curriculum.[52] Commercial education—a major interest of Methodist schools—had been carried out mainly by private schools without any official regulation; the 1927 Provisional Plan of Studies was the first pedagogical attempt to systematize it.[53]

New educational concerns emerged during the third decade. The state assumed the responsibility of maintaining kindergartens; the Pedagogical Institute opened a special section devoted to the preparation of teachers in special education; interest in women's education led to the creation of high schools for girls in Lima, Cajamarca, Trujillo, Tacna, Huaraz, and Puno; there was a general preoccupation with the training of teachers.[54] However, in spite of the rhetoric of La Patria Nueva, the social situation of the indigenous people was unaffected.

The entire school system remained middle-class oriented, rural masses did not have access to formal education, and secondary education was an ante-chamber for university studies.[55] Between 1895 and 1930, the public school system was only partly able to produce skills, particularly those that the introduction of imperialist capitalism into Peru required. Ideological reproduction was fulfilled with difficulties. There were complaints about the poor preparation of teachers, a lack of concern for building the character of the students, and the emphasis on memorization, particularly in the high schools. The results of Ley Organica de Ensenanza of 1920 were, as in the case of earlier educational initiatives, disappointing. The gap between the written law and educational practice was a persistent characteristic of Peruvian educational policy. American borrowings did not help since they were not integrated into a coherent educational theory. The uneven and combined character of the Peruvian socio-economic formation, the subsequent structure of political power in which pre-capitalist and capitalist elements co-existed, creating an educational bureaucracy tainted by political favoritism, framed public educational practices.   To this one needs to add the permanent confusion created by new laws, decrees, and reforms.   The entire situation opened doors to private schools.   Methodists, for example, would develop their own school system and provide needed skills by such means as commercial training (here the state could not compete, since it lacked a corps of adequate staff), as well as instilling the ideological content thought desirable by many Peruvian critics of the public system.

References

[1]Roberto MacLean y Estenos, *Sociologia Educacional del Peru* (Lima: Imprenta Gil, 1944), The address is reproduced in part on p. 307.   Education and instruction are interchanged in the laws and speeches.   Also most of the authors consulted here use these terms very loosely.

[2]Manuel Vicente Villaran, "Las Profesiones Liberales en el Peru," in *Estudios sobre Educacion Nacional*, pp. 8-9 quoted in Jose Carlos Mariategui, *Seven Interpretative Essays on Peruvian Reality* (Austin and London: University of Texas Press, 1971), p. 80.

[3]Authors dealing with the impact of French educational views on the Peruvian educational system do not provide details. There is also a further complication: "El Reglamento General de Instruccion Publica de 1876" was issued at a time when France was reorganizing its own educational system.   Roberto MacLean y Estenos acknowledges the French influence on the "Reglamento" of 1876 but his treatment is extremely limited.   He says that the government hired French professors for the Universities, the School of Construction and Mining, and the Normal Schools in Cuzco and Lima.   He also mentions the importance given to the "French spirit."   Roberto MacLean y Estenos, *Sociologia*, pp. 281 and 288. The *Ley Organica de Ensenanza* (1901) lasted only one year.   This law divided secondary education between "Liceos" and "Colegios." The law transplanted to Peru the French organization of the "Liceos."   Ibid., p. 326.

[4]Jose Carlos Mariategui, *Seven Interpretative Essays*, pp. 76-77.   See also Roberto MacLean y Estenos, *Sociologia*, pp. 375-376.

[5]Augusto Salazar Bondy, *Historia de las Ideas en el Peru Contemporaneo. El Proceso del Pensamiento Filosofico*, 2nd Edition. (Lima: Francisco Moncloa Editores, 1967), Vol. I, pp. 130-131 and 131-143.

[6]Ibid., p. 136.

[7]Ibid., pp. 138-142.   "Illustration" refers to the level of instruction.

[8]Ibid.

[9]Ibid., p. 139 and also pp. 147-148 and 149-221. See also:

Jack Himelblau, *Alejandro O. Deustua, Philosophy in Defense of Man* (Gainesville: University Press of Florida, 1979), Chapters I and II; and Ernesto Yepes del Castillo, *Peru 1820-1920. Un Siglo de Desarrollo Capitalista* (Lima: Instituto de Estudios Peruanos, 1971), pp. 186-189.

[10]Jack Himelblau, *Alejandro O. Deustua*, p. 14.

[11]Ernesto Yepes del Castillo, *Peru 1820-1920*, pp. 187-188.

[12]Augusto Salazar Bondy, *Historia*, Vol. 1, p.140.

[13]"In order to cut off the evil at its roots, Deustua advocates reform of the University before that of the primary school because the leaders of the country will come from the former and not from the latter. He proposes a plan of reforms that includes: 1) reorganization of the ruling institutions; 2) concentration of University teaching in Lima; 3) the preparation of high school teachers; 4) reduction in number and centralization of high schools; 5) preparation of inspectors to divulge the new ideas and pedagogical procedures all over the country; 6) the hiring of foreign educators; 7) the dispatch of teachers and students to foreign countries; 8) the training of elementary teachers in a way suited to the needs of the country; 9) an increase in the budget allocated for teaching." Roberto MacLean y Estenos, *Sociologia*, p. 340.

[14]Alejandro Deustua, *El Problema Pedagogico Nacional* (Lima, November, 1904). A booklet quoted in Roberto MacLean y Estenos, *Sociologia*, p. 339.

[15]Jose C. Mariategui, *Seven Interpretative Essays*, p. 115. Mariategui characterized Deustua's concept of work as medieval and aristocratic. He supported his argument with the following quotation from Deustua, "Values and work, virtue and self-interest, are essential to the formation of character but they play very different roles in that process. Just as they play different roles in the process of education. Freedom is a value that educates; education consists of the realization of values. Work does not educate; it enriches and instructs; with practice it confers skills. But it is motivated by self-interest, which enslaves the soul." Quoted in Jose Carlos Mariategui, *Seven Interpretative Essays*, p. 116.

[16]Jorge Basadre, *Historia de la Republica del Peru*, Vol. IX (Lima: Ediciones Historia, 1964), Chapter CLXXXII, p. 4295.

[17]Jose Carlos Mariategui, *Seven Interpretative Essays*, p. 88.

[18]This is a reference to the rural population, mostly constituted by indigenous people. Ibid.

[19]Popular Universities are an early antecedent of today's programs of popular education, carried out in many Latin American countries. The development of political consciousness and critical awareness of social problems is a leading aim of these programs.

[20]Isabel Yepes and Estela Gonzalez, "La Auto Educacion Obrera." *Chaski*, No. 17 (Lima: April 1981), pp. 7-11.

[21]Montevideo Congress 1925, *Christian Work in South America*, 2 Vols. (New York-Chicago: Fleming H. Revell Company, 1925), Vol. II, pp. 262-263. "The boys of the old aristocratic families of Lima go to a school carried on by the French Fathers of the Recoleta. The Augustinian Fathers have a large school attended by middle-class boys. Then in a continuously descending scale, both in quality of work and type of pupil, are the schools of the Fathers of Mercy, the Salesians, the Dominicans, and the annex of the Roman Catholic Seminary. The Type of training given in Roman Catholic schools is essentially scholastic. The best educational standards are probably those maintained by the Jesuits. Two lines of progress may fairly be noted since 1916: 1) the Salesians have developed a scheme of industrial education with great success, both in Lima and in the provinces; and 2) a Catholic University founded in Lima, in 1917." Ibid.

[22]Roberto MacLean y Estenos, *Sociologia*, pp. 341-343.

[23]In June 1896 a resolution signed by President Nicolas de Pierola named a Committee, that included people like Pedro Labarthe and Francisco Garcia Calderon, to work on a project of law that culminated in the Law of Public Instruction of 1901. In an attempt to improve primary education, the "Direccion de Primera Ensenanza" was founded. Secondary schools were divided into "Liceos" and "Colegios"; Liceos taught practical courses in commerce, mining, and mechanics. Secondary education for girls was regulated and offered them the prospect of university attendance. Jorge Basadre, *Historia*, Vol. IX, Chapter CLXXXI, p. 4251; Robert MacLean y Estenos, *Sociologia*, pp. 323-329. The Law of January 1902, with which Alejandro Deustua was associated, distinguished, following the English model of organization, a gradual hierarchy in public education: Primary school (vocationally oriented) Grammar School (a primary school

that would prepare the child to proceed to secondary education);
the High School (which prepared the student for industrial or
commercial employment); and the "College" (which prepared the
students who intended to enter a liberal profession).   The Congress
changed the Law in 1903 and eliminated the Grammar School.
Roberto MacLean y Estenos, *Sociologia*, pp. 329-337.

[24]Ibid., p. 337.

[25]Meanwhile new schools had been founded by the state, by
private organizations, and by individuals.   Following a decree of
February 1, 1896 each municipality had to establish at least one
school of Arts and Trades.   In the same year, Liceo Grau was
offering elementary and secondary education, the latter including
commercial training.   Liceo Fanning, a private school for girls, was
founded by Teresa Fanning, who sponsored moral teaching and lay
education.   There were also new Roman Catholic schools such as
the Colegio San Agustin (1903) and the Colegio San Vicente de
Paul in Arequipa (1912).   In Callao, private initiative provided the
first high schools after the war, and also elementary schools.
Instituto Callao (1895) a high school, Colegio Bozano (1901)
offering elementary and commercial instruction for girls, Instituto
Chalaco for boys (1902), are some examples.   Jorge Basadre,
Historia, Vol. IX, Chapter CLXXXI, pp.   4274-4275.

[26]Ibid., p. 4259.

[27]Roberto MacLean y Estenos, *Sociologia*, pp. 341-342.   The
law is reproduced at the bottom of pp. 341-342.

[28]Ibid.

[29]Ibid.

[30]Jorge Basadre, *Historia*, Vol. IX, Chapter CLXXXI, p.
4262.

[31]Ibid., pp. 4263-4264.

[32]Ibid., Chapter CLXXXI, pp. 4263-4264.

[33]Ibid., pp. 4262-4263.

[34]Roberto MacLean y Estenos, *Sociologia*, pp. 341-342.

[35]Ibid., pp. 347-348   [36]Ibid., p. 348.

[37]Jorge Basadre, *Historia*, Vol. IX, Chapter CLXXXI, p. 4261.

[38]Panama Congress 1916, *Christian Work in Latin America*, 3 Vols. (New York: The Missionary Education Movement, 1917), Vol. I, p. 399 and p. 405.

[39]Jorge Basadre, *Historia*, Vol. IX, Chapter CLXXXI, p. 4266.

[40]Ibid., pp. 4268-4269   [41]Ibid., p. 4285.

[42]Ibid., pp. 4291-4293.

[43]Ibid., Chapter CLXXXII, p. 4291.

[44]Ibid., p. 4293.

[45]Roberto MacLean y Estenos, *Sociologia*, pp. 355 and 357.

[46]Ibid., p. 360.

[47]Roberto MacLean y Estenos, *Sociologia*, p. 376.

[48]Jorge Basadre, *Historia*, Vol. IX, Chapter CLXXXIII, pp. 4319-4320.

[49]Roberto MacLean y Estenos, *Sociologia*, p. 374.   The report on "Progress in Educational Legislation and Sentiment" presents the following assessment: "In 1921 the new American educators were duly installed in charge of these various branches of educational activity.   Unfortunately, most of them knew no Spanish, so that months passed without their being able to show many tangible results. By the end of 1921 many of them became the object of fierce attack in Congress and in the press, with the result that one by one they began to resign. A year ago, only one of the twenty-five remained in Peru. In connection with this educational experiment two great mistakes were made: 1) in securing so many experts at once, and 2) in contracting with men who had no previous contact with Latin American and no knowledge of Spanish." Montevideo Congress 1925, *Christian Work*, Vol. II, pp. 261-262.

[50]Roberto MacLean y Estenos, *Sociologia*, p. 374-375.

[51]Ibid., p. 379-389.   [52]Ibid., p. 380.

[53]Jorge Basadre, *Historia*, Vol. IX, Chapter CLXXXIII, p. 4330.

[54]Roberto MacLean y Estenos, *Sociologia*, pp. 377-378, 380-383.

[55]Between 1919 and 1929 primary schools increased in number from 3006 to 3553 (Basadre considered that, when the economic changes in Peru during this period are borne in mind, the rate of increase is too slow). By 1929, there were also thirty-six high schools, twenty-nine of them for boys and seven for girls. Jorge Basadre, *Historia*, Vol. IX, Chapter CLXXXIII, p. 4322.

CHAPTER VI

Methodist Schools

Methodist Educational Ideas

A consideration of the ideas that lay behind practice in Methodist missionary schools leads us to pay particular attention to the way in which missionary education was discussed and understood at an interdenominational level. Many Protestant denominations that sustained missionary agencies in Latin America shared a basic conception of education.

The Congress on Christian Work in Latin America held in Panama from February 10 to 20, 1916, is the richest and earliest source, since the Congress devoted a great deal of time to missionary education and received the impressive co-operation of fifty denominational organizations, including English missionary boards.[1] It was organized by the still incipient Committee on Cooperation in Latin America (1913) "for the thorough-going, scientific yet systematic study of the religious life and needs of the Latin American republics."[2] Certainly,

> the closer political relations which have sprung up between some of the Latin American states and the United States tended to develop and cement a friendly relationship of increasing significance.[3]

The hour was opportune for such a meeting; the international political framework—and obviously the economic network—was already in place.

The conclusions reached at this congress allowed the reconstruction of the educational theory that would give shape, at least to some extent, to the educational policy followed by many denominations engaged in educational activities in Latin America. It is easy to recognize in those conclusions ideas put forward by the Methodists in Peru, although as a rule they did not present them in a systematic form but interwove them with practical proposals or doctrinal assertions.

Education was defined as a process: the interplay of the will of the individual and the will of the social group, the interaction of a person and the environment.[4]

> Education is the formation of habits, the acquisition of knowledge, the development of character, all these and more according to the needs and opportunities arising from adjusting a person to his environment.[5]

But,

> an adequate education of whatever type must be a training for the entire man, and hence must rationally include as an integral part of it moral and religious training.

The aim of education appears synthesized in this manner: "Mental and spiritual fellowship among men, mental and spiritual initiative and independence in the individual constitute its goal."[6]

The vagueness and lack of conceptual precision are readily apparent; this is not unusual among religious people dealing with secular issues, particularly where, as reformers, they owe many of their ideas, as Donald Meyer has observed, to people around them.[7] Although the educational ideas of American evangelical Protestantism rested primarily on the requirements of a church based on close reading of the Bible, with conversion as a major goal, its basic conceptions were firmly nourished, from the middle 1890s onward, by elements of Social Gospel and doctrine and American progressivism.

John Dewey's ideas appeared scattered in denominational (including Methodist) and interdenominational writings. This is not unexpected since, as Lawrence Cremin puts it, "Dewey's most seminal contribution was to develop a body of pedagogical theory which could encompass the terrific diversity of the progressive education movement."[8] In 1920, *El Mensajero*, the Methodist periodical, published an article written by Evelyn Dewey (John Dewey's daughter) in order to familiarize Methodist mothers with new ideas on children's education.[9] George A. Coe's early book, *Education in Religion and Morals*, was highly praised in an article published in *El Mensajero* in 1918.[10] The book, originally published in 1904, had been translated into Spanish in 1917. It was devoted to an examination of the teaching of religion from the perspective of "the new psychology." The interesting point here is that Coe, a Methodist, a member of the Social Service Federation, and deeply committed to the interdenominational movement, was a student and follower of John Dewey.[11] In another book, *A Social Theory of Religious Education*, published in 1917, Coe integrated progressive theories, pragmatism in particular, with Social Gospel doctrines. The book was dedicated to "Harry Ward who sees and makes others see."[12] Coe was, like Ward, on the staff of the Union Theological Seminary until 1922, when he went to Columbia Teachers' College;[13] he was back again at the Union Seminary in the late 1920s. The dedication of the book to Harry Ward is eloquent. This Methodist minister has been described as "the most active clerical participant in secular organizations of any of the prophets."[14] Ward's name or signature appears in many letters addressed to the Methodist mission in Peru, and he was also the author of numerous texts used in its Sunday schools. Although the extent of the influence of radical exponents of the Social Gospel like Ward on missionaries in Peru is not easy to assess directly, certainly Coe's books were being welcomed eagerly well into the 1930s.[15] His ideas were presumably discussed in those lectures and seminars on pedagogy frequently mentioned, but without great detail, in Methodist mission reports.

It is useful now to describe, although briefly, the basic ideas of *Social Theory of Religious Education*,[16] a book that became the main source of reference when Social Gospel leaders discussed educational theory.[17]

G.A. Coe believed that the basal process in education was social interaction and that the isolation of the school experience from other experiences had to be overcome.[18] This basic conception was in line with the conclusions reached at the Panama Congress and with policies implemented in the main Methodist schools in Peru. At the heart of his interpretation there was a "genetic analysis of the mind as a functional instrument displaying growth and phases of development";[19] Donald Meyer considers that human nature as explained by Coe's theory was pure potentiality.[20] Coe wrote on the teaching of religion,

> gradually there is a dawning of realization that our social experience is a sphere of communion with God, that here children can share religion with adults and grow in religion without any forcing whatever.[21]

He was referring here primarily to the growth of will.

It is meaningful to return now to the definition of education expounded at the Panama Congress; in that definition the emphasis was on the adjustment of a person to his or her environment.

What kind of adjustment is being referred to, within the doctrinal context of the Social Gospel?   Coe, using a combination of Dewey's thought and the religious vision he embraced, tried to make clear what must be understood by adjustment of the child to the environment. He wrote,

> adjustment of a child to society just as it is does not satisfy the educational conscience, or even the conscience of society in general. . . . Thus, education is not only society's supreme effort at self-preservation; it is also society's supreme effort at self-improvement . . . and our thinking, as was indicated at the beginning of the chapter, grows within practice, not in a different world. . . . Nevertheless the idealization of life, which implicitly if not explicitly condemns our actual life, is of the essence of educational practice.[22]

The Montevideo Congress took a mature approach to educational theory, enriched by a critique of the practice and by Coe's more systematic analysis.   When dealing with religious education the emphasis was on the understanding of "the educational process not as one of knowledge primarily but of life and conduct."[23]

> As already indicated, the validity of depending upon moral instruction, upon information concerning right and wrong, upon precept and example as the method of securing character must be questioned. Common sense has always insisted that we learn in and through experience.[24]

The report remarked on the need to recognize that the educational process should be "pupil-centered" rather than "material-centered."[25] As the report continued,

> Clearly we cannot accept the third principle [the educational process not one of knowledge primarily but of life and conduct] without its corollary—that the curriculum activities and material must meet the pupil's present moral and religious needs; they must be based on what he already knows and does; they must be in contact with all his environment and experience; they must use such methods as are suited to his experience and capacity.[26]

The next important principle was that the process of character-training of the pupil should be unified. "As far as possible," stated the report, "the process of character education must be so unified that each part of his training builds upon the others and is not a contradiction, a confusion, or an unreal duplication"[27]

The report on religious education presented at the Montevideo Congress demonstrates that, in spite of the arguments about attempts to relate religion to social practice and the consequent religious crisis that took shape during the 1920s, progressive educational conceptions prevailed in the educational work of those denominations associated with the Committee on Cooperation in Latin America. It is noticeable, however, that the Montevideo Congress was not representative of all missionary boards working in Latin America. Indeed, it can safely be said that, from a theoretical perspective and with the reservations already noted, Methodist schools possessed a notable continuity from the early years of the second decade until the end of the period under consideration.

Methodist missionaries manifested an extraordinary faith in the transforming power of education. A report written in 1921 reads, "We believe that the schools established by Methodists in North Andean republics were destined to be a potential force for the intellectual and moral uplifting of these nations."[28] This faith converged with the vision of Christianity as a source for world transformation which implied changes at societal and individual levels.

> If the work of Christ has to be done, life must be consecrated and educated. . . . The work of the Department of Religious Education at the elementary schools and high schools as in Christian Colleges is vitally related to that aim.[29]

Also, missionaries supporting Social Gospel views realized that they needed to have political points of reference if they were to attempt to exert influence on the development of new political parties or on potential social movements. *La Nueva Democracia* is an example at an interdenominational level. Missionary educators, in turn, faced the necessity of determining the social goals to be taught (the accomplishment of which transcended the school and the Church) and, therefore, the need to specify the kind of adjustment of the child to society proposed by the schools and to clarify the place of indoctrination in their theories and practices. Notably, missionaries claimed the political neutrality of their teaching practices (in spite of the presence of Aprista teachers in Methodist schools, particularly at Callao High School in the middle 1930s). However, Methodist missionaries used to remark that their schools were truly liberal centres (meaning that they helped to awaken thought, develop personally independent attitudes on religious and social matters, and prepare citizens for a democratic society). In fact, Social Gospel doctrinaires also acknowledged "useful contributions" from liberalism.[30] The positive tendencies of liberalism, Coe wrote, could be reinforced with the defects avoided by developing in the student a radical will within a Christian atmosphere.[31] Thus, the apparent contradiction between individualism and fellowship among people could be eluded and the internal individual tensions generated by the struggle between selfishness and unselfishness could be reduced to a moral problem dealing with unification and integrity of the self.[32]

The theoretical bases of Methodist education work in Peru and that of a number of other denominations sustaining missions in Latin America depended on an uneasy combination of the Social Gospel postulates (that also involved the entire American Protestant tradition), the progressive movement within education, and John Dewey's pedagogical theories. The limits to the envisioned goals were set by the characteristics of the Peruvian socio-economic formation, by the North-Americanism pervading the missionary work, and consequently by the attempt to export cultural and religious principles while underestimating the creativity of other people with their own histories.

The Educational Policy from an Interdenominational Perspective

The school work sustained by the American Methodist Episcopal Church was impressive. In 1916, there were more than 93,000 students attending missionary schools and 47,000 students attending Methodist schools in the United States.[33] Formal education had a significant part in the Methodist missionary enterprise and in that of other denominations as well. The report presented at the Panama Congress gives the following descriptions of the aims of the mission:

"to make disciples of all nations" to raise up in every nation a truly Christian people, nourished by all the fellowships and institutions of self-propagating Christian civilization and living in mutually helpful relations with every other people.   To this end schools are an indispensable means.[34]

At the same congress, participants working on the Education Committee paid particular attention to the ends to be achieved by all missionary schools. Thus, they pointed out:

The bringing of children and youth under influences by which they may be led to adopt the Christian principles, the upbuilding of the Christian community including the development of Christian leaders of spiritual power, the permeation of the community at large with the highest Christian ideas and ideals making for the application of these ideals to all phases of human life. The provision of an opportunity for the natural and spontaneous expression of the spirit of Christianity in its care for all human welfare.[35]

The Panama Congress was held in 1916; it is noteworthy that, a year later, George A. Coe published *A Social Theory of Religious Education*, and Benjamin S. Winchester published *Religious Education and Democracy*. Winchester's book was specially prepared for the Commission on Christian Education of the Federal Council of Churches of Christ in America, over which he presided. It examined the relationship of religious education to democracy, and also examined and recommended changes in the teaching of religion.[36] Social Gospel doctrine had reached its highest point at that time and exerted a strong influence on educational conceptions.

At the Panama congress, there was a serious attempt to outline an educational policy to be shared by all the denominations working in Latin America; however, the final conclusions did not surpass the level of recommendation. It was suggested that all mission boards working in the field come together to study educational problems and design a common set of educational arrangements for primary and secondary education leading up to the creation of a central educational organization (the form that the latter might take would be submitted for discussion).[37] This co-operative effort could be carried out by co-ordinating courses, by combining and merging existing schools, by the placing of Christian leaders at national universities, and by the use of endowed lectureships.[38] This general framework was in line with the policy developed by the Committee on Cooperation in Latin America and later with the guidelines followed by *La Nueva Democracia*: the creation of solidarity at inter-American levels, under the "benevolent" guidance of the United States. In fact, the Congress was the most comprehensive effort ever made by evangelical Protestantism to export North American cultural principles; the crusade was carried out in the name of "brotherhood" (at the same time as American capitalism was rapidly penetrating Latin America).

Naturally, the relationship with national governments was also considered an important point. It was agreed that missions should not engage in needless competition with the state, and school administrators were advised to recognize the official plan of studies—while of course maintaining high standards so that their schools might be regarded as exemplars—since the goal was to vitalize the national educational process.[39] (The evolutionary concept of change is at the basis of this idea.)

At the Montevideo Congress of 1925, two committees were set up, one dealing with education in general and the other with religious education. There were, of course, a good number of recommendations for the improvement of co-operative work among the various denominations and between these and the interdenominational agencies. However, very much in contrast to the Panama Congress, there were no recommendations intended to lead to a common educational policy. Educational aims were examined in the context of religious education and not education in general, as happened at the Panama Congress. In answering the self-posed question, "What Religious Education May Mean in the Life of a Nation,"[40] the committee report stressed the importance of religious education as a means of generating social consensus through a unifying ideology with strong apparent ties to the capitalist model of democracy. It reads:

> The thoughtful citizen's first concern is for that combination of freedom and order that is the foundation of modern national life. This foundation must be cemented by a widespread loyalty to the common weal. Upon this the patriotic citizen would see built a glorious

superstructure—an intelligent and active citizenry, the decline of drudgery, poverty, and disease, moral leadership in the councils of the nations, wise use of leisure, the rise of genius in arts and sciences.

But the basis of all these hopes is the character of the individual citizen. Freedom and order, the cornerstones of democracy, are not maintained by police forces but by the ability of the citizen to govern himself among his fellows with justice, honor, and good-will—and these are traits of character. Loyalty to the common weal must be not a passing emotion but a trait of character. Colonel Lawrence said rightly, "the art of government wants more character than brains."[41]

At the Panama Congress, the Committee on Education stressed the importance of elementary schools as evangelical agencies. However, by this time there were mission schools in Latin America with widely differing mandates, from the Presbyterian Instituto Ingles in Santiago, Chile, through the Presbyterian popular schools in Valparaiso (south of Chile), characterized by low fees, and the schools for Indians in Paraguay, founded by the American Missionary Society of the Anglican Church, to the various Methodist schools in Peru, which were mainly vocationally oriented.[42] The emphasis placed by Methodist missionaries in Peru on vocational education (the teaching of English and commercial subjects), while responding to the needs created by foreign capital, was nevertheless in line with one of the conclusions reached by the Committee on Education:

While the first business of education is to give right conceptions of life, and to instill principles which assure the living of a life worthwhile, yet every man should be trained to do well some particular thing.[43]

The Methodist Educational Policy

The Location and Programs of the Methodist Schools

The main Methodist schools were located in Lima and Callao, in the coastal region, and in Huancayo, the capital city of the department of Junin, in the mountain region. Commercial courses, English, and the Bible were also taught in smaller localities on the coast or in the Sierra.[44]

Early documents described Callao High School as the Department of Secondary Education of the Escuelas Anglo-Americanas (Anglo-American Schools) in Callao. (The school work began in Callao in 1891.) The report presented to the annual conference of 1920 explained its situation as follows: "Callao High School and the primary sections are in two separate houses having two different principals but both work together towards the same goal."[45] The primary school will be referred as the Escuela Anglo-Americana del Callao, and the secondary school as Callao High School, as became the usual practice. Both were co-educational schools;[46] the Escuela Anglo-Americana, from 1904 onward, also operated a kindergarten. The latter grew from a few students to a registration of 544 by 1930.[47] There were complaints about low enrolment figures in 1910, general poverty and the hostility of the Roman Catholic Church being pointed out as the causes.[48] However, enrolment rose from 196 in 1917 to 354 in 1919;[49] this was attributed to the growing popularity of English and the good reputation of a school that insisted on high standards, punctuality, and regular attendance.

Callao High School was mainly a commercial school serving the province of Callao and the seaport of the same name, which had increased its commercial importance as a result of the establishment of foreign companies from the beginning of the century. Enrolment rose from sixty in 1916 (no figures are available for earlier years) to 151 in 1930.[50]

The Escuela Anglo-Americana de La Victoria (Anglo-American School of La Victoria, a poor district of Lima) was founded in 1915. It was also a co-educational primary school with a special kindergarten section. Registrations increased from thirty-four in 1916 to 266 in 1930.[51] As the missionaries put it, this school attracted pupils who were not Protestant Christians because of "its courses in English and emphasis on character training."[52]

Lima High School was founded in 1906 by the American educator Elsie Wood-Schofield, Thomas Wood's daughter, and functioned under the sponsorship of the Methodist Women's Foreign Missionary Society. It offered kindergarten, elementary and high school programs, and had a commercial section. It also had a boarding department for girls coming from outside of Lima.

The English Academy was established in the little town of Tarma, in the mountain regions, in 1904. This school was moved to Huancayo in 1913, and its name was changed to Colegio Norteamericano de Huancayo. However, the Mission continued to run a small elementary school in Tarma; it had twenty-five registrants in 1916 and seventeen in 1923.[53]

The Colegio Norteamericano de Huancayo (American School of Huancayo) was opened in 1913.[54] In 1920 its name was changed to Instituto Andino (Andean School). It was located in Huancayo, 11,000 feet above sea level. It had kindergarten, elementary, and commercial departments, and made provision for boarders (a secondary department lasted only for four years, from 1920 to 1924). Numbers in registration rose from eighty-nine in 1914 to 259 in 1930 (indeed, enrolment reached the latter level as early as 1920, but decreased when the secondary department was closed because of financial problems).[55]

In the mountains, there were schools placed within the mining circuit, in Cerro de Pasco, Goyllarisquisga, Smelter, and La Oroya. These schools had difficulties in becoming established, and appear and disappear in the annual reports. The school in La Oroya appears to have been the most firmly founded, surviving until the early 1940s.

There was also a school in Chincha Alta, on the coast, founded in 1917 under the sponsorship of the National Missionary Society; the principal, a Miss Algorta, was Methodist.

The Instituto Norteamericano de Varones (North American Institute for Boys) was founded in Lima by the Methodist Mission in 1920, but merged with the Colegio Anglo-Peruano (Anglo-Peruvian School) four years later, the latter name being retained. The Colegio had been organized in 1916 by Dr. John Mackay; Spanish was the chief medium of instruction, and the school followed the public curriculum.[56] This differed from the Methodist practice. However, Dr. F. Stanger, a Methodist missionary, became vice-principal following the merger. The Colegio Anglo-Peruano had in operation all the grades of a primary as well as of a secondary department.

Methodist Schools and Peruvian Official Regulations

The Methodist mission organized its school work in the ways described in Chapter III. Although there was a special committee on educational policy, the Financial Committee took a substantial part in deciding on a new plan of studies or the creation of new courses. School principals reported on achievements and difficulties at the annual meetings; superintendents usually reported on the activities of small schools under their jurisdiction. There were close ties with the Board of Foreign Missions of the Methodist Episcopal Church, which also had its Board of Education.

The relationship between the Mission and the Peruvian Ministry of Instruction was not one of conflict, although fluctuations in the equilibrium of political power meant a greater influence of the Roman Catholic Church in educational matters from time to time. This made itself felt in the issuing of regulations concerning religious education and in the inspection of private schools; but these did not hamper missionary schools to any marked extent. However, archbishops used their pastoral letters to urge parents not to send their children to Protestant schools. (The Pastoral Letter issued by the Archbishop of Huancayo in 1921 tried to prevent attendance at the Methodist school in Huancayo.)

There is strong evidence that, from the beginning of missionary educational work in Peru, Protestant schools were viewed favorably by many governmental leaders and business representatives. Out of considerations of prudence, public officers were reserved in their expressions of support. The Lima Chamber of Commerce and the foreign companies displayed open interest, a good example being when the American Mercantile Bank asked Lima High School in 1919 to open classes for its employees.[57]

Methodist school administrators were free to organize their schools and develop their own curriculum. Although from 1905 onwards public instruction, elementary in particular, was centralized under the direction of the national government (during the Presidency of Jose Pardo), they obtained licenses to operate schools from the Ministry of Instruction without great inconvenience. However, Methodist schools did not obtain official status until the early 1920s, since they did not follow the official plan of studies, their organization and curricula were modelled after the American school system, and English took precedence over Spanish. The minutes of the twelfth annual meeting, called to assess progress during 1921, state:

> Since the Directorship of Public Instruction is preparing a new program and it has not been published yet, we cannot recommend its application in our schools, but we

do advise that our plan of study be adjusted as much as possible to the official program.[58]

The Mission was anxious from the beginning to be able to provide official diplomas, so that graduates from Methodist high schools might be admitted to the national university,[59] and later take up influential positions in Peruvian life, or perhaps become leaders of Peruvian Protestantism. (The Committee on Education at the Panama Congress expressed the same concern.)[60] The Missionaries' aspiration to provide the national church's leaders with a university education and more generally to prepare suitable young people for advanced studies is still expressed in 1926.[61] Access to public high schools was facilitated by a law of 1917 enabling graduates from private elementary schools to take official examinations to qualify for admission.[62]

Even after adopting the official plan of studies, Methodist schools were able to maintain considerable independence, not only with respect to their organization but also where basic educational theory, teaching methods, and the approach to the subjects taught were concerned. Even at the Panama Congress it was acknowledged that some schools, while adopting national programs, had modernized their interpretation and execution to the point that no apparent disadvantages followed.[63] In Peru, in any case, once the decision had been made to follow the official plan, Methodist school administrators only had to fulfill formal legal requirements to obtain recognition. The religious issue was periodically inconvenient, but, in spite of some mild incidents, schools carried out their tasks without interruptions even before 1915, the year in which religious freedom was granted.[64] The number of students steadily grew (as the reader can observe in Figure 1).

Buildings and Financial Resources

All Methodist schools shared a common past, in that they began their activities in rented buildings that were gradually improved and adapted. Later the schools had their own buildings financed out of mission funds and through funding campaigns in the United States. In some cases, this process took many years. Lima High School moved from rented quarters (the location changed twice) into a new building in 1932.[65] The building was constructed and equipped at a cost of two hundred thousand American dollars

Figure 1

Total number of students from 1916 to 1940 attending urban Methodist schools: Colegio Norte-Americano, later Instituto Andino (Huancayo); Escuela Anglo-Americana (Victoria, Lima); Callao High School (Callao); Escuela Anglo-Americana (Callao); Lima High School (Lima).

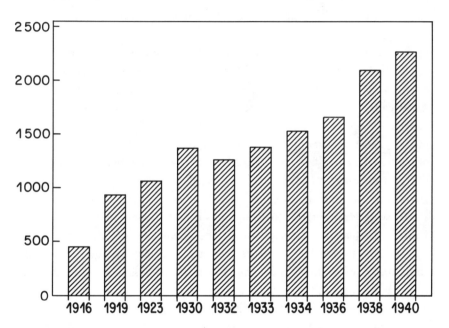

Sources: *Actas Officiales de la Conferencia Misionera Andina del Norte de la Iglesia Metodista Episcopal,* November-December 1916, September 1919, January-February 1924, December 1930, December 1931; *Actas Oficiales de la Conferencia Misionera del Peru de la Iglesia Metodista Episcopal,* December 1933, December 1934, February 1937, February 1939; *Actas Oficiales de la Conferencia Anual Provisional del Peru de la Iglesia Metodista,* December 1940.

($200,000.00); it provided a spacious gymnasium, a beautiful auditorium seating 500, boarding accommodation for forty pupils, laboratories for the Sciences and Home Economics, a library, and other facilities.

The Colegio Norteamericano of Huancayo (later Instituto Andino) moved into its own building in 1924. At that point the largest Methodist property in Peru, it was built with funds from the "Centenary,"[66] and included boarding facilities and a Biblical Institute. In 1939, it was still considered that the Andino had the best school facilities of any school in the mountains.[67]

It is difficult to trace the rental arrangements and location changes of the Callao High School and the Escuela Anglo-Americana del Callao. (Later, the two schools merged, forming Colegio America.) The annual report of 1920 made clear that the primary section occupied two houses, one on Colon Street and the other on Union Street. The Mission also occupied the buildings that, according to the original deed of trust and regulations governing the management of the English Church and Schools in 1897, were transferred to the Consuls of Great Britain and the United States of America and the manager of Pacific Steam Navigation as trustees for the use and benefit of the Protestant community of Callao.[68] In the 1940s the Mission bought one of these buildings, the one occupied by the secondary school in Calle Teatro 153. The present building was inaugurated in 1948.[69]

The main financial resources came from the United States; the missionary budget made provision for the payment of the missionaries and teachers, and provided for other needs when required. The estimated sum requested by the mission for the year 1925 was $26,796.00 ($1,082.00 less than in 1924).[70] In addition, sizeable sums were regularly obtained through private donation and funding campaigns in the United States. This money was mainly applied to the construction of new buildings and the acquisition of equipment. However, since the schools charged fees and received donations within Peru, progressively they became able to cover maintenance expenses, including in some instances the payment of non-missionary teachers and the rental charges, from their own resources. For example, in 1919 the Escuela Anglo-Americana del Callao provided scholarships and discounts from its own funds to poor children attending Sunday schools; the money also covered the cost of American desks for 210 pupils.[71] Moreover, the report assessing the school work during 1921 said:

> until this year the school had been a burden for the
> Mission since it still received money for its expenses.
> During this year we have been able to pay all the
> expenses with the school money and to have a profit of
> $5,000.00.[72]

It can also been seen in a letter dated November 1924:

> all our day schools are self supporting with the aid of the
> Mining Company subsidies. The only exception this past
> year (1923) has been Victoria School in Lima and next
> year it will be entirely self supporting.[73]

A year later the school was able to save $700 American.[74]

It is difficult to obtain systematic information about school
fees paid by parents. A letter concerning the financial situation of
the mission in 1924 says, "Please remember also that many of our
families are paying quite high fees to educate their children."[75] At
the end of the century, monthly tuition ranged from one Sol in the
first grade to four Soles for the high school (the latter amount was
approximately $1.00 in American currency).[76] In 1921 the average
fee (taking into account discounts for parents registering two or
more children) at Callao High School was 8.90 Soles monthly per
student (approximately $4.00 U.S.).[77] In 1931, a manuscript list of
those receiving bursaries who were members of La Victoria Church
and another list with the names of those belonging to the Central
Church in Lima indicates that an annual scholarship covered $70.00
in fees ($7.00 per month). There is no information about the
schools for which they had been selected. In 1940, the Escuela
Americana in La Oroya required fees that ranged from three Soles
per month (Preparatoria) to 6.50 Soles (for the fifth year); in
addition, pupils were required to pay registration and examination
fees.[78]

The policy with respect to scholarships had undergone
changes during the period under consideration. At the beginning
the children of church members were favoured, but progressively
regulations became very strict and more selective.[79] In 1913, fee
payment for the Escuelas Anglo-Americanas del Callao (Callao High
School presumably included) was as follows: no payment for
children of members of the Methodist Conference in Peru (the

number of national members of the Conference was small); discounts of one Sol for two students from the same family and two Soles for three or more students from the same family; discounts of one Sol for a monthly payment of three Soles and two Soles for a monthly payment of five Soles in the case of children of Evangelical non-Methodist missionaries. Scholarships (a different item in the report) were limited to twenty; these were paid by the Mission to the church. They were requested by petitioning the Conference, meetings of which took place every three months; to qualify, the applicants had to show proof of their financial status.[80] In 1921, the Instruction Committee specified that in order to obtain a scholarship at any Methodist school it was necessary that the child or one of the parents had been a member of the church for at least one year and had attended Sunday school for one year and continued to do so on a regular basis.[81] In 1940, the Prospectus of the Escuela Americana de La Oroya reads:

> The school maintains itself through its own tuition fees; the monthly fee that parents pay for the instruction of their children is a cumulative investment for their future; therefore the payment will be made in advance to enable the payment of the teachers' salaries at the right time. The pupil who has not paid the fees five days after the month following the due date will be suspended until he pays. The receipt will be the only proof of payment.[82]

The number of scholarships was small, both at elementary and secondary levels, when compared with the number of registered students. For example, when in 1921 the Escuela Anglo-Americana del Callao provided ten full scholarships and thirty-one half scholarships for $1,910, there were 530 registered pupils.[83] In 1924 the Escuela Anglo-Americana de La Victoria, located in one of the poorest districts of Lima where only three per cent of the population lived in good conditions (according to a 1931 survey),[84] had twenty-four scholarships for 161 pupils.[85] This school presumably attracted a good number of students from other parts of the city.

Teaching Staff

From the beginning, missionaries realized the necessity of educating the national teaching staff of the schools. In 1917, an evaluative appraisal reads, "But the imperious need is to create a department that might produce especially skilled teachers who sympathize with our ideas and efforts."[86] The year before (1916), missionaries had proposed the establishment of courses in pedagogy for teachers in Methodist schools.[87] The preoccupation appeared again in 1924:

> Although the Organic Law of Teaching does not recognize private Normal Schools of any kind, in order to serve the Evangelical Schools and other private schools in a better way, it is important to create in the upper years of Lima High School a Normal Section. If it is not possible there, the project should be under consideration for development at Callao High School.[88]

Missionaries formed the core of the teaching staffs, which included, nevertheless, numbers of national teachers who were either Protestant or sympathetic to Protestant causes. For example, Lima High School had on its staff in 1921 four missionary teachers, four full-time national teachers, two part-time national teachers, and two specialist national teachers for piano and drawing.[89] Most of the national teachers were graduates from Methodist High Schools or from the Anglo-Peruvian School. Some of these were sent to the United States to be trained as teachers. Otherwise seminars and reading courses on pedagogy attempted to compensate for the lack of an Evangelical Normal School. Missionary leadership at the schools was strong and decisions were highly centralized. Here is an illustrative statement:

> We insist that the teaching staff of an institution of instruction has to govern itself by the fundamental and educational principles and the plans of action of those who direct the institution. It is clear that the results that we all look for will not be achieved if the auxiliary teachers do not appreciate the imperative necessity of co-operative joint action, sharing the ideals of those who direct the schools and a profound appreciation of the things that are of value in education.[90]

Curriculum

The schools owed their success to the kind of curriculum missionaries taught and to the plan of studies, which may be roughly but distinctively characterized as an emphasis on the teaching of English and commercial subjects. Thus, they met the needs for skilled bilingual personnel created by the presence of foreign companies, especially in Lima and Callao. Public schools could hardly provide programs of the same quality; in fact, until 1927 there were not attempts there to systematize commercial education.

In the early years, Methodist schools in Peru followed American models.[91] From the early 1920s, as already indicated, they adopted the official plan of study at both elementary and secondary levels.   However, their approach to organization, teaching, and teacher-pupil relationships remained unique, Christian in principle but modified by American progressive thought.   The addition of courses and the emphasis on extra-curricular activities were also distinctive features.

Methodist missionaries were always anxious to-be-up to date in their educational work.   Thus, in 1918 missionaries urgently recommended an in-depth study of educational reforms already carried out in the most progressive nations, and requested that particular attention be given to their potential relevance to Peru; it was also acknowledged that properly modern curricula, especially in the elementary grades, should take into account local social problems.[92] The annual report of the Instruction Committee continued,

> Changes in thought and in commercial life that we see today and the great popularity of our schools make imperative the use of all our strength for an immediate and complete occupation of the educational field.[93]

The Mission was referring here to vocationally oriented education.

At the beginning, the emphasis was primarily on the teaching of the English language; later, commercial subjects were equally or even more greatly emphasized.   An advertisement published in 1917, which sought to direct the attention of parents to the Anglo-American schools of Lima and Callao, said: "In these English schools, the English language is taught better than in other schools in Peru.   This year we have three more foreign professors."[94] By 1920 the main schools were offering well-established commercial programs.

F. Stanger, then principal of Callao High School, stated in 1923 that the school was, and had mainly been in the past, a commercial school. In that year the curriculum was re-organized in an attempt to obtain official accreditation. A five-year commercial program leading to a high school certificate and a less advanced, two-year program were also approved.[95] Both programs worked out well since business classes were very popular.[96] The existence of the two-year program did not interfere with enrolment in the five-year one.[97] In 1924, the school opened a night program for young people who worked during the day; it offered English, typewriting, bilingual shorthand, and accounting courses.[98]

The work in the Sierra was within the boundaries of what Methodists named the Central District. It included the Colegio Norteamericano de Huancayo and the schools of the mining circuit. The Mission had great hopes for this area. The report presented to the fifteenth annual meeting said:

> There is a great opportunity for the evangelical faith. The district had experienced a very rapid commercial growth which stimulates a great interest in education and offers increased opportunities for educated men and women. It seems to me that the next quarter of the century will see an interesting increase in the district of the Sierra in education, in business, and also in evangelical religion. We need preachers for our churches, we need businessmen dedicated to Christ.[99]

It is remarkable that this sanguine statement, which ignores the economic limitations imposed on the Sierra region by the special character of foreign investments applied to create economic enclaves and of the dominance of great landowners, was actually written by a socially and politically strong-minded missionary. The statement, in which evangelical faith, business, and education appear closely associated, makes it clear that one of the aims of the Mission was the transmission of capitalist social structures within the Social Gospel doctrine.

The Colegio Norteamericano de Huancayo offered commercial courses and taught English in all the sections of the school. However, from 1919, under the direction of W. J. Dennis, the school adopted Spanish as the main language and began to teach the national course of study as a first step toward official accreditation.[100] In 1923, out of ninety-one pupils from the elementary section taking the official examination, seventy passed; in 1925, seventy-five out of eighty-one passed.[101] However, the teaching of English was still considered important in the three sections of the school.   Daily English lessons were given in the three-year commercial program; the second-year courses were taught partly in English and partly in Spanish, and the third year was taught wholly in English except for the course in Mercantile Law[102] The regular high school had daily English classes during its brief period of existence (it closed in 1924), and had proposed to attempt the teaching of history and geography in English, to the extent that this might be possible.   The intent was to have students read and write English fluently by the end of the program.[103]

The schools located within the mining circuit were highly dependent—to judge by missionaries' comments—on the stability of the work force and the degree of collaboration provided by the Cerro de Pasco Copper Corporation and the Peruvian Railway Corporation; but this cannot altogether explain the variations in the number of registered pupils or the high proportion of children leaving school.   For example, the school in Cerro de Pasco had 120 pupils in 1914 while by 1916 there were twenty-one;[104] the four schools (in Cerro de Pasco, Smelter, Goyllarisquisga, and La Oroya) had, taken together, 201 pupils in 1923, seventy in 1924, and 191 in 1925.[105]   The rate of withdrawal may have been high in particular years.   For example, in 1936 out of 143 original registrants at Colegio Americano de La Oroya, fifty-nine withdrew, and only sixty-seven eventually passed their courses.[106]   These schools followed American models closely, and this may have had something to do with attendance fluctuations.   The teaching of English, for instance, is puzzling, since the children of the proletariat of mining centres and smelting plants spoke Quechua, not Spanish.

At Lima High School there was a great preoccupation with the quality of teaching, American schools always being used as a reference point.   School administrators stated in 1925, "and finally we are doing everything humanly possible and it is within our reach to offer to our students the program equal to that of any higher college in the United States."[107] Lima High School was an elementary and high school and also a commercial school.   In 1916, the program of studies began with kindergarten and continued until Grade Nine; from 1917 onwards two additional years were provided.[108] A 1917 advertisement introduced the school as follows,

In this Institute the plan of studies is in conformity with
that followed in the United States; we provide instruction
in all sections including kindergarten, leading up to a
complete knowledge of English.   Also, we offer a special
boarding department for a limited number of girls, which
has been organized with the greatest possible care.[109]

Missionaries thought of their schools as a power for the
moral uplifting of the nation and expressed joy once North Andean
Methodism had gained acknowledged distinction through its
teaching institutions and the promotion of educational reforms.[110]
There were attempts to develop social centres, with the school as
the nucleus, the purpose being, on the one hand, to strengthen ties
between church and school, and on the other, to induce co-
operation between parents and teachers[111] (a co-operation that did
not require a parental religious affiliation).   This policy, in line
with a curriculum that attempted to develop a youth leadership
with a new Christian mentality, a modern one, intended to exert
influence on the community at large.

Methodists often praised their teaching methods; children,
they said, were taught to ask why and how, and a "finer"
discipline, strict but humane, prevailed, and was supported by
student councils.[112]   As they remarked, this pattern was the
opposite to that found in public schools.   Certainly, the
organization of the classroom, to judge by references scattered in
annual reports, moved away from coercion and encouraged self-
control and consensus.   This approach implied the collective
assumption of the values and principles transmitted by the teacher,
who in turn necessarily took the individual characteristics of
students into account in classroom planning.   This is in accordance
with the report on religious education presented at the Montevideo
Congress that recommended that the educational process be pupil-
centred rather than material-centred.   In addition, co-education
gave Methodist schools a distinctive feature.

The introduction of innovative courses and emphasis on
extra-curricular activities helps to illustrate, to some extent, the
Methodist approach to curriculum.   For example, in 1920 there was
introduced at Callao High School a course on political science for
the higher grades.   (Apparently it was addressed to boys.)[113]   In
the same year there were visits to factories and prisons, among
other places.   The comment on these visits written in the annual

report of the school says: "There is no question that these youths were deeply moved and that with those experiences they will be better prepared than if they devoted that time strictly to commercial studies.[114] A parallel course on home economics was organized for girls in the upper grades, as well as a course in nursing and first aid.[115] Other schools did not supply detailed information on the courses that were taught, but there was mention of the advisability of their building links with the community.   Of course, Bible classes were always taught as a means to the development of the spiritual life of the students; they were considered fundamental for the growth of personal freedom (which was mainly equated with the acquisition of a modern mentality) and for the rebuilding of Peruvian society.   Many students were motivated to attend Sunday schools and participate in the Epworth League (Youth League), in spite of being nominally Roman Catholic.

Relationships with Peruvian teachers from public schools and from other private schools arose mainly from the participation of Methodist schools in extra-curricular activities, for example in the Temperance Leagues.   The report of 1920, written by the administrator of the Colegio Norteamericano de Huancayo, contains, however, information on further involvement: "Now we are creating an association of professors from this province and we hope that a lot can be done to improve instruction, particularly in public schools."[116] Although it was not possible to trace this initiative further, it is important to notice that missionaries were trying to exert influence on Peruvian teachers at a moment when public authorities were inspired by American educational models.[117]

Methodist students participated in campaigns against cruel sports, such as bullfighting and cockfights.   When the Society for the Protection of Animals was created in Lima, the Committee on Instruction of the Methodist Mission recommended that the schools co-operate with the Society whenever possible.[118] The schools also used national commemorations as opportunities to participate in parades and competitions and to organize artistic presentations that attracted influential people.

Students also engaged in activities more directly associated with their schools.   For example, from 1925 onwards there was a savings bank at the Instituto Andino.   The report written by the missionary working in the school included a comment that illustrates once more the contradictions of the missionary work: "It is a pity that in Peru today a great part of business requiring big capital is in foreign hands and it should not be that way."[119] Students from Callao High School ran their own periodical, *Sentinel of Progress*, from 1919. The Graduate Student Association of the Lima High School, founded in 1922 on the initiative of Miss G. Hanks, principal of the school, aimed at maintaining solidarity with school ideals, at continuing association with the school, and at the preservation of the friendship that originated in the classrooms.[120]

As in American schools, sports and athletic activities were strongly fostered; they were a means to promote student involvement and also to generate friendship among students attending Methodist schools.[121] All the schools had baseball, football, and basketball teams. Girls from Lima High School played volleyball and were particularly active. Physical culture was understood in the context of better health; thus, medical examinations of all the students were carried out in Lima on an annual basis at the Anglo-American Clinic from 1921; students from the Andean School and the schools from the mining circuit were examined at the Clinica Evangelica de Huancayo that opened in 1925.[122] The parents received reports on their children's health. (There are no details extant on the health care of students or information concerning the procedures—if any—followed after a diagnosis.)

Many of the texts used in the schools were American, sent from the United States, often by the American Book Company, for example, Stewart and Coe's *First Days in School*.[123] The schools bought in bulk consignments and sold them to the students. Other books were published by Inca, the Peruvian Evangelical Publishing House. The Methodist Publishing House, which had been in business in the United States since 1879, supplied religious literature, particularly for the Sunday schools, such as group-grades lessons.[124] Some religious books and booklets were translated into Spanish and others were written and published in Peru. The literature published by the Committee on Cooperation in Latin America was widely distributed. *La Nueva Democracia* was at the hand of all Methodist high school students.

Literature and Evangelical Christianity was the topic of one of the committees working at the Montevideo Congress. The reports included detailed lists of publishers, critical reflections on the material in use, and new proposals. One, for example, concluded:

> We have in the past probably been too trustful of the necessarily religious effects of a tale when adorned with a moral. We may have been too trusting of the good results of all literature properly tagged as Christian and given too little consideration to the elevating effects of the noble poetry and prose written by "secular" writers. We may now be missing the fine line of new children's books appearing in Spanish, which give proper play to the imagination, stories of adventures for boys and girls, books on the home, on the place of womanhood, on modern social questions, on science, and especially on ethical and moral questions.[125]

Among the books that were recommended we find *El Sermon de la Paz* by Zorrilla de San Martin; *Desolacion* by Gabriela Mistral; *El Hombre Mediocre* by Jose Ingenieros; *Positivismo e Idealismo* by Caso; the poems of Amado Nervo; *Os Deveres das Novas Geracoes Brasileiras* by Carneiro Leao; *Horas y Siglos* by Navarro Monzo; *El Sentimiento Tragico de la Vida* by Unamuno; and even older books like those of the "fiery moral prophet of Argentina", Agustin Alvarez.[126]

It is now time to examine the ideological content of the curriculum and look at the general educational aims of Methodist schools in Peru as stated and pursued by school administrators. The minutes of the annual meeting held in 1916 provided some details,

> In our schools we place special care not only on the physical, mental and moral development of the students but also on inculcating healthy ideals of ambition and work. Of our graduates, some not only enjoy positions of importance but, separated from viciousness and animated by a healthy ambition, they continue towards other better achievements; while others, drawn along by the insatiable thirst for knowledge acquired in our schools and by the noble aspiration of obtaining a career, have gone to the great nation of the north.[127]

An advertisement praising the qualities and advantages of Methodist schools emphasized character building and advised people not to pay too much attention to the program (the schools did not follow official plans at that time) but instead to the character and success of the graduates. It also said:

> if the graduates have good positions and can count on the confidence of the public, the school is then a good school. Anglo-American schools of Callao offer a good plan of studies and pay particular attention to the formation of good habits in their students.[128]

It is also known that Methodists expressed their intention to form "good citizens" who might contribute with their honesty, intelligence, and hard-working nature to the welfare of society. Women were included among these "good citizens"; the Mission addressed their education in such a way as to integrate them into the labour force and to encourage them to accept "civic responsibilities towards the community without prejudices and discriminations."[129]

These aims, which emphasized individual achievement, were often praised by Peruvians interested in the modernization of Peru. Such a one was Manuel Vicente Villaran, who talked of an education capable of promoting capitalism in Peru and a rejection of the feudal heritage. But the "good habits" inculcated by Methodist educators—punctuality, dependability, trustfulness—were highly appreciated by foreign companies (although of course also by national entrepreneurs and even by governmental authorities). Moreover, the expansion of Methodist schools did not exceed the absorptive capabilities of the economy.

The curriculum was then framed by contradictory goals. On the one hand, it aimed to develop spiritual life, that is, to uplift the individual and the nation through the free development of the potential of the individual and the cultivation of a freer personality. On the other hand, it aimed to provide practical skills and an ideology of corporative efficiency.[130] The emphasis on vocational education and the creation of short-term programs were at odds with equality of opportunity, a principle highly praised by missionaries. However, regular high school programs, although vocationally oriented, did not close doors to university studies, which were regarded as fundamental to the creation of an evangelical leadership. For example, the report on Peru presented to the Education Committee at the Montevideo Congress noted that:

> Where Evangelical resources are limited, it is more logical
> to specialize on the kind of schools which can most vitally
> touch the national life.   Commercially and industrially
> trained men certainly offer an open field for missionary
> service, but in a Latin country these are not the men who
> form the country's ideals and policies.   The national and
> spiritual center of gravity lies in the professions and
> especially among literary men and statesmen.   The
> Evangelical forces ought to keep open the avenues to
> higher education and to encourage young men and women
> to thoroughly prepare themselves for service to their own
> country.[131]

However, Peruvian missionaries were well aware that their students
would not become open Evangelical converts and hence considered
the "spiritual impression" the schools could make on their lives
extraordinarily important.[132]

Methodist Schools and Social Class

It is a difficult task to assess the social origin of the students
attending Methodist schools without having at hand detailed
records of parental occupation.

In considering the social classes reached by the educational
work it is necessary to take into account the missionary doctrinal
background, the preoccupation with building a Christian Evangelical
leadership, the search for recognition, legitimation, and expansion,
and the variety of skilled positions that the schools would be able
to provide.

The reports presented at the annual meetings in the period
under consideration underline with particular emphasis the fact that
children from "distinguished" families also attended Methodist
schools.   For instance, it is said in 1910, with reference to the
schools placed in Tarma, a small city in the Sierra, that "almost
all the students come from distinguished families, including that of
a senator, a colonel, and a number of rich land-owners."[133]

Administrators from Lima High School, a modern school for
girls that challenged women's traditional social status, clearly
stated, in 1917:

> Among the families represented in the school, many are

influential and kindly make good references to the school on all occasions. Among these, there are ministers of state, diplomatic representatives, senators, deputies, professors, doctors, and many others that occupy important positions in the state. The school is considered very fortunate in having these powerful friends.[134]

The reports from the Escuela Anglo-Americana de La Victoria and from the Instituto Andino did not comment on the social origin of students; but in the case of the latter there are references to public presentations that attracted influential people. The reports from the Anglo-American School of Callao repeated on various occasions that "the kind of children attending the schools improved every year."[135] One of these reports also reads, "this shows us that the public is convinced that we are providing a solid education that is practical and useful at the same time."[136] There are other similar statements which comment on the attendance of children belonging to notable families.

There are some differences here with Methodist retrospective literature of the 1930s and 1940s which give assurance that the Escuelas Anglo-Americanas of Lima and Callao (including Callao High School) fulfilled their aims by keeping fees low enough so that children from poor families could prepare themselves to do office work in two languages, and thus raise the economic level of their homes.[137] A change is noticeable in that which the missionaries emphasized with respect to the social work of the schools and their place in the Peruvian society. As it has already been observed, at the beginning the Mission tried to gain recognition and support from the dominant classes and, in particular, from those sectors inclined to modernize Peru. Progressively, and in accordance with the orientation being worked out by the Committee on Cooperation in Latin America, the Mission tried to identify new social and political currents, welcoming especially populist political leaders emerging from the petite bourgeoisie, like Haya de la Torre, and other non-official intellectual voices. This political shift became better defined in the 1930s and 1940s; during the 1920s the Mission moved with great political ambiguity.

The quotations that have been reproduced above do not necessarily lead to a general conclusion that *only* children from higher social classes attended the schools. However, it can be inferred that the curriculum was particularly attractive to bourgeois and petit-bourgeois parents, a number of whom were of immigrant origin to judge by some of the registered names.   Lima High School always had a number of children with foreign parents, and eventually a relatively high proportion of Jews.   It is observed in Figure 2 that in 1930 two per cent of the student body was Jewish; the percentage had increased to fourteen per cent in 1943, while that of Protestants—from various denominations—reached only twelve per cent.   Also the liberal but practical characteristics of the curriculum became a source of expectations for many displaced social sectors that tried to remain in the middle class, examples being small landed proprietors, and impoverished artisans, many of whom had already become proletarians.[138]   The programs developed at Callao High School, the Instituto Andino and even Lima High School responded to this situation.   The economic context provided few avenues to the middle-class, but the state bureaucracy—particularly during the 1920s—and the bureaucracy associated with financial institutions, especially those linked to foreign companies, offered certain possibilities.[139]   The fact that most of the students were Catholics also indicates that the religious motivation for attendance was not primary.   There are only scattered data for early years.   In Callao High School in 1919 only twenty-seven of ninety-four pupils were Protestants, and even some of these were recent converts.   Figure 2 shows that in 1930 eighty per cent of the pupils at Lima High School, a girls' school were Catholics.

It has already been remarked that attendance at Methodist schools remained relatively constant through years of economic and political crisis, a finding of some importance since the schools were fee-paying.   In 1930, the report from Escuela Anglo-Americana del Callao says:

> As everybody knows, the finances are in a very critical state in Peru; however, the number of students who abandoned studies for lack of money are few.   Peruvian parents have observed that their children need a Christian education, both practical and constructive, and they are ready to sacrifice everything in order that their children receive a good education.   We have received more special donations than in other years.   These donations are used for the education of poor children and those who need help.[140]

Figure 2

Percentage distribution of students following religious beliefs at Lima High School (girls school); years 1930 and 1943.

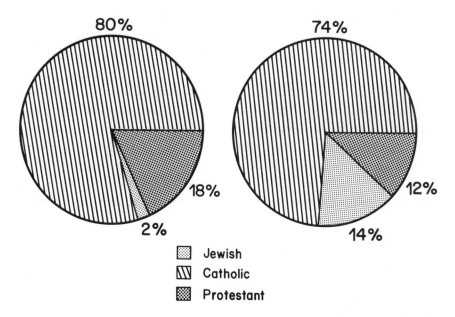

Sources: *Actas Oficiales de la Conferencia Misionera Andina del Norte de la Iglesia Metodista Episcopal*, 1930; *Actas Oficiales de la Conferencia Anual Provisional del Peru de la Iglesia Metodista*, 1943.

The number of scholarships did not increase.   The percentage of scholarships at Escuela Anglo-Americana de la Victoria, located in one of the poorest districts of Lima, decreased from 15 per cent in 1924 to 13.7 per cent in 1931.   (See Table 1.)   The percentage of withdrawals for the same school (shown in Table 2) decreased from 22.4 in 1924 to 13.7 in 1931.   The percentages of withdrawals from the Escuela Anglo-Americana del Callao (Table 3) shows slight changes from 1924 to 1933; the percentage decreased in 1933.   The Instituto Andino, at high school level, showed a high percentage of withdrawals in 1933, 32.7 per cent (no other data are available). The data laid out in Tables 1, 2, and 3 suggest that the great majority of the students paid their fees during the years of economic crisis (1930-1933).   This circumstance reinforces previous considerations regarding the social classes appealed to by Methodist schools, and tends to confirm that the programs provided skills highly regarded by parents as a means of maintaining middle-class status.

The educational work in the mining circuit was addressed, reports say, to the workers and employees of the mining compounds; the goal was to evangelize the workers and employees and to provide schools for their children, or to evangelize the children in order to convert their parents.   The report presented to the annual meeting assessing progress during 1925 stated that the schools placed in La Oroya, Cerro de Pasco, and Goyllarisquisga together had 191 pupils and operated without financial aid from the Mission.   It continues: "The concessions provided by the Peruvian Corporation, the Cerro de Pasco Copper Corporation, and the Cerro de Pasco Railway Company helped us in our work and we are deeply grateful."[141]   However, the Cerro de Pasco Copper Corporation, which provided the building for the Escuela Americana de La Oroya, became hostile to the school work in the late 1930s.   First, it stopped making repairs; then in March 1941, after the school had opened for registration, it asked the Mission to leave.[142]   No discussion of these episodes can be found in any Mission documents, but some church leaders attributed them to the increasing association of church members and even missionaries with the Aprista Peruvian Party.[143]

Documents and reports do not provide specific information on the social origin of pupils.   Children of employees attended these schools, but Methodists, on occasion, also mentioned their

Table 1

Scholarship distribution percentages (including
full, half, and quarter scholarships). Escuela Anglo-
Americana (Victoria-Lima)

YEAR	REGISTRANTS	SCHOLARSHIPS	PERCENT
1924	161	24	15.0
1931	278	38	13.7
1936	306	30	10.0

Source: *Actas Oficiales de la Conferencia Misionera Andina del
Norte de la Iglesia Metodista Episcopal*, December 1924, December
1931; Actas de la *Conferencia Misionera del Peru de la Iglesia
Metodista Episcopal*, February 1937.

Table 2

Percentages of withdrawals - Escuela Anglo-Americana (Victoria-Lima)

YEAR	REGISTRANTS	WITHDRAWALS	PERCENT
1924	161	36	22.4
1931	278	38	13.7
1936	306	48	15.7
1938	380	64	16.8

(La Victoria was a poor district of Lima.)

Source: *Actas Oficiales de la Conferencia Misionera Andina del Norte de la Iglesia Metodista Episcopal,* December 1924, December 1931; *Actas Oficiales de la Conferencia Misionera del Peru de la Iglesia Metodista Episcopal,* February 1937, February 1939.

Table 3

Percentages of withdrawals - Escuela Anglo-Americana del Callao (primary school)

YEAR	REGISTRANTS	WITHDRAWALS	PERCENT
1919	354	49	13.8
1923	413	55	13.3
1924	436	39	8.9
1925	467	34	7.3
1931	480	42	8.8
1933	413	28	6.8
1936	478	48	10.0

Sources: *Actas Oficiales de la Conferencia Misionera Andina del Norte de la Iglesia Metodista Episcopal*, September 1919, January-February 1924, December 1924, January 1926, December 1931; *Actas Oficiales de la Conferencia Misionera del Peru de la Iglesia* Metodista Episcopal, December 1933, February 1937.

efforts to expand instruction and education among the Indians in the mining centres (mining workers were mostly proletarianized Indian peasants).[144] However, it is observable that the schools that became established valued formal procedures and insisted on high standards, trying to increase their prestige and broaden their social influence.   The Escuela Americana de La Oroya (Institucion Norteamericana) is an example.   A prospectus published in 1940 detailed the way the school worked, mentioning discipline, personal appearance, care of the building and the furniture, punctuality, and the use of uniforms, as well as the teaching of English and the high teaching standards that gave students a solid basis for high school.[145] In spite of missionary claims that the teaching was equally addressed to the children of the workers and white collar employees, a school organized as described above responded to the backgrounds and possibilities of the children of white collar employees and merchants rather than to those of the children of the workers.

Women's Education

The Methodist Episcopal Church was regarded at the Panama Congress as a pioneer in women's education.   At that time, in 1916, the Women's Foreign Missionary Society that sponsored Lima High School also ran four boarding schools and a number of day schools in Mexico, including an industrial school for poor girls in Mexico City.   This society also maintained a school in Montevideo, Uruguay, with about 100 day pupils, a school in a well-equipped new building at Rosario, Argentina, with 125 boarding and day pupils, and another in Flores, outside Buenos Aires.   Other schools for girls were sustained by the Methodist Church in Iquique, Santiago, and Concepcion, all located in Chile.   The school in Santiago developed kindergarten, primary and secondary sections with additional courses and, besides, offered an eight-year program in music and a four-year program in fine arts.[146]

Methodist schools in Peru were co-educational until 1939, when co-education was prohibited by law.   The experience was described

> as years of healthy life with boys and girls together in the classroom at a time when co-education was practically unknown in other parts of the country and people were

saying, but Peruvians are different, co-education will not work here. It did work and the forces of the school, organizations of parents and graduates are once again hoping to lead in the reform of this law as a new and reputedly liberal government takes over the command this year.[147]

The positive response to co-education by the parents is clearly expressed in the number of girls attending Methodist schools. Figure 3 shows the sex distribution at important urban schools in Lima and Callao, Escuela Anglo-Americana de La Victoria, a primary school, and Escuela Anglo-Americana del Callao (the data include Callao High School); female enrolment was very high from the early years, in spite of the conservative influence of the Roman Catholic Church. Even at Colegio Norteamericano de Huancayo, located in the Sierra, girls constituted 48 of 128 pupils by 1918.

The Methodist Mission in Peru was constantly preoccupied with the improvement of women's social condition and also with their preparation for the labour market. Lima High School (later Colegio Maria Alvarado) has a dedication written on a bronze plaque saying that "lovers of education in North America have contributed to its edification with the noble proposal of exalting in the girl the ideals of Jesus Christ."[148] The aims are explained by Jane Hahne on the occasion of the celebration of the fiftieth anniversary of the school:

> Thus, we have tried to guide them to choose a noble and serving vocation, to inculcate in them the highest ideals of the dignity of the home, to cultivate good habits of self-discipline and intellectual independence, to awaken in them respect towards all races, to recognize the right of each individual to enjoy social, economic and religious freedom and finally to teach them to accept their social responsibility without prejudices or discriminations, with love to humanity in its entirety.[149]

In the Peruvian social context these aims meant a challenging and courageous approach.

It is remarkable that women missionaries working in education were close to the Peruvian pioneers in women's education from the very beginning. Elsie Wood taught at the Liceo Fanning School and shared ideals with Teresa Gonzalez de Fanning. Gertrude Hanks, principal of the school for twenty-five years

Figure 3

Student sex distribution at Escuela Anglo-Americana del Callao (primary school) and Callao High School, and Escuela Anglo-Americana de la Victoria (primary school)

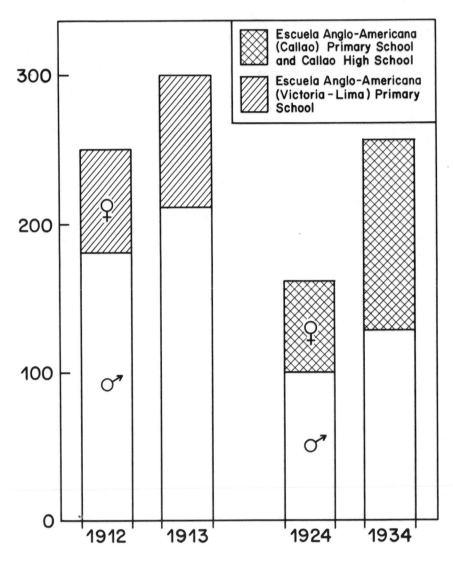

Sources: *Actas Oficiales de la Conferencia Misionera Andina del Norte de la Iglesia Metodista Episcopal*, December 1912, December 1913, December 1924; *Actas Oficiales de la Conferencia Misionera del Peru de la Iglesia Metodista Episcopal*, December 1934.

(1921-1946) was very close to the celebrated Peruvian educator Elvira Garcia y Garcia. The school was also well accepted by Evolucion Femenina, a society organized in 1914 which had as it purpose the establishment of public high schools for women, the spreading of practical knowledge about child care and household management, the provision of industrial work suitable for women, the development of the idea that all honest labour is dignified and honourable, and the securing for women of civil equality, and of their right, when married, to run their own financial affairs.[150] Evolucion Femenina publicly recognized the work accomplished by Gertrude Hanks when she retired in 1946.

> Because she has been a competent teacher and a kind friend to all young women of Peru, we sent to Miss Hanks this cordial message of deep friendship and eternal appreciation.[151]

However, women missionaries apparently did not associate with such outstanding women (characterized by the audacity of their social criticisms) as Dora Mayer or Magda Portal, or with female artists committed to an attack on wider social problems and to the problems of national identity,[152] although they knew of their work.

In general, missionaries considered that the progress of the Mission was often held back by the Peruvian women, who were frequently trapped within an unthinking conservatism.[153] However, the conception of women's role in society greatly differed between missionaries and Peruvian converts, and there were also differences among missionaries themselves. The Mission was also aware of the difficulties it faced here, and did not follow the advice of progressive Social Gospel preachers like Coe (who believed in the democratic family as a support of political democracy).[154] Although Coe's proposals sounded extremely idealistic (rooted in his faith in the health of American bourgeois democracy), it must be recognized that the revision of women's roles in Peru was not an easy process. In Peruvian society, conventionalism and social patterns were dramatically rigid and compulsive; by the same token, there were no drastic economic changes of the kind that had occurred in the highly industrialized societies. Consequently, articles published in *El Mensajero* by Peruvians, whether converts or guest writers, were amazingly conservative in tone. It published in 1920 an article by Emilio Delboy (reproduced from *Hogar*) in which he denied that women had the *capacity* to be creative writers;[155] he even had the audacity to include among those intruders into men's natural domains the Chilean writer Gabriela Mistral, who would later receive the Nobel Prize for literature.   Nevertheless, most Peruvian Methodist literature expressed a wish to dignify women and provide them with education; the central point was, however, that women needed this education to fulfill in the best manner possible their role as mothers.   An article published in *El Mensajero* said:

> that your daughter, your wife and your mother be wiser in their mission, less ignorant to understand and help their husbands, brothers and fathers. . . .   The woman needs culture to become the interpreter of the man, knowing his qualities and defects, to learn to be mother and to know that her mission is not only to feed their children but to be an artist in shaping the body and soul of her children.[156]

The raising of children, the main role ascribed to women (that involved, to use current terminology, the reproduction of the labour force), was fundamental to the ideological changes that missionaries tried to generate.

Of course, the Methodists went much further than these articles would suggest, largely because of the commitment to preparing girls for the labour market.   Callao High School and the Andean School produced skilled girls who were in demand by business houses.   And it is clear that Lima High School, in particular, had consciously determined on a policy of transculturation affecting the life of the girls.   Clyde Brewster described the educational work of the school in 1924 in the following terms:

> The school has a teaching force of five American girls, all college graduates, and they are doing a work for the advancement of this country that can hardly be established. . . . But in this school the Peruvian girls are coming in contact with the very finest type of American womanhood and are being influenced by a newer and finer type of good wholesome culture than they have ever known before.[157]

The ethnocentric quality of these judgments needs no extended comment; they depend on an imported conception of womanhood that presumed universality and ignored its historical and social foundations. However, the life of the school, it must be admitted, was intellectually rich, although flawed by the contradictions running through missionary activities in Peru. Thus, socially and politically committed Peruvian writers, especially those associated with the Committee on Cooperation in Latin America, and Social Gospel advocates like George Howard were frequently invited to speak to the pupils. (Luis Valcarcel, a pro-Indian voice, was also among the guest speakers.) Nevertheless, the school showed a strong tendency to approach social problems paternalistically, and always stressed the importance of charity.

In the Peruvian social context it is not surprising to find that Lima High School was the Methodist school that most appealed to petit-bourgeois and bourgeois parents; a sizeable number of foreigners, Jews in particular, also attended. The reports mention the daughters of diplomatic representatives and high-ranking members of government.[158] Even as late as 1956 attendance statistics show the dominance of girls with petit-bourgeois backgrounds.[159]

The number of graduates from Lima High School was small; from 1916 to 1930 there were only 49 graduates from the regular high school and commercial programs (registration figures in all the sections rose from 83 in 1916 to 190 in 1930).[160] There are no reports on the number of withdrawals for the high school section, but general references indicate that the number was not high. It seems likely that the school maintained extremely selective standards, especially in the upper grades. Almost all graduates moved into important executive secretarial positions, most of them in foreign companies. Those with a commercial specialization, working in foreign houses in Lima and elsewhere, were held to have distinguished themselves by their preparation and competence. Moreover, missionaries claimed that graduates from Lima High School were the first women to hold important secretarial positions in companies.[161] In 1957 a review of the positions held by some graduates mentioned the following: secretary to the regional manager of Panagra; secretary to the manager of Anderson Clayton and Co. S.A.; secretary to the director of Mission of Operations from Outside Service in Peru (USOM), and director of the Cooperative Service Production of Food (SCIPA); and secretary to the vice-manager of the First National City Bank of New York in

Lima.[162]

Lima High School was one of the first female institutions in Peru that was afforded the privilege, in 1956, of celebrating its Bodas de Oro (Golden Anniversary).

Conclusion

The second part of this chapter has shown the independence of Methodist schools from the public system in Peru and the extent to which, in the period under review, they constituted a system on their own.

Methodist schools in Peru were established when Peruvian authorities were trying to rebuild the public school system. The different Peruvian governments between 1895 and 1930 were only able to organize the infrastructure of primary education; no major changes or improvements occurred in secondary education. Foreign influence was present in every educational reform sponsored by the state, but it was particulary strong during Leguia's Oncenio (1919-1930) when American educators played an active but ultimately unsuccessful role. In spite of many laws and decrees and innumerable committees and debates, no articulated theory of education appeared to shape educational policy, which instead fell victim to the vicious ways of the official political life. In the background economic and social development followed its uneven path, being conditioned by the imperialist presence, and a pervasive seigniorial mentality remained strong. Meanwhile, during the 1920s progressive intellectuals and elements within the working class embarked on their own educational projects through the Popular Universities.

Methodist educators held to a theory of education in which American progressivism (including John Dewey's pedagogical ideas) was interwoven with Christian doctrine; their educational policies in Peru were distinct from those of the public system in almost every respect. In due course their schools conformed to the official plan of studies, but the practical consequences for missionary educational work was negligible, relationships with the Ministry of Education being entirely formal. When decisions of importance had to be made their source was local missionary administrative bodies, or sometimes the Board of Foreign Missions. In the case of Lima High School the Women's Foreign Missionary Society made the ultimate decisions. Major recommendations for innovation came from various quarters: important inter-denominational meetings like the Panama and Montevideo Congresses, the writings of church specialists in education like Coe, as well as directly from the missionaries themselves, who were highly practical people preoccupied with the expansion of their educational activities. The schools adopted foreign names or otherwise indicated their foreign origin; in turn, the public recognized them as American schools.

The Methodist schools were able to prepare people to work at various levels in a capitalist-dependent economy in a way that the public schools could not. They produced the qualified personnel required by foreign companies and their subsequent local networks such as skilled commercial employees, administrators, and intermediate leaders related to the financial bureaucracy. An assessment of Callao High School written in 1939 claimed that the male and female graduates from the school had always been in demand by leading business houses and could be found in many positions of trust and confidence, not so much because of their thorough training as because of their knowledge of English and, above all, their sense of responsibility and great trustworthiness.[163] The Instituto Andino graduates received similar appraisals, although the commercial program extended for only two years beyond the primary school. Lima High School was one of the most praised Methodist schools. These schools achieved, although on a limited scale, the training of personnel and, to a certain extent, the ideological formation required following the introduction of imperialist capitalism into Peru; they played their part in an uneven economic and social context in which a conservative education, like that provided by the Catholic Church, also had a place.

Methodist schools not only provided trained personnel, however; with results that are difficult to assess, they were also agencies for trans-culturation. Within the context of an ideologically conflicting atmosphere, in which the "North Americanism" of the Social Gospel and other more conservative views shared ground with nationalist Peruvian standpoints, they helped to generate political expectations from the perspective of the middle-class and the petite bourgeoisie; and these expectations would eventually be in contradiction with the oligarchic state,

where, given the lack of space for political intermediation, middle
sectors could only aspire to professional bureaucratic positions.[164]

References

[1]Panama Congress 1916, *Christian Work in Latin America*, 3 Vols. (New York: The Missionary Education Movement, 1917), Vol. I, p. 3.

[2]Ibid., p. 3.   [3]Ibid.

[4]Ibid., p. 501.   [5]Ibid.

[6]Ibid.

[7]"The pastors in whom the self-consciousness developed were reformers and, as such, were indebted to an age of reform. Many of their ideas they owed to men around them. This has been true among the earlier Social-gospel leaders, between the Civil War and the First World War. Edward Bellamy and Henry George, Richard Ely and Simon Patten, Lester Ward and Herbert Croly, Populists and Progressives and socialists all had formulated economic, political, and social ideas more fully and clearly than the pastors, as Thorstein Veblen, John Dewey, and spokesmen for the New Deal were to continue to do so. The pastors were therefore a kind of register of the penetration of the religious community by ideas from more secular headquarters." Donald B. Meyer, *The Protestant Search for Political Realism, 1919-1941* (Berkeley and Los Angeles: University of California Press, 1961), p. 2.

[8]Lawrence Cremin, "John Dewey and the Progressive Education Movement, 1915-1952" in Reginald D. Archambault, ed., *Dewey on Education* (New York: Random House, 1966), p. 13.

[9]Evelyn Dewey, "En el Mundo de los Juegos," *El Mensajero*, VI, No. 68 (Lima: December 1920), p. 6.

[10]Jorge P. Howard, "La Educacion Religiosa: Como la Entiende la Iglesia Evangelica," *El Mensajero*, IV, No. 43 (Lima, July 1918), p. 4.

[11]Donald B. Meyer, *The Protestant Search*, p. 137.

[12]George A. Coe, *A Social Theory of Religious Education*, 1927 rpt., 1917 1st edition (New York: Arno Press and The New York Times, 1969).

[13]Donald B. Meyer, *The Protestant Search*, p. 137.

[14]Ibid., p. 145.

[15]The author consulted letters and bills from the American Book Company, 88 Lexington Avenue, New York, N.Y. One of the letters addressed from the company, dated on February 16, 1933 says "We wish to thank you for your order of January 25th which reached us on February 8th for twelve of our Stewart and Coe's *First Days in School* . . . . ." Signed by C. Abruzzi, Department of Accounts.

[16]Coe's book is divided into five parts: Part I, The Social Standpoint in Modern Education; Part II, The Social Interpretation of Christianity Requires Social Reconstruction in Religious Education; Part III, The Psychological Background of a Socialized Religious Education; Part IV, The Organization of a Socialized Religious Education; Part V, Existing Tendencies in Christian Education Viewed from the Social Standpoint."

[17]For example in considering religious education at the Montevideo Congress. Montevideo Congress 1925, *Christian Work in South America*, 2 Vols. (New York-Chicago: Fleming H. Revell Company, 1925), Vol. II, pp. 77-158.

[18]George A. Coe, *A Social Theory*, pp. 18-24. "To bring society and the individual child together is the aim. This means that what we have to teach the child is humane and just living in the various relationships, and also active, well directed labor that contributes to the common life of the present and likewise to the improvement of it. It might seem superfluous, but the history of schools proves that it is not, to point out that, in the last analysis, social experience is the only thing that can thus socialize anyone." Ibid., pp. 18-19.

[19]Donald B. Meyer, *The Protestant Search*, p. 137; see also George A. Coe, *A Social Theory*, Chapter III.

[20]Donald B. Meyer, *The Protestant Search*, p. 138.

[21]George A. Coe, *A Social Theory*. p. 327.

[22]Ibid., p. 18. According to Lawrence Cremin: "Dewey had no illusions about the school changing society on its own; that educational and political reform would have to go hand in hand was the progressive view from the beginning. Nor did the notion of adjusting the school to society imply that the school would have to accommodate itself to all institutions and practices. Dewey wanted schools to use the stuff of reality to educate men and women intelligently about reality. His notion of adjustment was an adjustment of conditions, not to them, a remaking of existing

conditions, not a mere remaking of self and individual to fit into them. And as for the corrupting influence of life itself, Dewey was no visionary; the problem for him was not to build the perfect society but a better society. To this he thought a school that educated for intelligence about reality could make a unique contribution." Lawrence Cremin, "John Dewey and the Progressive," p. 23.

[23]Montevideo Congress 1925, *Christian Work*, Vol. II, p. 87.

[24]Ibid., pp. 87-88. "Our contrasting practices are indicated thus:

Based chiefly on knowledge.	Based on more complete activity.
a. "Opening exercises" conducted entirely by the superintendent of the Sunday school with the pupils only singing hymns.	Young People's Society religious meetings where the whole service is conducted by the young people themselves.
b. Learning how to teach by studying a book and by writing correct answers to questions.	Learning how to teach by practice teaching combined with observation, study, and guidance.
c. Lesson instruction consisting chiefly in reading a Biblical passage, asking the pupils what it means, telling them what it means, asking questions to see if they "know their lesson."	Discussion of the purposes of characters in a lesson resulting in a debate requiring the pupils to look up material and form judgments; planning and doing some act of service based on discussion of characters.
d. Continued use of the catechism with memorization of question and answer.	Discussion in class groups of problems in the actual life of the pupils, the pupils themselves, with the leader's co-operation, deciding upon Christian solutions.
e. Study a lesson arbitrarily selected by an overhead committee with lesson helps prepared by writers far removed from the actual local situations in which the lesson is used.	The selection by the class of a project which will require individual initiative, choice, and constructive activity on the part of each member.

Even these items still remain as activities within the church only. They must become dynamically related to the everyday experiences of boys and girls and young people, if the religious education is to be effective. There seems yet little understanding that the church must directly influence home and school and play." Ibid., pp. 89-90.

[25]Ibid., p. 90.

"In practice we find both principles tried:

a. Uniform lessons for all ages;	Lessons specifically adapted to groups of pupils with common interests, needs, and at common state of development;
b. A system of lessons which undertake to bring the entire Bible to the pupil in historical sequence;	A program of religious education which takes its point of departure from the experience of the pupil looking to the Bible and to other sources for material to enrich and direct experience;
c. Hymns and prayers, undoubtedly Christian, but expressing adult religious experience, "taught" to children.	Hymns and prayers which express the experience of the pupils;
d. Memorization of passages, not understood, but which will be "useful later."	Memorization of passages only as they are understood by the pupils and can be used in present experience."

[26]Ibid., p. 91.

[27]Ibid., p. 92.

[28]*Actas de la Cuarta Reunion de la Conferencia Misionera Andina del Norte de la Iglesia Metodista Episcopal*, Callao, December 18 to 21, 1912.

[29]James I. Vance, "Movimiento Interdenominacional en el Mundo," *El Mensajero*, VI, No. 59 (Lima, March 1920), p. 12.

[30]"Here, then, are three points in which liberalism has obvious significance for a theory of religious education: The effort to develop in each person an individual of independent attitude in

all religious matters; the awakening of thought as contrasted with mental habituation; and the fusion of rightness toward God with rightness toward men. . . . The educational problems of liberalism: Liberalism opens the way to the most vital materials and methods of instruction, but it encounters the danger of intellectualism. . . . Liberalism cultivates respect for man as man, but it does not so readily appreciate institutional organizations of the good will as the church. . . . These three positive educational tendencies of liberalism can be reinforced, and the correlative defects avoided by identifying religious freedom with the positive purpose of the democracy of God." George A. Coe, *A Social Theory*, pp. 338-341.

[31]Ibid.

[32]Donald B. Meyer, *The Protestant Search*, p. 139; George A. Coe, *A Social Theory*, Chapter III.

[33]Henry A. Nordahl, "El Metodismo y la Educacion," *El Mensajero*, II, Nos. 19-20 (Lima, July-August 1916), pp. 4-5.

[34]Panama Congress 1916, *Christian Work in Latin America*, 3 Vols. (New York: The Missionary Education Movement, 1917), Vol. I, p. 504.

[35]Ibid.

[36]Benjamin S. Winchester, *Religious Education and Democracy* (New York-Cincinnati: The Abingdon Press, 1917).

[37]Panama Congress 1916, *Christian Work*, Vol. I, p. 526. Repercussions at the Panama Congress can be traced in the Minutes of the 1919 Annual Conference. Missionaries recommended the merging of evangelical schools in Peru and the creation of an articulated educational system at interdenominational level. *Actas de la Octava Reunion*, November 30 - December 3, 1916.

[38]Ibid., p. 527.   [39]Ibid., pp. 508-509.

[40]Montevideo Congress 1925, *Christian Work*, Vol.II, pp. 81-82.

[41]Ibid.

[42]During the discussions at the Panama Congress, one of the missionaries on the Committee on Education had suggested that most of the disappointment in educational work had arisen from the attempt to combine two types of schools, those created for the

sake of the church, and those schools with the goal of overcoming prejudices against Protestantism among the higher classes. Panama Congress 1916, *Christian Work*, Vol. I, p. 467.

[43]Ibid., p. 511.

[44]Details of early school developments at the end of the century are not included. Concerning this issue see: Paul E. Kuhl, "Go Ye Into All the World and Teach Arithmetic to Every Creature: Thomas Bond Wood and Methodist Schools in Peru, 1891-1902", paper presented at the Interdisciplinary Conference on Latin America and Education sponsored by the Center for Latin American Studies of Tulane University, New Orleans, Louisiana, April 28-30 1983.

[45]*Actas de la Decima Segunda Reunion*, February 3-8, 1921. Early reports (1912-1913 and 1914) merged the data for both the Anglo American School of Callao and Callao High School.

[46]At the beginning, the schools did not follow co-educational practices; there were separate schools for boys and girls.

[47]*Actas de la Segunda Reunion*, January 13-17, 1911.

[48]Ibid.

[49]*Actas de la Novena' Reunion*, December 8-10, 1917; *Actas de la Decima Primera Reunion*, September 18-22, 1919.

[50]*Actas de la Decima Segunda Reunion*, February 3-8, 1921; *Actas de la Octava Reunion*, November 30 to December 3, 1916; *Actas de la Vigesima Segunda Reunion*, December 2-8, 1930.

[51]Ibid.

[52]*Actas de la Decima Quinta Reunion*, January 30 to February 3, 1924; Clyde W. Brewster, Supplementary Report in ibid., pp. 319-320.

[53]*Actas de la Octava Reunion*, November 30 to December 3, 1916; *Actas de la Decima Quinta Reunion*, January 30 to February 3, 1924. The author could not follow ulterior developments of this school. *Actas de la Novena Reunion*, December 8-10, 1917.

[54]*Actas de la Quinta Reunion*, December 16-21, 1913. Some pamphlets indicate that it was founded in 1912.

[55]*Actas de la Octava Reunion,* November 30 to December 3, 1916; *Actas de la Decima Primera Reunion,* February 3-8, 1921; *Actas de la Decima Septima Reunion,* January 6-9, 1926; *Actas de la Vigesima Segunda Reunion,* December 2-8, 1930.

[56]Letter of John MacKay addressed to Dr. F. Stanger (Methodist Mission in Peru) dated in Buenos Aires, Argentina, August 14, 1923.

[57]*Actas de la Decima Primera Reunion,* September 18-22, 1919.

[58]*Actas de la Decima Tercera Reunion,* December 28, 1921 to January 1, 1922.

[59]*Actas de la Decima Reunion,* November 5-10, 1918.

[60]Panama Congress 1916, *Christian Work,* Vol. I, p. 527.

[61]*Actas de la Decima Septima Reunion,* January 6-9, 1926.

[62]*Actas de la Decima Reunion,* November 5-10, 1918.

[63]Panama Congress 1916, *Christian Work,* Vol. I, p. 441.

[64]One notices that courses on religion were sufficiently general to permit official tolerance.

[65]The land was bought in 1925. It had an area of 5000 square metres located on 28 de Julio Street. The school expected to receive contributions from the "Christian American Youth" during 1927 and 1928 in order to build the school. *Actas de la Decima Septima Reunion,* January 6-9, 1926.

[66]In 1919, the Methodists celebrated the centenary of their first mission. The Methodist Centenary became a gigantic fund-raising program; by June 1919 the Methodist Episcopal Church and the Methodist Episcopal Church South had collected subscriptions of $140,000,000.00. Donald B. Meyer, *The Protestant Search,* p. 8.

[67]*The Methodist Church . . . in Peru* (pamphlet, 1939).

[68]Letter of the Methodist Episcopal Mission in Peru addressed to Dr. Harry Farmer dated in Lima, May 15, 1922. Personal communication from Dr. Carlos Carrasco, ex-principal of Callao High School.

[69]The Anglo-American School of Victoria eventually had its own new building (inauguration date unknown). In 1919 the Mission expected to build a new school with a donation of $4,000.00 that it had received from private sources in the United States. However, in 1925 the school had not yet been built. *Actas de la Decima-Primera Reunion*, September 18-22, 1919.

[70]Letter of F. Stanger (Methodist Episcopal Mission in Peru) addressed to R. E. Diffendorfer (Board of Foreign Missions) dated in Lima, October 6, 1924.

[71]*Actas de la Decima Primera Reunion*, September 18-22, 1919.

[72]*Actas de la Decima Tercera Reunion*, December 28, 1921 to January 1, 1922. We do not know if $5,000.00 refers to American or Peruvian currency.

[73]Letter of Methodist Episcopal Mission in Peru addressed to Bishop F. J. McConnell, Pittsburg, Pa., dated in Lima, November 14, 1924.

[74]Letter of the Methodist Episcopal Mission in Peru addressed to Dr. R. E. Diffendorfer (Board of Foreign Missions) dated Lima, October 6, 1924.

[75]Letter of the Methodist Episcopal Mission in Peru addressed to Bishop F. J. MacConnell, Pittsburg, Pa., dated in Lima, November 14, 1924.

[76]Paul E. Kuhl, "Go Ye Into All the World," p. 4.

[77]In 1924, one Sol was worth about 45 cents in American gold.

[78]*Escuela Americana de La Oroya* (formerly Colegio Americano), Institucion Norteamericana de Instruccion Primaria, (Mixta) con Valor Oficial. Director General de Colegios Americanos, Howard Yoder, A. B., BA, Prospectus. (1940).

[79]Paul Kuhl argues that Thomas Wood "adjusted the fee to the ability to pay, insisting only that the student pay something and pay regularly." Paul E. Kuhl, "Go Ye Into All the World," p. 5.

[80]*Actas de la Quinta Reunion*, December 16-21, 1913.

[81]*Actas de la Decima Tercera Reunion*, December 28, 1921, to January 1, 1922. "Article 2: The conditions specified in Article 1 must be proven by means of a certificate issued by the pastor of the church in charge of the Sunday School which the applicant attends. Article 3: The scholarship will cover only fifty per cent." Ibid.

[82]*Escuela Americana de la Oroya*, Prospectus.

[83]*Actas de la Decima Tercera Reunion*, December 28, 1921 to January 1, 1922.

[84]Baltazar Caravedo Molinari, *Burguesia e Industria en el Peru, 1933-1945* (Lima: Instituto de Estudios Peruanos, 1976), p. 38.

[85]*Actas de la Decima Sexta Reunion*, December 8-11, 1924.

[86]*Actas de la Novena Reunion*, December 8-10, 1917.

[87]*Actas de la Octava Reunion*, November 30 to December 3, 1916.

[88]*Actas de la Decima Sexta Reunion*, December 8-11, 1924.

[89]*Actas de la Decima Tercera Reunion*, December 28, 1921, to January 1, 1922.

[90]*Actas de la Decima Reunion*, November 5-10, 1918.

[91]"A contrast of the typical curricula will be of interest. For this, we have chosen American Institute, La Paz, Bolivia to represent the schools following governmental standards, and *Instituto Ingles*, subjects of the six year course in the Bolivian School are compared to those of the four year elementary and the two year intermediate courses of the Chilean School.

AMERICAN INSTITUTE	INSTITUTO INGLES
La Paz and Cochabamha, Bolivia	Santiago, Chile
English—Reading, Conversation, Grammar, Composition	English—Conversation, Spelling Translation of Charts, Reading
Spanish—Writing, Reading, Spelling, Grammar, Composition	Spanish—Spelling, Writing, Reading
Metric System and Calculation	Arithmetic

Geometric Forms and Drawing

Normal Work
Drawing
Object Lessons and Natural
Science

Geography	Geography
History and Constitution Law	History—General Principles and National Civics (Derecho Chileno)
Gymnastics	Gymnastics
Games Elementary Hygiene Writing	Writing
Moral and Social Usage	Sacred History

"It would seem that either of these courses might find parallels in the United States. Our most modern socialized curricula certainly include some of the subjects listed by the Bolivian school and omitted by the "Instituto Ingles." Whatever advantage there is in one system over the other must lie chiefly in the interpretation of the curriculum, in the equipment and in teaching methods and personnel. An interesting characteristic of the national programs of most Latin American countries is the inclusion of very elementary teaching in geometry, physics and other sciences from the earliest years. Often in these schools science is taught in the intermediate grades purely from text-books, there being not the simplest laboratory apparatus available. The work thus resolves itself largely into a memorization of definitions and formulas. The influence of North American Schools has done much to stimulate a more practical type of instruction." Panama Congress 1916, *Christian Work*, Vol. I, p. 443.

[92]*Actas de la Decima Reunion*, November 5-10, 1918.

[93]Ibid.

[94]"Interesante Aviso Escolar," *El Mensajero*, III, Nos. 25-26 (Lima, January-February 1917), no page number.

[95]*Actas de la Decima Quinta Reunion*, January 30 to February 3, 1924.

[96]*Actas de la Decima Sexta Reunion*, December 8-11, 1924.

[97]Ibid.   [98]Ibid.

[99]*Actas de la Decima Quinta Reunion*, January 30 to February 3, 1924.

[100]*Actas de la Decima Primera Reunion*, September 18-22, 1919.

[101]*Actas de la Decima Sexta Reunion*, December 8-11, 1924; *Actas de la Decima Septima Reunion*, January 6-9, 1926.

[102]*Actas de la Decima Quinta Reunion*, January 30 to February 3, 1924.

[103]*Actas de la Decima Septima Reunion*, January 6-9, 1926.

[104]*Actas de la Sexta Reunion*, November 12-16, 1914; *Actas de la Decima Tercera Reunion*, December 28, 1921, to January 1, 1922.

[105]*Actas de la Decima Quinta Reunion*, January 30 to February 3, 1924; *Actas de la Decima Sexta Reunion*, December 8-11, 1924; *Actas de la Decima Septima Reunion*, January 6-9, 1926.

[106]*Actas de la Vigesima Octava Reunion*, February 17-21, 1937.

[107]*Actas de la Decima Septima Reunion*, January 6-9, 1926.

[108]*Actas de la Octava Reunion*, November 30 to December 3, 1916.

[109]"Lima High School," *El Mensajero*, III, Nos. 25-26 (Lima, January-February 1917), advertisement, no page number.

[110]*Actas de la Cuarta Reunion*, December 18-21, 1912.

[111]*Actas de la Octava Reunion*, November 30 to December 3, 1916.

[112]"Documento Evaluativo." Manuscript (Lima, July 1945).

[113]*Actas de la Decima Segunda Reunion*, February 3-8, 1921.

[114]Ibid.   [115]Ibid.

[116]Ibid.   [117]Ibid.

[118]*Actas de la Decima Tercera Reunion.* December 28, 1921 to January 1, 1922.

[119]*Actas de la Decima Septima Reunion.* January 6-9, 1926.

[120]*Lima High School.* Prospectus (Lima, 1928) in *Blue and Gold.* Special Number. Fiftieth Anniversary (Lima, June 21, 1956).

[121]*Actas de la Decima Reunion.* November 5-10, 1918.

[122]*Actas de la Decima Sexta Reunion.* December 8-11, 1924.

[123]Letter of the American Book Company, signed by C. Abruzzi (Department of Accounts) addressed to Mr. C. W. Brewster (Director North Andean Mission of the Methodist Episcopal Church) dated New York, February 16, 1933. There are many invoices, but they do not mention the names of the books.

[124]The Methodist Publishing House, *Methodist Church School Literature* (U.S.A.: booklet, 16 pages, no date).

[125]Montevideo Congress 1925, *Christian Work*, Vol. II, p. 179.

[126]Ibid., p. 180.

[127]*Actas de la Octava Reunion*, November 20 to December 3, 1916.

[128]"Interesante Aviso Escolar," *El Mensajero*, III, Nos. 25-26 (Lima: January-February 1917), no page number.

[129]Jane Hahne, "A Todas y Cada Una de las ex Alumnas del Lima High School," *Blue and Gold*, Special Number, Fiftieth Anniversary (Lima, June 21, 1956), p. 16.

[130]For example, the well known Argentinian Jorge (George) Howard, whose career might be paralleled with that of Harry Ward, wrote in 1918, while discussing the need to prepare experts in religious education: "Why then do we not accomplish our goal with the care, intelligence and assertiveness of a modern corporation dealing with its commercial affairs." Jorge P. Howard.

"La Educacion Religiosa," p. 4.

[131]Montevideo Congress 1925, *Christian Work*, Vol. I, p. 283.

[132]Ibid., p. 297.

[133]*Actas de la Primera Reunion*, January 21-25, 1910.

[134]*Actas de la Novena Reunion*, December 5-10, 1917.

[135]*Actas de la Decima Tercera Reunion*, December 28, 1921, to January 1st, 1922.

[136]*Actas de la Decima Septima Reunion*, January 6-9, 1926.

[137]"Colegio America para Mujeres," *Report*, typed version (Lima, July 1945).

[138]See Anibal Quijano Obregon, "Imperialismo, Classes Sociales y Estado en el Peru: 1895-1930," in Raul Benitez Zenteno (Coordinador Seminario de Oaxaca), *Clases Sociales y Crisis Politica en America Latina* (Mexico: Siglo XXI, 1977), p. 134.

[139]"However, the question was that the concentration of the property and the control of the resources of production whether in the capitalist or pre-capitalist field pushed more and more groups of people toward a middle social position; meanwhile, the economic activities did not broaden to a great enough extent so that those people could find their own socio-economic place." Anibal Quijano Obregon, "Imperialismo, Clases Sociales y Estado," p. 156.

[140]*Actas de la Vigesima Segunda Reunion*, December 2-8, 1930.

[141]*Actas de la Decima Septima Reunion*, January 6-9, 1926. Report signed by C. W. Brewster.

[142]Letter of Julio C. Sanchez (Principal of the Escuela Americana de La Oroya) addressed to Dr. Alfonso Villanueva Pinillo (General Director of Instruction, Lima) dated La Oroya, March 5th, 1941. The principal of the school demanded that the authorities intervene on behalf of the school with the American Company.

[143]Personal communication from Dr. Carlos Carrasco.

[144]Letter of Julio C. Sanchez (Principal of the Escuela

Americana de La Oroya) addressed to Dr. Alfonso Villanueva
Pinillo (General Director of Instruction, Lima) dated La Oroya,
Peru, March 5, 1941.

[145]*Escuela Americana de La Oroya* (formerly Colegio
Americano).

[146]Panama Congress, 1916, *Christian Work*, Vol. II, pp.
147-148.

[147]"Colegio America para Mujeres," *Report*.

[148]Jane Hahne, "A Todas y Cada Una de las ex Alumnas,"
p. 16.

[149]Ibid.

[150]Panama Congress 1916, *Christian Work*, Vol. II, p. 166.

[151]Wenceslao O. Bahamonde, "Establishment of Evangelical
Christianity in Peru," manuscript copy, incomplete materials on
developments after 1900, not included in thesis of the same title
(Lima, 1952), p. 51. The quotation has been taken from *World
Outlook*, (June 1946), p. 267. Neither the name of the author nor
the title of the article were given. Miss Gertrude Hanks received
special recognition from the government. When she retired the
resolution said: "Whereas, Miss Gertrude Hanks has completed
twenty-five years of service as the principal of Lima High School in
this capital: Be it resolved: 1) That we congratulate this
distinguished teacher for her beautiful and fruitful valorous
contribution to the educational work in our country. Signed.
Valcarcel, Minister of Education, Lima, 1946, quoted in Wenceslao
O. Bahamonde, "Establishment of Evangelical," p. 52.

[152]See Cecilia Bustamante, "Intelectuales Peruanas de la
Generacion de Jose Carlos Mariategui," *The Canadian Journal of
Latin American and Caribbean Studies*, VII, No. 13 (1982), pp.
111-126.

[153]Letter of Clyde W. Brewster addressed to "My Dear
Friends," dated in Huancayo, Peru, March 1, 1924. This letter
was printed for distribution in the United States. Number of
copies: 200.

[154]George A. Coe, *A Social Theory*, p. 211.

[155]Emilio Delboy, "Las Mujeres que Escriben," *El Mensajero*,

VI, No. 60 (Lima, April 1920), pp. 15-16.   The article had been published in *Hogar*.

[156]Elena Hansen, "La Deficiencia en la Educacion de la Mujer," *El Mensajero*, VI, No. 66 (Lima, October 1920), pp. 1-2.

[157]Letter of Clyde W. Brewster addressed to "My Dear Friends," dated in Huancayo-Peru, March 1, 1924.

[158]*Actas de la Novena Reunion*, December 8-10, 1917.

[159]*Statistics Colegio Maria Alvarado* (formerly Lima High School) for the year 1956.   Number of High School students not including Commercial, Home Economics and Special students: 351.

Father's occupation	Secondary	Elementary
Businessmen	67	39
Private Employment	46	54
Engineers	21	15
Lawyers	13	8
Doctors	13	9
Military men (army)	16	15
Teachers	3	13
Newspapermen	1	2
Navy	2	2
Farmers	1	2
Barbers	2	1
Dentists	4	3
Government employees	10	1
Book-keepers		16
Salesmen		12
Photographers		7
Evangelical Pastors		3
Textile		4

[160]*Actas de la Octava Reunion*, November 30 to December 3, 1916; *Actas de la Vigesima Segunda Reunion*, December 2-8, 1930; *Actas de la Trigesima Reunion*, February 8-13, 1938.

[161]Wenceslao Bahamonde quotes a report presented by Miss Carn to the Conference on Missions in Latin America, held in 1913.   This report appears to be in contradiction with documents that do not mention the commercial section at that time.   The Report says: "Today there are sixteen women in the various departments of the government University.   Of these, nine are from our school. . . .   At the graduation exercises of our school last December, more young women secured high school and commercial

diplomas at one time than had ever been so honored in any past year in the history of peru.   His Excellency, President Billinghurst, has expressed his deep gratification over the work this school is doing."   Wenceslao Bahamonde, "Establishment of Evangelical," p. 51.

[162]*Lima High School.*   Prospectus.

[163]*The Methodist Church. . . In Peru.*

[164]See   Anibal   Quijano   Obregon,   "Imperialismo,   Clases Sociales y Estado," pp. 147-149.

BIBLIOGRAPHY

PRIMARY SOURCES

Government Documents

Anuario de la Legislacion Peruana. Legislatura 1916, Vol. I. Edicion Oficial.

Censo de las Provincias de Lima y Callao levantado el 13 de Noviembre de 1931. Trabajo ejecutado por la Junta Departamental de Lima Pro-Desocupados. Republica del Peru.

Respuesta a la Circular del Poder Ejecutivo de la Provincia de Buenos Aires del 20 de Agosto de 1827 y al Mensaje del mismo del 14 de Setiembre de 1827. Setiembre 24, 1827. In Sergio Bagu, *El Plan Economico del Grupo Rivadaviano 1811-1827. Su Sentido y sus Contradicciones, sus Proyecciones Sociales, sus Enemigos,* "Seccion Documental," No. 163, p. 475.

Letters

Thomson, James Diego. *Letters on the Moral and Religious State of South America, Written during a Residence of Seven Years in Buenos Aires, Chile, Peru and Colombia.* London: James Nisbet, 1827.

Masonic Literature

A.L.G.D. *Liminar de los Anales Masonicos de la RESP . . LOG . . SIMB . ., Concordia Universal No. 14. Apuntes Sinopticos al Conmemorar Cien Anos de su Fundacion.* Callao, Peru: Talleres Graficos Quiros, 1949.

Medina, Casimiro and Jose B. Ugarte. "Dictamen," *Revista Masonica del Peru,* XI, No. 125 (Lima, March 31, 1892), 60-62.

"Seccion Official." *Revista Masonica del Peru,* X, No. 113 (Lima, March 31, 1891), 58.

Methodist and Interdenominational Sources

1. Proceedings of Conventions and Meetings, Reports.

Actas Oficiales de la Conferencia Misionera Andina del Norte de la Iglesia Metodista Episcopal (the conference was renamed during the

1930s, Conferencia Misionera del Peru and from 1940 Conferencia Anual Provisional del Peru). Peru. Annual Reports presented in January 1910, January 1911, December 1912, December 1913, November 1914, November-December 1916, December 1917, November 1918, September 1919, February 1921, December 1921-January 1922, February 1923, January-February 1924, December 1924, January 1926, February 1929, December 1930, December 1931, January 1933, December 1933, December 1934, February 1937, February 1938, February 1939, December 1940 and 1943.

Anglo-American Committee. *Anglo-American Hospital Report Presented to a General Meeting of the Anglo-American Community on April 5, 1920.*

Annual Report of the Missionary Society of the Methodist Episcopal Church for the Year 1903. New York.

Annual Report of the Board of Foreign Missions of the Methodist Episcopal Church for the Year 1929. New York: Board of Foreign Missions of the Methodist Episcopal Church.

Antay, Federico. *Informe desde Julio 17 de 1895 a Enero 12 de 1896.* Lima: Plaza de la Inquisicion 213, Imprenta y Libreria, 1896.

Committee on Cooperation in Latin America. *Report of Secretary.* New York: 1933.

Montevideo Congress 1925. *Christian Work in South America.* 2 Vols. New York-Chicago: Fleming H. Revell Company, 1925.

Panama Congress 1916. *Christian Work in Latin America.* 3 Vols. New York-Chicago: The Missionary Education Movement, 1917.

Penzotti, Francisco. *Spiritual Victories in Latin America. The Autobiography of Rev. Francis G. Penzotti.* New York: American Bible Society, 1916.

Students and the Present Missionary Crisis. Addresses Delivered before the Sixth International Convention of the Student Volunteer Movement for Foreign Missions, Rochester, New York, December 29, 1909, to January 2, 1910. New York: Student Volunteer Movement for Foreign Missions, 1910.

"Visiting the Central Mountain District from La Oroya to Smelter and Cerro de Pasco including the Villages of Huarancaca and Colquilja." Internal report, undated, but probably written in the 1920s.

Wheeler, Reginald W., Robert Gardner McGregor, and Others (members of a commission appointed to visit Chile and Brazil by the Board of Foreign Missions of the Presbyterian Church in the United States). *Modern Missions in Chile and Brazil.* Philadelphia: The Westminster Press, 1926.

2. *Non Classified Church Documents, Letters and Memorandums From the Collection of the Official Correspondence of the American Methodist Mission in Peru.*

"Anglo-American School of La Victoria: Report: Salaries and Expenses." Lima, July 1933.

Callao High School 1891-1966. 75th Anniversary. Pamphlet, 1966.

"Carta Circular a los Pastores del Distrito del Centro." Huancayo, March 22, 1933.

"Colegio America para Mujeres." Report. Lima, July 1945.

Colegio America para Varones. *Report on Property Now Being Used for Media and Commercial.* Callao, Peru: Calle Teatro 153, February 1, 1944.

"Documento Evaluativo." Manuscript. Lima, July 1945.

Escuela Americana de La Oroya (formerly Colegio Americano). Institucion Norteamericana de Instruccion Primaria (Mixta) con Valor Oficial. Director General de Colegios Americanos, Howard Yoder A.B., B.A. Prospectus (1940).

The Federal Council of Churches Speaks. Pamphlet. July 1940.

Iglesia de La Victoria. Iglesia Central. "Lista de Estudiantes Becados." Manuscript. Year 1933.

Iglesia de La Victoria. "Lista de Miembros Oficiales." Manuscript. November, 1924.

Informe de la Seccion de Justicia. Re: Directorio de Misiones Extranjeras de la Iglesia Metodista Episcopal en el Peru. Signed: Alfredo Maguina, Jefe de la Seccion de Justicia. Lima, February 2, 1923.

Instituto Misional de Maestros de la Provincia de Yauli. Cuestionario Pedogogico. This questionnaire was answered by the principal of "Escuela Americana," La Oroya, September 22, 1941.

Lima High School. Prospectus. Lima, 1928.

Mackay, John.   "Peruvian Social Problems and Protestantism." Manuscript. No date available. Possible date: 1923.

The Methodist Church . . . In Peru. Pamphlet. 1939.

Methodist Church School Literature.   Methodist Publishing House. United States: booklet, no date.

North Andes Mission. "Merrit Thompson: Salary: Gain in Exchange on Salary for 1921."

"Obreros Metodistas en Peru." Incomplete list of active converts.

Watlington, Elton. *Peru: Land of the Incas. The Methodist Church at Work in Latin American Countries.* New York: Pamphlet published by the Editorial Department, 1963.

"Wolfe, Frederic Fay" (Biography). Typed Version. No author. No date available.

Letter of Hays Archerd (Methodist Episcopal Mission in Peru, Central District) addressed to Mr. Smith, dated Huancayo, Peru, May 14, 1920 (copy).

Letter of G. Fowles (Treasurer of the Board of Foreign Missions) addressed to Mission Treasurers and Finance Committees, dated New York, October 26, 1920.

Letter of H. Farmer (Board of Foreign Missions) addressed to F. Stanger (Lima) dated New York, August 11, 1921.

Letter of Frank Mason North (Board of Foreign Missions) addressed to F. Stanger (Lima) dated New York, August 31, 1921.

Letter of the Methodist Episcopal Mission in Peru addressed to Dr. Harry Farmer (Board of Foreign Missions) dated Lima, May 15, 1922 (copy).

Letter of the Methodist Episcopal Mission in Peru addressed to Bishop W. P. Thirkield (Mexico) dated Lima, May 22, 1922 (copy).

Letter of the Methodist Episcopal Mission in Peru addressed to Dr. Harry Farmer (Board of Foreign Missions) dated Lima, October 5, 1922 (copy).

Letter of A. W. Greenman (Methodist Episcopal Mission in Peru) addressed to Dr. Harry Farmer (Board of Foreign Missions) dated Lima, November 21, 1922 (copy).

Letter of the Treasurer of the Methodist Episcopal Mission in Peru addressed to Mr. Chas. E. DeVesty (Board of Foreign Missions,) dated Lima, November 22, 1922 (copy).

Letter of the Methodist Episcopal Mission in Peru addressed to Dr. Harry Farmer (Board of Foreign Missions) dated Lima, January 23, 1923 (copy).

Letter of the Methodist Episcopal Mission in Peru addressed to Mr. H. Archerd (Central District) dated Lima, March 22, 1923 (copy).

Letter of F. Stanger (Methodist Episcopal Mission in Peru) addressed to Mrs. W. T. T. Millham (Cuzco, Peru) dated Lima, April 16, 1923 (copy).

Letter of A. W. Greenman (Methodist Episcopal Mission in Peru) to Bishop Luther B. Wilson, D.D. (Secretary of Board of Bishops, Methodist Episcopal Church, New York) dated Lima, April 5, 1923 (copy).

Letter of E. Cherrington (The Anti-Saloon League of America, Ohio) addressed to Mr. F. Stanger (Methodist Episcopal Mission in Peru) dated Ohio, April 30, 1923.

Letter of Robert Speer (Committee on Cooperation In Latin America, New York) addressed to the Members of the Committee on Cooperation in Latin America and the Mission Boards and Missionaries interested in the Montevideo Congress, dated New York, May 2, 1923.

Letter of the Methodist Episcopal Mission in Peru addressed to Dr. Titus Lowe and Dr. Harry Farmer (Board of Foreign Missions) dated Lima, May 7, 1923 (copy).

Letter of the Methodist Episcopal Mission in Peru addressed to Dr. Harry Farmer (Board of Foreign Mission) dated Lima, May 22, 1923 (copy).

Letter of Mr. F. Stanger (Methodist Episcopal Mission in Peru) addressed to Mr. H. Archerd, dated Lima, June 13, 1923 (copy).

Letter of the Methodist Episcopal Mission in Peru addressed to Dr. Titus Lowe, Dr. Harry Farmer, Bishop W. F. Oldham, and Bishop

W. P. Thirkield, dated Lima, June 15, 1923 (copy).

Letter of F. Stanger (Methodist Episcopal Mission in Peru) addressed to Dr. Titus Lowe dated Lima, July 4, 1923 (copy).

Letter of Titus Lowe (Board of Foreign Missions) addressed to F. Stanger dated July 31, 1923. Original not received. Copy sent to Dr. Fleck.

Letter of John Mackay addressed to Mr. F. Stanger, dated Buenos Aires, August 14, 1923.

Letter of H. Archer (Methodist Episcopal Mission in Peru) to Dr. H. Farmer (Board of Foreign Missions) dated September 19, 1923 (copy).

Letter of F. Stanger (Methodist Episcopal Mission in Peru) addressed to Dr. John Mackay, dated October 17, 1923 (copy).

Letter of F. Stanger (Methodist Episcopal Mission in Peru) addressed to Dr. Harry Farmer (Board of Foreign Missions) dated Lima, October 18, 1923 (copy).

Letter of the Methodist Episcopal Mission in Peru addressed to Dr. Harry Farmer (Board of Foreign Missions) dated Lima, October 19, 1923 (copy).

Letter of the Methodist Episcopal Mission in Peru addressed to Harry Farmer (Board of Foreign Missions) dated Lima, October 23, 1923 (copy).

Letter of F. Stanger (Methodist Episcopal Mission in Peru) addressed to Bishop W. P. Thirkield (Board of Foreign Missions) dated Lima, November 6, 1923 (copy).

Letter of F. Stanger (Methodist Episcopal Mission in Peru) addressed to Mr. J. C. Field, dated in Lima, November 9, 1923 (copy).

Letter of Dr. Harry Farmer (Board of Foreign Missions) addressed to F. M. Stanger, dated November 12, 1923.

Letter of Dr. Harry Farmer (Board of Foreign Missions) addressed to F. Stanger (Methodist Episcopal Mission in Peru) dated New York, November 30, 1923.

Letter of F. Stanger (Methodist Episcopal Mission in Peru) to Dr. Harry Farmer (Board of Foreign Missions) dated Lima, December

2, 1923.

Letter of H. Archerd to Mr. F. Stanger (Lima) dated Cerro de Pasco, Peru, December 11, 1923.

Letter of Fidel Ferrer addressed to F. M. Stanger (Lima) dated Huancayo, Peru, December 19, 1923.

Letter of Clyde W. Brewster addressed to "My Dear Friends," dated in Huancayo, Peru, March 1, 1924. This letter was printed for distribution in the United States (200 copies).

Letter of F. Stanger (Methodist Episcopal Mission in Peru) addressed to R. E. Diffendorfer dated Lima, October 6, 1924 (copy).

Letter of the Methodist Episcopal Mission in Peru addressed to Bishop F. J. McConnell, Pittsburg, Pa., dated Lima, November 14, 1924 (copy).

Letter of the Methodist Episcopal Mission in Peru addressed to Sr. Andres Munoz (Goyllarisquisga, Peru) dated December 17, 1924 (copy).

Letter of the General Manager of the "Ferrocarril Central del Peru" addressed to F. F. Wolfe (Methodist Episcopal Mission in Peru) dated Lima, December 17, 1924.

Letter of the Methodist Episcopal Mission in Peru addressed to Dr. and Mrs. Rader, dated January 6, 1932 (copy).

Letter of Howard Yoder (Instituto Andino) addressed to Mr. C.W. Brewster, dated Huancayo, Peru, April 15, 1932.

Letter of the Methodist Episcopal Mission in Peru addressed to Miss Serena Johnson, dated June 3, 1932 (copy).

Letter of the Methodist Episcopal Mission in Peru addressed to Miss Semeramis Kutz, dated May 24, 1932 (copy).

Letter of D. C. Heath and Company (Spanish-American Department) addressed to Mr. C. W. Brewster (Director Escuela Anglo-Americana de La Victoria) dated February 14, 1933.

Letter of the American Book Company, signed by C. Abruzzi (Department of Accounts) addressed to Mr. C. W. Brewster (Director North Andes Mission) dated New York, February 16, 1933.

Letter of the Methodist Episcopal Mission in Peru addressed to Senor Baldomero Santa Maria de Aliaga (Director de Estudios y Examenes, Lima) dated Lima, September 27, 1934 (copy).

Letters between Rev. Howard Yoder (Lima) and the principal of Colegio Andino, formerly Instituto Andino (Huancayo), from April to December 1939.

Letter of the Vice-President for Foreign Works of the World Association of Daily Vacation Bible Schools addressed to Mr. Howard Yoder, dated New York, June 20, 1940.

Letter of Julio C. Sanchez (Principal of the Escuela Americana de La Oroya) addressed to Dr. Alfonso Villanueva Pinillo (Director General de Instruccion Lima) dated La Oroya, Peru, March 5, 1941 (copy).

Letter of W. Crawford Barclay (Organizer, Conference on Christian Literature for Latin America to be held Mexico City July 1941) addressed to Rev. Howard Yoder, dated New York, April 14, 1941.

Letter of the Methodist Episcopal Mission in Peru addressed to Bishop George Miller (Oakland, California) dated January 25, 1942.

Memorandum to the Board of Bishops from the Missionaries forming the Financing Committee of the North Andes Mission, dated in Lima, March 28, 1923. Signed by H. P. Archerd (Supt. Central District), A. W. Greenman (Supt. Coast District), Dr. Warren L. Fleck, F. M. Stanger (Sec. Financial Committee), Clarence Snell and Ruperto Algorta (copy).

Memorandum to the Hon. Miles Poindexter, United States Ambassador to Peru. Re: "Confirming conversation of Friday evening last with F. M. Stanger," dated Lima, July 17, 1923 (copy).

3. *Documents, Pamphlets from the Wolfe Memorial Library. Archivo Vertical.*

Presencia de la Iglesia Metodista en Nuestra Patria y su Contribucion. Peru, 1964.

Reunion de la Comision Organizadora Central del Primer Congreso de la Juventud Evangelica de America Latina del 5 al 9 de Abril de 1939. *Report.*

Vasquez, A. T. "Datos Historicos de la Iglesia Metodista Episcopal." Personal Testimony. Lima, September 1, 1937.

Watlington, Elton. *El Rol del Misionero en la Iglesia Metodista del Peru.* Iglesia Metodista del Peru: Junta de Publicacion y Comunicaciones, pamphlet, 1969.

4. Non Classified Documents under "Archivo Historico."

"La Educacion en los Colegios Metodistas del Peru." October 1975.

"Methodist Missionaries in Peru: 1910-1930." Incomplete list.

Ritchie, John, ed. *Guia Evangelica Peruana.* Lima, 1924.

5. Letters, Literature, General Information from the Files of Colegio Maria Alvarado (formerly Lima High School).

Blue and Gold. Special Number. Fiftieth Anniversary of the Colegio Maria Alvarado (formerly Lima High School), Lima, June 21, 1956.

Letter of Mr. Anthony Armenta (American Vice-Consul in Peru), Foreign Service of the United States of America, addressed to Colegio Maria Alvarado, dated American Embassy, Lima, February 21, 1961.

Statistics Colegio Maria Alvarado (formerly Lima High School) for the years 1947-1948; 1950-1951-1952; 1956; 1958-1959.

6. Methodist and Interdenominational Literature.

a. Methodist and Ecumenical Periodicals

Alma Latina (Methodi, 1926-1928).

Accion y Fe (Methodist Monthly, 1935-1960; from 1960, occasional numbers.)

Ecos Metodistas (from 1980).

El Heraldo. Union Evangelica de Sud-America, 1911-1916.

El Heraldo Cristiano. Union Evangelica de Sud-America, 1916-1921.

El Mensajero (from 1923 *El Mensajero Cristiano.* Methodist, 1914-1924).

Incaland (Methodist, 1924-1941).

La Nueva Democracia. Committee on Cooperation in Latin America,

1920-1964.

Peru Calling (Methodist, 1957-1970).

Renacimiento (Interdenominational: Evangelical   Union   of   South
America,   Christian   and   Missionary   Alliance,   Free   Church   of
Scotland.   It began publication in 1921.)

The World Sunday School News

b.   *Selected Articles*

"A Nuestros Lectores de Cerro de Pasco y Smelter." *El Mensajero*, VI,
No. 59 (Lima, March 1920), 18.

Algorta, Ruperto. "El Congreso Internacional Antialcoholico Reunido
en Washington, D. C." *El Mensajero* VI, No. 67 (Lima, November
1920), 2-3.

"Articulos Constitucionales Racientemente Aprobados por el Congreso."
Renacimiento, XXI, No. 11 (Lima, November 1932), 198.

"El Asunto del Arzobispado de Lima." *Renacimiento*, XXII, No. 6
(Lima, June 1933), 110.

A. T. V. "El Matrimonio Civil." *El Alba*, No. 33 (Lima, February
1920), no page number.

A. T. V. "El Matrimonio Civil Obligatorio." *El Mensajero*, VI, No. 67
(Lima, November 1920), 16.

Baez, E. "Los Problemas Presentes y sus Causas." *Renacimiento*,
XXII, No. 6 (Lima, June 1933), 122.

"El Bolchevismo Desmoraliza al Obrero y Destruye la Industria." *El
Mensajero*, VI, No. 66 (Lima, October 1920), 11.

Brackenridge, David C. "La Obra de la Sociedad Biblica Britanica y
Extranjera en el Peru." *Renacimiento*, X, No. 7 (Lima, July 1921),
8.

Brewster, C. W. "Dr. Howard in Peru." *Incaland*, IX, No. 4 (1933),
4-5.

Browning, Webster. "La Educacion de la Ninez." *El Mensajero*, VI,
No. 57 (Lima, January 1920), 13-14.

Butler, J. W. "La Guerra con Mexico seria Injustificada." *El Mensajero*, II, No. 21 (Lima, September 1916).

"Carta Abierta al Episcopado Peruano." *Renacimiento*, XXI, No. 5 (Lima, May 1932).

"El Catolicismo y la Libertad de Religion." *El Mensajero*, II, No. 21 (Lima, September 1916), 2-3.

"El Centenario Metodista. Anuncio de un Gran Acontecimiento." *El Mensajero*, VI, No. 64 (Lima, August 1920), 4.

"Conferencia de Julio Navarro Monzo." *El Mensajero Cristiano*, XI, No. 122 (Lima, May 1923), 11.

"La Conferencia de la Iglesia Metodista Episcopal." *El Mensajero*, III, No. 18 (Lima, June 1916), 2.

"La Conferencia General de la Iglesia Metodista Episcopal." *El Mensajero*, VI, No. 63 (Lima, July 1920), 2.

"La Cooperacion en La America Latina." *El Mensajero*, II, No. 35 (Lima, November 1917), 8.

Cornelison, Bernice. "Girls." *Incaland*, XX, No. 1 (1925).

"La Cuestion Universitaria." *Renacimiento*, X, No. 11 (Lima, November 1921), 161-162.

Delboy, Emilio. "Las Mujeres que Escriben." *El Mensajero*, VI, No. 60 (Lima, April 1920), 15-16.

Dewey, Evelyn. "En el Mundo de los Juegos." *El Mensajero*, VI, No. 68 (Lima, December 1920), 6.

"Una Emboscada." *Renacimiento*, XI, No. 8 (Lima, August 1922), 115.

Garcia Calderon, Francisco. "La Originalidad Intellectual de America." *La Nueva Democracia*, III, No.1 (January 1922) 13-15.

Garcia y Garcia, Elvira. "Valor de la Educadora." *La Nueva Democracia*, IX, No.5 (May 1928), 27 and 30.

Go Ahead. "La Iglesia en el Departamento de Ica." *El Mensajero*, VI, No. 60 (Lima, April 1920), 2.

Go Ahead. "El 1ero de Mayo." *El Mensajero*, VI, No. 61 (Lima,

May 1920), 2.

Go Ahead. "El Congreso Internacional Contra el Alcoholismo." *El Mensajero*, VI, No. 65 (Lima, September 1920), 2.

Go Ahead. "Al Terminar la Sexta Jornada." *El Mensajero*, VI, No. 68 (Lima, December 1920), 2.

Hansen, Elena. "La Deficiencia en la Educacion de la Mujer." *El Mensajero*, VI, No. 66 (Lima, October 1920), 1-2.

Harada, Tasuko. "The Present Position and Problems of Christianity in Japan." *International Review of Missions*, I, no issue number available (1912), 79-97.

Howard, Jorge. "La Educacion Religiosa: Como la Entiende la Iglesia Evangelica." *El Mensajero*, IV, No. 43 (Lima, July 1918), 3-4.

"Las Ideas Pedagogicas de Haya de la Torre." *La Nueva Democracia*, IX, No.2 (February 1928), 12.

"Iglesia Metodista Episcopal. Reuniones Semanales." *El Mensajero*, VI, No. 64 (Lima, August 1920). Advertisement.

"Imperialismo y Decadencia." *La Nueva Democracia*, VII, No. 9 (September 1927), 3-5.

"Interesante Aviso Escolar." *El Mensajero*, III, Nos. 25-26 (Lima, January-February 1917). Advertisement.

"El Instituto Biblico." *El Mensajero*, III, No. 28 (Lima, April 1917), 8.

J. O. G. "El Movimiento Interdenominacional." *El Mensajero*, VI, No. 57 (Lima, January 1920), 11-13.

J. O. G. "Que es el Comite de Cooperacion en la America Latina?" *El Mensajero*, VI, No. 62 (Lima, June 1920), 16.

"La Labor Moralizadora de los Evangelistas." *El Mensajero*, V, No. 39 (Lima, March 1918), 11-12.

"La Nueva Democracia." *El Mensajero*, VI, No. 61 (Lima, May 1920), 20. Advertisement.

"La Ley de Divorcio que ha sido Vetada per el Gobierno Peruano." *El Mensajero*, VI, No. 68 (Lima, December 1920), 15.

"Lima High School." *El Mensajero*, III, Nos. 25-26 (Lima, January-February 1917). Advertisement.

"Lo Que Pasa: Construccion del Templo de la Iglesia Metodista de La Victoria." *El Mensajero*, III, No. 33 (Lima, September 1917), 4.

"Lo Que Pasa: Ecos de la Inauguracion del Templo de la Iglesia Metodista de La Victoria." *El Mensajero Cristiano*, X, No. 161-162 (Lima, December 9, 1924).

Mackay, John.   "Renacimiento." *Renacimiento*, X, No. 7 (Lima, July 1921), 101.

Mathews, Shailer.   "Missions and the Social Gospel." *International Review of Missions*, III, No. 27 (1914), 432-446.

"Mensaje a los Jovenes Evangelicos de America Latina." *Accion y Fe*, III, No. 1 (January 1938), 10-12.

"Metodologia de la Geografia." *El Mensajero*, VI, No. 62 (Lima, June 1920), 13.

Meza Chavez Nemesio.   "Nuestra Beldad es mas que la Joya." *El Mensajero*, VI, No. 64 (Lima, August 1920), 12.

Miller, George.   "Conferencia Central de la Iglesia Metodista." *El Mensajero Cristiano*, IX (Lima, August 1923), 4.

Miller, George.   "Day Break in Peru." *Incaland*, VIII, No. 6 (November-December 1932), 89-91.

Millham, Guillermo.   "La Obra de la Union Evangelica en el Peru." *Renacimiento*, X, No. 7 (Lima, July 1921), 106-108.

Mott, John.   "The Continuation Committee." *International Review of Missions*, I, no issue number available (1912), 62-78.

Mott, John.   "El Programa de los Proximos Cien Anos." *El Mensajero*, VI, No. 57 (Lima, January 1920), 9.

Nordahl, Henry A. "El Metodismo y la Educacion." *El Mensajero*, II, Nos. 19-20 (Lima, July-August 1916), 4-5.

"La Necesidad de Construir Cementerios Protestantes." *El Mensajero Cristiano*, IX, No. 117 (Lima, January 1923), 2.

"Noticias del Callao." *El Mensajero*, VI, No. 62 (Lima, June 1920), 19.

Osuna, Andres.   "El Latinismo y el Nacionalismo en la Iglesia Metodista." *El Mensajero Cristiano*, X, No. 153 (Lima, July 1924), 8.

"Progresando." *El Mensajero*, III, No. 31 (Lima, July 1917), 2.

"La Propaganda Protestante en el Peru." *Renacimiento*, XI, No. 8 (Lima, August 1922), 116.

"Por Que el Cristianismo no Puede Fracasar." *El Mensajero*, VI, No. 66 (Lima, October 1922), 2-3.

"Los Proyectos Financieros del Gobierno." *Renacimiento*, X, No. 11 (Lima, November 1921), 161.

P. W. D. "Miscelanea.   Hechos muy Significativos."   *El Mensajero*, VI, No. 60 (Lima, April 1920), 10.

R. A. "La Tercera Jornada." *El Mensajero*, III, Nos. 25-26 (Lima, January-February 1917), 2.

R. A. "El Instituto Biblico." *El Mensajero*, III, No. 29 (Lima, May 1917), 2.

"Rasgos Biograficos del Reverendo Thomas B. Wood." *El Mensajero Cristiano*, IX, No. 120 (Lima, March 1923), 2.

"The Recent Revolution of the Indian Government on Education Policy." *International Review of Missions*, II, no issue number available (1913), 430-441.

"La Religiosidad Peruana y les Problemas Nacionales." *El Mensajero*, III, No. 33 (Lima, September 1917), 2.

"La Republica y Nuestros Deberes Ciudadanos." *El Mensajero Cristiano*, X, No. 153 (Lima, July 1924), 3.

Ribeiro, Maria Rosa de.   "Evolution of the Peruvian Woman." *Incaland*, XII, No. 1 (1936), 1-5.

Ritchie, John.   "Apuntes para la Historia del Movimiento Evangelico en el Peru durante el Primer Siglo de la Republica.   La Extension del Movimiento de Lima y Cuzco."   *Renacimiento*, X, No. 10 (Lima, October 1921), 150 and 160.

Ritchie, John. "Apuntes para la Historia del Movimiento Evangelico en el Peru durante el Primer Siglo de la Republica. La Extension del Movimiento de Lima y Cuzco." *Renacimiento*, X, No. 11 (Lima, November 1921), 166 and 171.

Sanchez, C. "El Centenario Metodista." *El Mensajero*, VI, No. 66 (Lima, October 1920), 7.

Saulo. "El Indigena y el Evangelio." *El Mensajero*, VI, No.61 (Lima, May 1920), 14.

Saulo. "Injusticias Sociales." *El Mensajero*, VI, No. 68 (Lima, December 1920), 11.

"Seccion del Centro." *El Mensajero*, VI, No. 61 (Lima, May 1920), 13.

"Seccion Doctrinal. Los Articulos de Fe." *El Mensajero*, VI, No. 57 (Lima, January 1920), 8.

"Seccion Femenina. Cuando los Ninos Dominan a sus Padres." *El Mensajero*, VI, No. 57 (Lima, January 1920), 11-12.

"El Senor Haya de la Torre: En Panama Pronuncia Bellisima Pieza Oratoria en la Iglesia Metodista." *El Mensajero Cristiano*, IX, No. 136 (Lima, November 1923), 8.

"La Separacion de la Iglesia y el Estado." *El Mensajero Cristiano*, IX, No. 131 (Lima, August 1923), 3-5.

"La Separacion de la Iglesia y Estado en el Peru y *El Comercio*." *Renacimiento*, XXI, No. 5 (Lima, May 1932).

Shedd, W. A. "Christianity and Islam. The Vital Forces of Christianity and Islam." *International Review of Missions*, I (1912), 294-311.

"Sociedad Misionera Nacional." *El Mensajero*, II, No. 18 (Lima, June 1916), 7-8.

"Sociedad Misionera Regional. Palabras del Obispo Oldham." *El Mensajero*, IV, No. 39 (Lima, March 1918), 8-9.

"Sublevacion Indigena." *Renacimiento*, X, No. 11 (Lima, November 1921), 162.

"Los Sucesos de Caraz. Documentos para la Historia." *Renacimiento*, XI, No. 8 (Lima, August 1922), 123.

Tallon, A. G. "Nacionalizacion de la Iglesia." *El Mensajero*, III, No. 31 (Lima, July 1917), 5.

"Temperancia: La Prosperidad de la Clase Obrera." *El Mensajero*, II, No. 22 (Lima, October 1916), 5.

"Temperancia: Constitucion de la Liga Mundial Contra el Alcoholismo." *El Mensajero*, VI, No. 61 (Lima, May 1920), 7-8.

"Temperancia.   La Municipalidad de Lima y La Campana contra el Alcoholismo."   *El Mensajero*, VI, No. 68 (Lima, December 1920), 7.

"Topicos del Mes: La Conversion de los Bolcheviques." *Renacimiento*, X, No. 7 (Lima, July 1921), 97.

"La Universidad Catolica." *El Mensajero*, III, No. 28 (Lima, April 1917), 2.

Vallejo, Senefelder. "La Libertad." *El Mensajero Cristiano*, X, No. 153 (Lima, July, 1924), 7.

Vance, James I. "Movimiento Interdenominacional en el Mundo."   *El Mensajero*, VI, No. 59 (Lima, March 1920), 12.

W. O. S. "La Libertad y el Progreso."   *El Mensajero*, III, No. 34 (Lima, October 1917), 11.

Interviews

Heysen, Luis. Personal interview. Lima, Peru, July 1977.

SECONDARY SOURCES

Articles

Bustamante, Cecilia.   "Intellectuales Peruanas de la Generacion de Jose Carlos Mariategui." *The Canadian Journal of Latin American and Caribbean Studies*, VII, No.13 (1982), 11-126.

d'Epinay, Lalive.   "Les Protestantismes Latin-Americains.   Un modele typologique." *Arch. Social des Rel.*, 30 (1970), 33-57.

North, Lisa.   "Origenes y Crecimiento del Partido Aprista y el Cambio Socio-economico en el Peru." *Desarrollo Economico*, XXXVIII, No. 10 (1970), 163-214.

Yepes, Isabel and Estela Gonzalez. "La Auto educacion Obrera." *Chaski* (Boletin de Educacion Popular), No. 17 (Lima, April 1981), 7-14.

Unpublished Papers

Kuhl, Paul E. "Go Ye Into All the World and Teach Arithmetic to Every Creature: Thomas Bond Wood and the Methodist Schools in Peru, 1891-1902", unpublished paper prepared for delivery at the Interdisciplinary Conference on Latin America and Education sponsored by the Center for Latin American Studies of Tulane University, New Orleans, Lousiana, April 28-30, 1983.

Books

Alexander, Robert J. *Aprismo. The Ideas and Doctrines of Victor Raul Haya de la Torre.* Ohio: The Kent State University Press, 1973.

Archambault, Reginald D., ed. *Dewey on Education.* New York: Random House, 1966.

Arms, Goodsil F. *El Origen del Metodismo y su Implantacion en la Costa Occidental.* Santiago de Chile: Imprenta Universitaria, 1923.

Bagu, Sergio. *El Plan Economico del Grupo Rivadaviano 1811-1827. Su Sentido y sus Contradicciones, sus Proyecciones Sociales, sus Enemigos.* Rosario-Argentina: Instituto de Investigaciones Historicas, 1966.

Basadre, Jorge. *Historia de la Republica del Peru,* 2 Vols. 3rd ed. Lima: Editorial Cultura Antartica, 1946.

Basadre, Jorge. *Historia de la Republica del Peru,* 10 Vols. Lima Ediciones Historia, 1964.

Bastian, Jean Pierre. *Breve Historia del Protestantismo en America Latina.* Mexico: Casa Unida de Publicaciones, 1986.

Benitez Zenteno, Raul., ed. *Clases Sociales y Crisis Politica en America Latina.* Mexico: Siglo XXI, 1977.

Bonilla, Heraclio. *Guano y Burguesia en el Peru.* Lima: Instituto de Estudios Peruanos, 1974.

Bourricaud, Francois. *Ideologia y Desarrollo. El Caso del Partido Aprista Peruano.* Jornadas No. 58. Mexico: El Colegio de

Mexico, 1966.

Caravedo Molinari, Baltazar. *Burguesia e Industria en el Peru 1933-1945.* Lima: Instituto de Estudios Peruanos, 1976.

Carey, James C. *Peru and the United States, 1900-1962.* Indiana: University of Notre Dame Press, 1964.

Coe, George A. *A Social Theory of Religious Education.* rpt. 1927; 1st ed. 1917. New York: Arno Press and The New Times, 1969.

Copleston, Frederick, S. J. *A History of Philosophy.* Vol. VIII, *Modern Philosophy. Bentham to Russell.* New York: Image Books, 1965.

Cotler, Julio and Richard R. Fagen, eds. *Latin America and the United States: The Changing Political Realities.* California: Stanford University Press, 1974.

Ebaugh, Cameron D. *Education in Peru.* U. S. Office of Education. Security Agency. Bulletin 1946, No. 3. Washington: Government Printing Office, 1946.

Garcia Salvatecci, Hugo. *El Pensamiento de Gonzalez Prada.* Lima: Editorial Arica, 1972.

Himelblau, Jack. *Alejandro O. Deustua. Philosophy in Defense of Man.* Gainesville: University Presses of Florida, 1979.

Hopkins, Charles Howard. *The Rise of the Social Gospel in American Protestantism.* 6th ed. New Haven: Yale University Press, 1961.

Inman, Samuel G. *El Destino de America Latina.* Trans. R. Elizalde. Santiago, Chile: Ediciones Ercilla, 1941.

Kaestle, Carl F. *Joseph Lancaster and the Monitorial School Movement.* New York: Teachers College Press, Columbia University, 1973.

Kantor, Harry. *The Ideology and Program of the Peruvian Aprista Movement.* New York: Octagon Books, 1966.

Klaiber, Jeffrey L., S. J. *Religion and Revolution in Peru 1824-1976.* Indiana: University of Notre Dame Press, 1977.

Klaren, Peter. *La Formacion de las Haciendas Azucareras y los Origenes del APRA.* Peru Problema No. 5. Lima, Instituto de Estudios Peruanos, 1970.

Mackay, John A. *The Other Spanish Christ.* London: Student Christian Movement Press, 1932.

Mackay, Juan (John). *El Otro Cristo Espanol.* Trans. G. Baez Camargo. Mexico and Buenos Aires: Casa Unida de Publicaciones and Editorial La Aurora, 1952.

MacLean y Estenos, Roberto. *Sociologia Educacional del Peru.* Lima: Imprenta Gil, 1944.

Mariategui, Jose Carlos. *Ideologia y Politica.* 2nd ed. Lima: Empresa Editora Amauta, 1971.

Mariategui, Jose Carlos. *Seven Interpretative Essays on Peruvian Reality.* Trans. Marjory Urquidi. Austin: University of Texas Press, 1971.

Martinez de la Torre, Ricardo. *Apuntes para una Interpretacion Marxista de la Historia Social del Peru.* 4 Vols. Lima: Editorial Peruana, 1947.

Martinez Zaldua. *Historia de la Masoneria en Hispano-America. Es o no una Religion la Masoneria?* 2nd ed. Mexico: Costa Amic, 1967.

May, Henry F. *Protestant Churches and Industrial America.* New York: Octagon Books, 1963.

Meyer, Donald B. *The Protestant Search for Political Realism, 1919-1941.* Berkeley and Los Angeles: University of California Press, 1961.

Miller, Robert Moats. *American Protestantism and Social Issues 1919-1939.* Chapel Hill: The University of North Carolina Press, 1958.

Milne, Ines. *Desde el Cabo de Hornos hasta Quito con la Biblia.* Buenos Aires: La Aurora, 1944.

Neely, Thomas B. *La Iglesia Metodista Episcopal en America del Sur.* Buenos Aires, 1906.

Novack, George. *Pragmatism versus Marxism. An Appraisal of John Dewey's Philosophy.* New York: Pathfinder Press, 1975.

Pike, Frederick B. *The Modern History of Peru.* New York: Praeger, 1967.

Quinley, Harold E. *The Prophetic Clergy: Social Activism among Protestant Ministers.* New York: John Wiley and Sons, 1974.

Ratner, Joseph, ed.   *Intelligence in the Modern World: John Dewey's Philosophy.* New York: Random House, 1939.

Richard, Pablo.   *Iglesia, Estado Autoritario y Clases Sociales en America Latina.*   Documentos.   DOCET.   CELAM   III.   No.10. CELADEC, 1975.

Salazar Bondy, Augusto.   *Historia de las Ideas en el Peru Contemporaneo.   El Proceso del Pensamiento Filosofico.*   2 Vols. 2nd ed.   Lima: Francisco Moncloa Editores, 1967.

Salazar Bondy, Augusto.   *Sentido y Problema del Pensamiento Filosofico Hispanoamericano.*   With English translation.   Occasional Publication No. 16.   Lawrence: Center of Latin American Studies, University of Kansas, 1969.

Sanchez, Luis Alberto.   *Haya de la Torre o el Politico.   Cronica de una Vida sin Tregua.*   3rd ed.   Santiago de Chile: Ediciones Ercilla, 1936.

Sulmont S., Denis.   *Historia del Movimiento Obrero en el Peru (de 1890 a 1977).* Lima: TAREA, 1977.

Valcarcel, Luis E. *La Ruta Cultural del Peru.*   Mexico: Fondo de Cultura Economica, 1945.

Winchester, Benjamin S. *Religious Education and Democracy.*   New York-Cincinnati: The Abingdon Press, 1917.

Yepes del Castillo, Ernesto.   *Peru 1820-1920.   Un Siglo de Desarrollo Capitalista.*   Lima: Instituto de Estudios Peruanos, 1972.

Theses - Unpublished Sources

Bahamonde, Wenceslao O.   "The   Establishment   of   Evangelical Christianity in Peru, 1822-1900."   Unpublished Ph.D.   diss., Hartford Seminary, 1952.

Bahamonde, Wenceslao O.   "The   Establishment   of   Evangelical Christianity in Peru."   Incomplete materials on developments after 1900, not included in thesis of the same title.   Lima: 1952.

Kuhl, Paul E.   "Protestant Missionary Activity and Freedom of Religion in Ecuador, Peru and Bolivia."   Ph.D.   diss., Southern

Illinois University, 1982.

Stanford, James Carlton. "Methodism in Peru 1900-1930." Master of Arts dissertation. Chapel Hill: University of North Carolina, 1968.

Stanger, Francis. "La Iglesia y el Estado en el Peru Independiente." Doctoral dissertation. Facultad de Filosofia, Historia y Letras. Universidad Nacional Mayor de San Marcos, Lima, 1925.

INDEX

SR SUPPLEMENTS

Note: Nos. 1, 3, 4, 5, 7, 8, 10, and 15 in this series are out of print.

2. *Martin Heidegger's Philosophy of Religion*
   John R. Williams
   1977 / x + 190 pp.
6. *Beyond Mysticism*
   James R. Horne
   1978 / vi + 158 pp.
9. *Developments in Buddhist Thought: Canadian Contributions to Buddhist Studies*
   Edited by Roy C. Amore
   1979 / iv + 196 pp.
11. *Political Theology in the Canadian Context*
   Edited by Benjamin G. Smillie
   1982 / xii + 260 pp.
12. *Truth and Compassion: Essays on Judaism and Religion
   in Memory of Rabbi Dr. Solomon Frank*
   Edited by Howard Joseph, Jack N. Lightstone, and Michael D. Oppenheim
   1983 / vi + 217 pp.
13. *Craving and Salvation: A Study in Buddhist Soteriology*
   Bruce Matthews
   1983 / xiv + 138 pp.
14. *The Moral Mystic*
   James R. Horne
   1983 / x + 134 pp.
16. *Studies in the Book of Job*
   Edited by Walter E. Aufrecht
   1985 / xii + 76 pp.
17. *Christ and Modernity: Christian Self-Understanding in a Technological Age*
   David J. Hawkin
   1985 / x + 181 pp.
18. *Young Man Shinran: A Reappraisal of Shinran's Life*
   Takamichi Takahatake
   1987 / xvi + 228 pp.
19. *Modernity and Religion*
   Edited by William Nicholls
   1987 / vi + 191 pp.
20. *The Social Uplifters: Presbyterian Progressives and the
   Social Gospel in Canada, 1875-1915*
   Brian J. Fraser
   Spring 1988 / 280 pp. estimated

EDITIONS SR

Note: No. 3 in this series is out of print.

1. *La langue de Ya'udi : description et classement de l'ancien parler
   de Zencircli dans le cadre des langues semitiques du nord-ouest*
   Paul-Eugène Dion, O.P.
   1974 / viii + 511 p.
2. *The Conception of Punishment in Early Indian Literature*
   Terence P. Day
   1982 / iv + 328 pp.
4. *Le messianisme de Louis Riel*
   Gilles Martel
   1984 / xviii + 483 p.
5. *Mythologies and Philosophies of Salvation in the Theistic Traditions of India*
   Klaus K. Klostermaier
   1984 / xvi + 552 pp.
6. *Averroes' Doctrine of Immortality: A Matter of Controversy*
   Ovey N. Mohammed
   1984 / vi + 202 pp.
7. *L'étude des religions dans les écoles : l'expérience américaine, anglaise et canadienne*
   Fernand Ouellet
   1985 / xvi + 666 p.

8. *Of God and Maxim Guns: Presbyterianism in Nigeria, 1846-1966*
Geoffrey Johnston
1988 / iv + 322 pp.

9. *A Victorian Missionary and Canadian Indian Policy:*
Cultural Synthesis vs Cultural Replacement
David A. Nock
Spring 1988 / 200 pp. estimated

10. *Prometheus Rebound: The Irony of Atheism*
Joseph C. McLelland
Fall 1988 / 360 pp. estimated

STUDIES IN CHRISTIANITY AND JUDAISM / ETUDES SUR LE CHRISTIANISME ET LE JUDAISME

1. *A Study in Anti-Gnostic Polemics: Irenaeus, Hippolytus, and Epiphanius*
Gérard Vallée
1981 / xii + 114 pp.

2. *Anti-Judaism in Early Christianity*
Vol. 1, *Paul and the Gospels*
Edited by Peter Richardson with David Granskou
1986 / x + 232 pp.
Vol. 2, *Separation and Polemic*
Edited by Stephen G. Wilson
1986 / xii + 185 pp.

3. *Society, the Sacred, and Scripture in Ancient Judaism:*
A Sociology of Knowledge
Jack N. Lightstone
1988 / xiv + 126 pp.

THE STUDY OF RELIGION IN CANADA / SCIENCES RELIGIEUSES AU CANADA

1. *Religious Studies in Alberta: A State-of-the-Art Review*
Ronald W. Neufeldt
1983 / xiv + 145 pp.

2. *Les sciences religieuses au Québec, 1972-1984*
Louis Rousseau et Michel Despland
Printemps 1988 / 146 p. estimé

COMPARATIVE ETHICS SERIES / COLLECTION D'ETHIQUE COMPAREE

1. *Muslim Ethics and Modernity: A Comparative Study of the Ethical Thought*
of Sayyid Ahmad Khan and Mawlana Mawdudi
Sheila McDonough
1984 / x + 130 pp.

2. *Methodist Education in Peru: Social Gospel, Politics, and American*
Ideological and Economic Penetration, 1888-1930
Rosa del Carmen Bruno-Jofré
1988 / xiv + 223 pp.

Available from / en vente chez:

Wilfrid Laurier University Press
Wilfrid Laurier University
Waterloo, Ontario, Canada   N2L 3C5

Published for the
Canadian Corporation for Studies in Religion/
Corporation Canadienne des Sciences Religieuses
by Wilfrid Laurier University Press